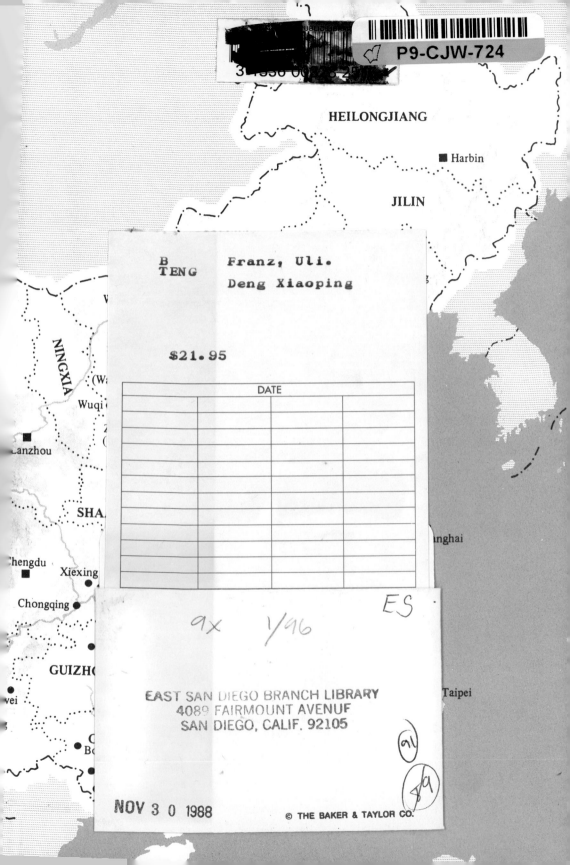

HEILONGJIANG

■ Harbin

JILIN

NINGXIA

(Wa

Wuqi

Lanzhou

SHA

Chengdu

Xiexing

Chongqing

GUIZHO

vei

Bo

anghai

Taipei

Deng Xiaoping

$(x+5)(x+1)$

x^2+6x+5

$=y=-x^2-5$

$2y+2x=-x^2-6x$

$x+3$

x

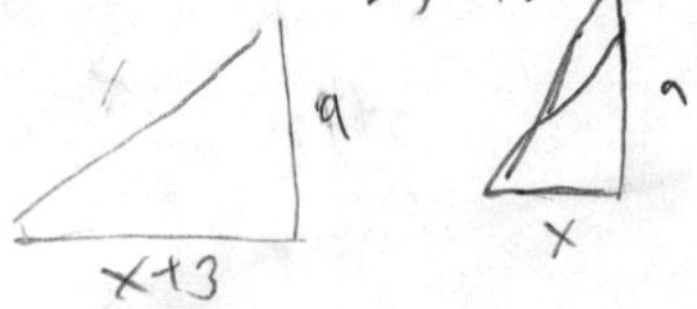

$$\frac{(x-3)(x+2)}{(x+9)(x+2)} \cdot \frac{4(x-6)}{(x+2)(x+9)}$$

$h(3.5)$

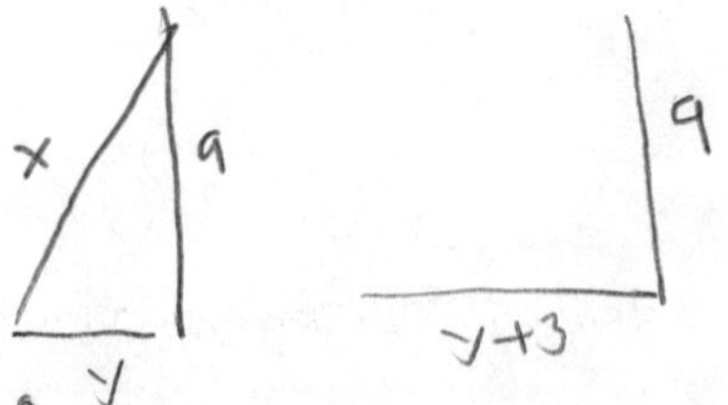

$\sqrt{x^2}=\sqrt{81+y^2}$

$x^2=y^2+81$

$y^2+81=y^2+6y+9$

$81=6y+9$

$6y=72$

$y=12$

x 9

9

$y+3$

$x=y+3$

Deng Xiaoping

Uli Franz

Translated by Tom Artin

HARCOURT BRACE JOVANOVICH, PUBLISHERS

Boston   San Diego   New York

Designed by Pascha Gerlinger
Printed in the United States of America

Library of Congress Cataloging-in-Publication Data

Franz, Uli.
[Deng Xiaoping. English]
Deng Xiaoping / Uli Franz; translated by Tom Artin.—1st ed.
p. cm.
Translated from German.
Bibliography: p.
Includes index.
ISBN 0-15-125177-0
1. Teng, Hsiao-p' ing, 1904–   2. Heads of state—China—
Biography.
I. Title.
DS778.T39F7313   1988
951.05'8'0924—dc19   88-11158
[B]   CIP

First edition
A B C D E

For Max and Panda

Contents

Foreword

*If a biography is to be written, it must
include the good as well as the bad one
has done, even the mistakes. So it is
better not to write a biography.*

—Deng Xiaoping

I HAVE DONE it anyway. May Deng Xiaoping forgive my violating a taboo, or, as the Chinese say, touching the tiger's tail.
The time is ripe to sketch out the course of Deng's life. The
Communist principle that great men should be honored only posthumously changes nothing. By now, the world public has a right
to find out more about Deng's career than his party has let us
know.[1]

Without question, Deng Xiaoping has made mistakes. Mistakes for which, after his death, the future would condemn him,
Mao Tsetung once prophesied. Weighing Mao's mistakes against
Deng's, however, would be more or less like throwing a handful
of rice into one scale, and a feather into the other. And Mao has
not yet been condemned.

A single service outweighs a hundred mistakes: Deng Xiaoping
has restored China. It is for that he has fought so long, perhaps
from the beginning of his political life. How else can we explain
the energy with which he has weathered three political falls and
a hundred intrigues, and has, nevertheless, each time, come a step
nearer his life's goal? I know of no politician of our century—
neither in the East nor in the West—who has traveled as tortuous,
as rocky, and yet as successful a life's course as Deng.

Common to the great Chinese Communist leaders is that they
can be more or less categorized: Mao Tsetung, the rebel; Zhou
Enlai, the diplomat; Liu Shaoqi, the bureaucrat; Lin Piao, the

soldier. But not Deng Xiaoping—the pragmatist, the "reed in the wind." His life is a kaleidoscope in which all these characteristics cluster.

The question remains: Why has so little been known to us for so long about this astonishing statesman who has been making world history? The explanation lies not in the enormous distance between China and the West, for in that country itself much less is to be learned about him for the most part than abroad. No, the explanation lies in the screening tactic of the Chinese Communist Party and its inconsistent relationship to its own history. If a party leader steps into the limelight, it must be not as an individual, but as a member of the collective. And its history is a history of power struggles, subjected still today to a continuing reassessment.

The present biography has a long prehistory that began in July 1977 more than 1500 kilometers north of Peking. I had been working just half a year as a lecturer in Peking when I got the chance to visit the oil field at Daqing. There I was surprised one night by the childlike abandon of jubilant oil drillers celebrating the comeback of the deposed Deng. I reacted with confusion, for I had come to China, after all, as a Maoist. I regarded the name Deng Xiaoping initially with considerable skepticism. But during the following three years of my life in Peking much changed in China, and, with it, in my consciousness as well.

To the extent that I learned to comprehend Chinese society as a society of "infinite impossibilities," I came to understand Deng's actions and motives. It was perhaps no accident that on one of my bicycle tours through the capital I ferreted out his highly secret residence. It was probably also no accident that one day, among the rice fields, I discovered his father's burial mound.

It was April 1986 before I finally had the confidence to put pen to paper. After widespread correspondence with sinologists in Germany, France, the USA, Japan, Taiwan, and Hongkong, I concentrated my attention on Hongkong and Taiwan. Hongkong feels China's pulse beat, Taiwan has the best accessible archives.

The present book is by no means the first work about Deng Xiaoping. It is, however, surely the first biography in the true sense of the word. All previous works that can to be taken seriously—I cite the books of Ching Hua Lee (Princeton-Taipei) and Han Shanbi (Hongkong)—are, examined in detail, historical representations in which Deng often appears as if by chance. The fault lies not with any inability on the part of the authors, but with appallingly incomplete documentation, especially for the years before 1949.

Anyone wishing to do research in China has to choose between two extremes: Either he seeks the green light from the very, very top, in which case archives and mouths open as though by magic, or he pursues "history from below," as inconspicuously as possible. I chose the latter path. I descended to the "grass roots," as they say in China, and interviewed contemporaries in Peking and Shanghai, and traveled throughout the province of Szechuan, Deng's birthplace, the village Xiexing, and many other places, way stations in his long life. France turned out to be a veritable mine of information. In Paris and Montargis, where Deng lived during most of his five-year stay, I dug up countless original documents.

Through dogged work on petty details, notes from my time in Peking, personal interviews, and source studies came together and finally revealed to me a remarkable flood of information. Now it has been channeled.

I could not have accomplished this task without the assistance of others. Many have helped, I name only a few: Winnie Lam (Hongkong), Nao Nakanishi (Tokyo), Christiane Kügeler (Köln), Manfred P. T. Peng (Taipei), Tien-min Li (Taipei), Geneviève Barman (Paris), Pater Jean Verinaud (Paris), André Fergani (Chalette), Wolfgang Bartke (Hamburg), Dieter Heinzig (Köln), Wolfgang Franke (Hamburg-Canton), and Anne-Marie Zhou (Hamburg). Finally, I thank my children, who understood me.

ONE

In a Jade-Green Landscape

THE HARD-SPRUNG INTERCITY bus took its time. "If a lot of people get on," the driver guessed, "it'll take six or seven hours." On the dot at seven in the morning, he starts his diesel motor; whoever hasn't got a ticket yet will have to wait till to-morrow morning.

Soon, the grey houses step apart, giving way to squares with trees, piles of brick, decaying rubbish, market stalls. The driver puts on the brakes. The first stop is in the outskirts of the Yangtze city Chungking, at a seemingly chaotic peasant market. Only now is the hand-painted sign marked "Guang'an" pasted onto the out-side of the windshield. It sticks, because the rain works like glue. Sprinkle, drizzle, streaming rain, pouring rain, rain without end— all these forms belong to Szechuan, as the sun belongs to Cali-fornia. If it is not raining, a milky mist veils the land and lies like gauze over the jade-green landscape. "When the sun shines, the dogs bark"—so runs an ancient Szechuan proverb, and it says everything about the weather.

Rotating windshield wipers and damp seats are the constant accompaniments to the journey through Deng's homeland. For the first thirty kilometers, we follow a powerful tributary of the Yangtze. Flooded roads give the traveler the impression of crossing a delta. At an iron bridge crossing the Chialing a peasant waves. The driver stops and opens the rickety door. The stop lasts a while—an empty basket, a yoke-shaft, another basket filled with apples, and a tied-up bundle are all handed in, after which their owner climbs aboard. In the bus, meanwhile, there is the smell of fish. Across the bridge, someone wants to get off; no one minds. So it goes. One hundred forty-eight kilometers in six hours—not a bad average for a long-distance bus in China. The "Guang'an" sign stays put—it is drizzling.

The bus struggles; the uppermost hairpin curve in the road disappears in a low-hanging cloud. In just a few, steep kilometers, China's "rice-bowl" transforms itself into a grey and black mountain landscape with luxuriant bamboo forests. But before anyone can become restless, back we go, freewheeling down to the level land of terraced fields that crowding each other in crescent, oval, rectangular, and semicircular shapes. Each apple tree, each banana plant, each cypress, each tea bush can be proud to have found some little place for itself in this cultivated hodgepodge. And scattered throughout, the peasant cottages that seem an organic part of the landscape. They are elongated, like barns; under overhanging roofs, golden ears of corn hang drying beside the variegated wash. The whitewashed mud walls hypnotize the eye in this chlorophyl sea.

Far in advance of the villages we are greeted by the brickyard chimneys billowing black smoke. A hectic building boom has set in here. The normally cautious driver brakes abruptly, not on account of the water buffalo grazing by the side of the road, but because the asphalt ribbon breaks off unceremoniously, and a red, swampy dirt track sets forth.

Deng Xiaoping's native region fairly vibrates with modernity. Japanese and Chinese trucks block each other's way, mopeds mingle with donkey carts, and in the crowds of people surprisingly many of the vizored caps are polyester. As we drive through Guang'an, the driver suddenly points to our right and says, not without pride, "Over there, the Japanese built a hunting rifle factory with us."

The city has long been known for its coal and limestone deposits. The newcomer sees not only many small mines, in front of which miniscule trucks stand congested, but also tall, billowing charcoal kilns.

No, traveling through Szechuan to the accompaniment of humming telegraph wires no longer bears any relation to the travels of a Ferdinand von Richthofen, who, in the year 1907 described this country:

Tung trees, sisyphus, fruit trees, mulberry trees, ree , pelal-shu, cypress—everything grows in fields and borders. From a distance, the peasant farms appear clean and prosperous—outside, white walls with dark timbers, in front, a wall containing a gate with tripartite ornamental roofs, inside, on three sides, the owner's dwelling with his entire household. Everyone is well-dressed, and the people are always friendly. The presence of a stranger does not surprise them; they approach him politely.

The province of Szechuan has built its agriculture on monoculture, primarily rice, but also wheat, oats, corn, and *kaoliang* (sweet millet). Tea plantations are rare; instead of cypress, bamboo thickets crowd the fields. The people are uniformly dressed in navy-blue or olive-green "Mao-jackets." They wear their pants rolled up high; their feet are bare, or clad in rust-brown plastic sandals. They approach strangers curiously. An enterprising individual calls out "hel-lou" or "gude-bai," and then the others laugh.

The Szechuanese are a peculiar, an independent stock. They approach foreigners as though they were their own. How pleasant that they lack the xenophobia of the Cantonese, that they are not as garrulous as the Shanghaiese, or as straightforward as the Pekingese. The people of the "four river land," Szechuan, pass long hours at play; they are never ill-natured or deceitful. But their thinking is quirky, complicated, and dodges around a thousand corners.

Contradict a fiery Szechuanese, and you provoke a pyrotechnical display of ten thousand words. Not without cause is Deng Xiaoping also known as the "peppery Napoleon." Much in the Szechuanese character is explained by a deep-seated humor, always leavened with self-irony. "Karl Marx," Deng once said, "is long since in heaven, to be sure, but he is still very powerful there. He looks down on me, and because what I have done and not done displeases him, he has punished me with deafness."

In Xiexing, a hamlet near Guang'an, stands the manor house of the Deng clan. It is whitewashed and roomy. Laid out in the form of a horseshoe, it offers a great deal of space with its 22 rooms. In the year 1986, its south wing was still occupied by Deng Xiaoping's deaf uncle, known to all in the village simply as "Lao

Deng" (old Deng), and Deng's half-deaf aunt, with her stunted lily-feet. Their rooms, across crude, high thresholds, seem small as garrets. The central room in the front of the main building serves during the day as an exhibition room and at night as the television room. The former room of Deng Xiaoping's eldest sister, Xianlie, adjoins this on the left. Up two worn stone steps and across the threshold of a wooden doorway with a carved latch the way leads to the holiest of holies: In the north wing on a hard-packed floor stands, just as it did then, the angular wedding bed in which Deng Xiaoping came into the world in 1904.

Since the land reform of 1953, beside Lao Deng and his wife, eleven families unrelated to the clan by blood or marriage have lived here in the birthplace of Deng Xiaoping. The traditional close family ties hardly exist in the China of today. When, for example, one of the residents of the house goes on foot to the eight-kilometer-distant district capital, Guang'an, to fetch medicine for the old Deng, he is paid for his trouble. But Lao Deng has money enough: as member of the Political Consultative Conference, he receives 70 yuan a month (about $22.00).

The color television set, the crank telephone, and the five naked 220-volt bulbs are there, thanks to the famous son of the house. In the village, where water is still fetched from the well and kerosene lamps are lighted at night, these things are luxuries—above all, *dianshi,* the television set. So at night the village children are there to see films like "Jade Butterfly" and "Gypsy Boy." They enjoy the fruits of Deng Xiaoping's opening politics in rooms that once were his father's.

Lao Deng, Deng Xiaoping's uncle, with the author.

Two

Father and Clan

MUCH HAS ALWAYS depended on the choice of a wife in China. It was crowned with success if the husband could bring home a "complete" wife, and only a woman who fulfilled the whole catalogue of exaggerated Confucian precepts deserved to be called complete: she was to be affectionate and submissive, and from defloration on her wedding night to the drawing of her final breath, the entire substance of her life was to concern herself solely with her husband.

Not only he, but the clan and society itself expected from her a generous measure of tact and wit in order to serve him without demeaning herself. The ideal of beauty included an oval face, and a small, round, cherry-red mouth.

Of course, no woman could fulfill all these requirements. The ancient Chinese knew this themselves, and therefore permitted concubinage as a practical way of realizing "the sublime completeness of woman" by gathering under one roof clever, beautiful, fecund, and demure mistresses. Concubines in ancient China were no ready-to-hand, scantily clad harem ladies; they were lifemates. A formal etiquette bound them to the family, and the children of the principal wife called them Mother.

Deng Xiaoping's father, the landholder Deng Wenming, possessed (in order to achieve the Confucian ideal of feminine completeness in his family) three concubines in addition to his first wife Zhang. It became clear only a matter of months after the wedding that Zhang was an "incomplete" wife—she was barren. Wenming therefore looked around for a concubine. His kin helped him in this. A second wedding was soon arranged in the Deng

7

house. Deng Wenming's first concubine, Tan, came from a good family and brought with her into the union a handsome dowry: the blood-red lacquered wedding bed was so bulky that only disassembled could it be fitted onto the bridal wagon. And to this day it stands in the place where Deng Wenming, according as his pleasure and his whim directed, visited his first "cushion of repose," as concubines once were called.

When Tan Shi Deng (Tan, Wife of Deng) conceived, and was viewed no longer simply as a supererogatory "cushion of repose," the clan looked hopefully to see whether this first concubine would confer life onto a boy or a girl. Relatives brought offerings of food, hopes were stirred, soothsayers consulted—everything pivoted on the birth of a son.

It was a girl, whom the father named Deng Xianlie. Soon, Tan was pregnant once more. Once more, hope sprang up among the impatient kin for a son and heir. Several days before lying-in, the wedding bed—with its sexual symbolism of phoenix and dragon, a true work of the South China carver's art—was arranged to receive an infant: the bamboo lattice that served as mattress was mended and stretched, the silk curtains arranged on the angular canopy. Success this time at last: On July 12 by the Chinese lunar calender, or August 22, 1904, by the Gregorian calender, in the hamlet of Xiexing, Deng Xixian—who would assume his Communist alias Deng Xiaoping twenty years later—first saw the light of day.[1]

Though the modern age was impinging powerfully on feudalism, mores still reigned in China at the turn of the century that had prevailed at the time of the first Emperor, especially in a village like Xiexing, lying isolated on a remote plateau 156 kilometers north of Chungking. In the year 1904, people still believed the birth of a son betokened good luck from the gods and the assumption of the family into the highest ranks of the ancestral cult. It was an ancient custom to announce the birth of a son to neighbors and visitors by hanging a bow and arrow on the house door. If a girl were brought into the world, a piece of cloth or a towel sufficed. A boy from a house as well-to-do as that of the Deng clan was given a jade scepter as his first toy; a girl, by contrast, would be given a cast-off spindle to rattle.

Deng Wenming now had a son, in the Chinese view a follower who would perforce be devoted to him. And for this filial de-

Marriage bed of the concubine Tan Shi Deng; here, on August 22, 1904, Deng Xixian (Deng Xiaoping) was born.

votion, in rigid conformity with Confucian rules, young Deng received every conceivable advantage such as millions of children in the destitute, often starving Ch'ing Empire dared dream of only on feast days.

Throughout his youth his ricebowl was full, replete with meat, vegetables, and all sorts of delicacies—always highly spiced, as is common in Szechuan. It was no hardship for father Deng to spoil the long-awaited son, for by Guang'an standards, he was a wealthy landowner. His servants, maids, and day laborers were able, after three harvests within the year, to heap up 13 tons of grain on the expansive threshing floor of the house. On the stately jigsaw puzzle of fields surrounding the manor house grew rice, but also wheat, oats, and kaoliang.

Soon, young Deng needed no longer play only with his older sister. He had just turned six when his brother Ken came into the world, and two years later, his brother Schuping, whom their father also called Xuchu. Deng Wenming wished for additional progeny—the proverb, after all, still holds that, "The jewel of heaven is the sun; the jewel of the house is the child." But after the birth of her fourth child, the concubine Tan grew sickly, and never regained her health. While the children were still young, Deng Xiaoping's mother died. His father was devastated: his principal wife barren, his second wife dead in the prime of her life. On the other hand, he was known in the village as a man with his feet on the ground. So it astonished no one when even as a rather elderly man he wed a certain Xiao, and ultimately—his third concubine—the very young daughter of a ferryman, Xia Bogen, who had reached just 32 years at the time of his death.

The father, Deng Wenming, was descended from an old Hakka lineage, developing already as a young man an aversion to everything Manchu—to the pigtail, and to the manners imposed by the Ch'ing Emperors. The Hakka, a pugnacious Chinese clan, had for centuries fought every form of foreign domination. They had at one time fled south from the Zhongyuan region at the lower reaches of the Yellow River to escape the invasions of the Mongols. After a lengthy exodus, the tiny, rather unpopular clan settled in the north of the province Guangdong. From here, the Dengs and many other Hakka families undertook a long odyssey west, eventually reaching the mighty Yangtze. The refugees followed the waterway upstream and landed in the "ricebowl" of the Middle Kingdom.

The father Deng Wenming had early on joined the nationwide secret society dedicated to fighting the Ch'ing Dynasty "Ge Lao Hui" (Society of Elder Brothers), which was famous in Szechuan under the name "Baoge" (Brothers in the Same Gown). As a religiously oriented rebel, he also played a leading role in the Taoist-Buddhist Society "Wu Zhi Jiao" (Faith of the Five Brothers).

Among the hundreds of secret societies of the seventeenth and eighteenth centuries, "Baoge" stood out as especially combat-effective. The egalitarian minded "Brothers" were inspired by the idea of shaking off the foreign domination of the Manchus and restoring Chinese rule.

In the twenties of this century, when the secret societies could function openly, their members were awarded important positions in local and provincial administrations. Deng Wenming was named leader of the "Baojia"[2] control system in his village, Xiexing. But Deng Xiaoping's father was not especially enamoured of the farmer's life, his true interests lying in the military and political realms. Thus, as a young man he had judiciously attached himself to the local military strongman, Yang Sen. He understood early that, even in the smallest hamlet—and Xiexing is tiny, even today—one can be successful only with military power at one's back. This insight turned to bitter reality following suppression of the Taiping uprising against the Manchu rulers in 1864: After the defeat of the Christianized rebels, who honored their leader as the Messiah, militarization in the Ch'ing Empire intensified. If the military powers once commanded their own mercenary armies on the provincial level, landholders now organized private militias of their own on the district and village levels. Out of this mostly ill-paid military rabble emerged a vagabond banditry that extorted ransoms and highway tolls, and plundered and murdered. Deng Wenming's wish for his own military power was, thus, pure self-defense.

Whoever had money and rice enough could pick up soldiers on the street or in the village inn. A person for whom this luxury was beyond reach placed his kin under the protection of a "war-lord," as the military strongmen also were known. Deng Xiao-

**Main section of the horseshoe-shaped Deng house in the
hamlet Xiexing, in the district of Guang'an.**

ping's father's only option was Yang Sen, least of the six great warlords of Szechuan, for Warlord Yang ruled over the Guang'an district where, in 1887, he had been born.[3] In the huge province of Szechuan, he was known by every peasant as a crude, yet glittering figure.

Yang Sen must have gotten on well with Deng's father, who adopted in many respects the progressive ideas of his military foster father and protector. Thus, the warlord favored the abolition of the Confucian educational institutions and the establishment of modern, cosmopolitan middle schools, and he proposed the idea of sending promising young people to study abroad. Even if it was his father who decided that the sixteen-year-old Deng should travel to France, this decision would certainly not have been reached without Yang Sen's influence.

In much the warlord was ahead of his time. He built parks within his domains and ordered sewers installed under the stinking village streets, which he also had widened. He wanted to bring modernity to isolated Szechuan by force: One day he stationed his soldiers at the city gates of Chengdu, where with large specially prepared scissors they cut off the ankle-length gowns of the traditionalists.

Deng Xiaoping's father was, thus, committed to this Yang Sen, for the warlord had extended his hand and helped him rise. Without him, Deng Wenming would not have been able in the year 1928 to become commander of recruit training in the Guang'an district, and commander of a battalion. In that year, Deng's father reached the summit of his power: He commanded 700 soldiers and one year later was military advisor to eight district militias.

To this day, "the Old Man" has a good reputation in his home district. The peasants report candidly that he often went to the teahouse, that he did not disdain liquor, and that he always lent a sympathetic ear to the troubles of the poor, the litter-bearers and the coolies, the day-laborers, and the debt-ridden tenant farmers. He is supposed to have had exceptional skill as an arbitrator and as an even-handed judge. He never broke his word; he never groveled in the dirt or kowtowed to his superiors.

In the stories of the Guang'anese, the man with the walrus moustache, likened to the horns of a water buffalo, lives, not as an *enfant terrible* like the warlord Yang Sen, but as a man commanding respect for all time as an honorable landlord with remarkable military, political, and judicial qualities.[4]

In the year 1938, when the Japanese overran Chinese positions with fixed bayonettes, a local feud cost Deng Wenming his head. The hale old man with his bald pate, which he sometimes tied in a turban Szechuan style, was returning from Chengdu to Xiexing. It was years since he had had to go on foot, and he could likewise eschew horseback, for as a village chief and prominent military personage he had access to a litter and eight bearers. Deng Wenming did not take the road to Chungking and the district capital Guang'an—the only way to reach Xiexing today—but chose instead the direct trail from Chengdu over Nanchong to his village on the east edge of the so-called "Red Basin." For the almost 450 miles, many days' march was required. The hilly and well-watered country forced myriad small detours. Above all, danger lurked everywhere. The traveler had to traverse the territory of brigands and pay passage tolls. Only a few kilometers from his manor, the party fell into an ambush by bandits, who beheaded Deng Wenming without much of a fight.

Deng's father had enemies, not among the poor and destitute, but among the wealthy and the ruthless, notwithstanding that he was known throughout the district as a well-meaning landlord, as a righteous village chief, and as an influential member of a secret society. The envious had been stalking him.

News of the murderous ambush of the renowned landowner spread quickly beyond the borders of the village. Twenty-six-year-old Deng Shuping rushed to the site of the atrocity to recover his father's sundered corpse. Since his older brothers Deng Xiaoping and Deng Ken were at the time pursuing their revolutionary activities, the task of sewing his father's head onto the trunk of his body and laying him out in his bed fell, as the oldest son present in the village, to him. It was equally Shuping's duty to summon the relatives to the wake.

In accordance with the status and position of the venerable old man, Shuping arranged for a group of Taoist monks to perform the ceremony of "Opening the Way," intended to release the soul of the departed. Days and nights on end the clean-shorn monks executed their march around the bier invoking the Buddha. The children, too, and the concubines and uncles and aunts, even the servants, carrying smoking sticks of pungent incense joined in the procession of noisy lamentation. When the hour for the sealing of the casket—a time compatible with the year of birth of the departed—had been determined (normally this took seven weeks), the cortège set out with the heavy wooden casket across the paved court south toward the place where today fruit trees adorn a gentle slope.

To the young Shuping, thrust now by the absence of his two older brothers to the highest position in the clan hierarchy, fell the unhappy task of presiding over the burial ceremony. He was spared at least the obligation of locating a geomantically suitable grave site. His father, in accordance with tradition, had searched this out himself long before his death, and had acquired the ground for an honorable burial mound from his neighbor Xiao Guitang.

Today, the grey gravestone with its three-pronged crown has been restored and inscribed from top to bottom in simple calligraphy with the name Deng Shaochang. Deng Wenming and Deng Shaochang are two names for one and the same person. The former and better-known name (by which his son Deng Xiaoping himself called his father) was used officially, while Shaochang was reserved for kin.

In old China, every child received at matriculation a special, official name for use by his schoolmates and teachers which he maintained all his life. The preference for—really, the overemphasis on—the social name went so far that today the public names—or, rather, the device of rule—of the Ming and Ch'ing emperors are mistakenly taken as their family names. The Chinese revolutionaries evolved their own wrinkle in the bestowal of names. They assumed aliases which in the course of the revolution lost their conspiratorial character and were elevated to public names. In France, as an organized Communist, the landowner's son Deng Xixian called himself Deng Xiaoping. The peasant's son and founder of the Republic Sun Wen assumed the alias Sun Yatsen.

The father had not only chosen his gravesite during his life, but had also ordered how he was to be named on the gravestone. Whether he went to much trouble over his final resting place outside the entrance to the village has not been handed down. But the old peasants in the village relate a legend: When the grave was dug in 1938, a red-gold snake, such as no one in the region of Guang'an had ever seen, wriggled from the soil into the daylight.

The burial mound of Deng Wenming near Xiexing.
The tablet bears the father's unofficial name:
Deng Shaochang.

Since the region lies on the river Qu, even today belief persists stubbornly in the river gods, which appear in serpent form. Particularly in Szechuan, which means, literally translated, "Four River Land," this superstition was widespread. In Chinese mythology, the god of the Yellow River appears as a delicate golden snake with a square head and red dots under its eyes.

Caught up in the serpent cult, the peasants of Xiexing digging the grave interpreted the strange snake slithering out of the bowels of the earth as a sign of the emergence of a great man in the Deng clan.[5]

On the sudden death of his father, this Deng Shuping, youngest son of Lady Tan, inherited the manor house and the ten hectares of land. Thirty-four-year-old Deng Xiaoping did not come into consideration as heir, for a career as a widely traveled Communist lay behind him, and a career as a revolutionary military leader still lay ahead of him. Tan's son, Deng Ken, also called Deng Xianxiu, already had one foot in the camp of revolution. As a socialistically minded teacher, he took part in the struggle against despotic landowners. So he, too, was excluded from consideration as heir.

The acquisition of the manor house would later be held against Deng Shuping by the Communists. This was all the easier for them, for Shuping had also played a managerial role in a district administration of the nationalistic Kuomintang (KMT), and had published the local KMT newspaper "Minsheng Ribao."

The Communist Deng Xiaoping did not rattle any skeletons in his family's closet and drew no class lines there. On the contrary, he used his ascension in the Chinese Communist Party (CCP) to assist his kin. At the beginning of the fifties he arranged for his brother, Shuping, his junior by eight years, and his wife, Lady Xie Jinbi, to be enrolled in a six-month traveling seminar in a so-called "revolutionary university," and to find temporary lodging with him in Chungking.

After the short and intense "denationalization," Shuping received the position of deputy district magistrate in a province neighboring Szechuan. During the Cultural Revolution, these months and years in the service of the Communists were suddenly no longer worth a fen (a penny). Deng Shuping's reactionary class origins, his KMT-membership, and his blood ties with Deng Xiaoping, the "second greatest capitalist despot" in China, made him the target of the Red Guard. Desperate, he committed suicide in 1967.

The life and career of Deng Xiaoping's brother Deng Ken ran a less tragic course. Following the antifeudal revolution of 1911, the authorities in the district capital Guang'an established a girl's school, where in the twenties Deng Ken found his first position. He longed to communicate, but not necessarily through teaching. Thus, he switched from the classroom to the editorial office of the local Kuomintang newspaper. The influence of his older brother, Deng Xiaoping, and the solidarity front between Communists and his party in the war against the Japanese resulted in Deng Ken's turning his back on the Nationalists in 1941, and throwing himself with sudden determination into the bosom of the revolution. Leaving Szechuan, he took his course toward the North to the desolate province of Shaanxi, where Mao Tsetung's base camp Yan'an drew revolutionaries like a magnet. In the "Red Capital" Deng Ken was celebrated as a defector who brought with him a solid professional training. Thanks to his qualifications as both "red and professional," he received the position of editor of what was at that time the most important Communist organ, "Xinhua Ribao," out of which grew the official news agency, "Xinhua" ("New China").

After the Communist seizure of power in 1949, in contrast to his younger brother, he had to submit to no "re-education." He was recognized as belonging to the Yan'an cadre, as among the earliest followers of Mao. Because of his many years of cultural-political activities, the Communist Party promoted him in 1954 to Deputy Director of the Chungking Cultural Office, and subsequently to Deputy Mayor of the city. Shortly before the start of the Cultural Revolution, the Central Party—presumably on account of incorrect politics—transferred him to the position of Assistant Mayor of the industrial city Wuhan. In 1986, Deng Ken was living as an ailing pensioner in Nanjing on the lower reaches of the Yangtze.

Deng Xiaoping's siblings followed differing paths, yet no scion of the great clan learned the farmer's trade, not even his youngest brother, heir to the land and power. Most achieved official posts, but remained always in the second or third rank. Only Deng Xiaoping represents an exception in the family. He worked his way up through perseverence. His star rose slowly, but higher eventually than any member of the Deng clan, even Deng Xiao-ping's ancestor Deng Shimin, had ever achieved.

The fall of the Manchu Ch'ing Dynasty was still far in the future when, barely thirty-five years old, Deng Shimin, also called Xunzhai, took part in the imperial civil service examinations in the imperial capital, and in the year 1736 passed the palace examination presided over by the emperor. On account of his exceptional aptitude, the Qianlong Emperor appointed the young man compiler of the second class in the National Academy. The career of Deng's ancestor at the imperial court evolved extraordinarily rapidly: In 1738 he was appointed examiner for the examinations of provincial capitals, and just seven years later, president of the supreme court. He resigned this office for family reasons and returned to Guang'an. But in 1766, the emperor recalled him to the court in Peking, and for eight years until he went into retirement Deng Shimin carried out the duties of the highest office in the empire.[6]

To this day, even progressive Chinese maintain that the children of concubines are more intelligent than those of a principal wife. The Deng clan does not confirm this widely held opinion unambiguously. After the founding of the new China, Deng Xiaoping's step-brother Xianqing—only child of the second concubine, Xiao—entered upon the career of financial bookkeeper in the Southwest Office of the CCP. His elder sister Xianlie was prostituted by their father to the landowner Tang Huiming in order to increase the power of his clan.

Deng Xiaoping's natural mother, Tan, doubtless had the warmest relationship to his father. She bore him a daughter and three sons. Two boys were born to his third concubine, Xia Bogen (of which the elder, Deng Xianrong, died in infancy), and two girls, whose names remain publicly unknown. Her second son, named Deng Xianqun, works today in the cadre of the CCP in the northern industrial city Tianjin. Xia Bogen brought her daughter from her first marriage, Deng Xianfu, into the Deng household. Perhaps the Deng clan would have evolved differently had the principal wife, Zhang, not been barren. What is certain is that thereby the Deng concubines assumed an unusually high status in the family.

Between 1950 and 1952, shortly after the Communist seizure of power, Deng Xiaoping used his position as chief functionary of the CCP in the southwest to bring his family to Chungking. Only his uncle and aunt remained in Guang'an. Even today, many relatives of the Deng clan live in the Yangtze city, or in Chengdu, provincial capital of Szechuan. In 1986, Deng Xiaoping's stepmother, the third concubine, Xia Bogen, was living with him and his family in Peking.

THREE

Precocious Abroad

THOUGH THE VILLAGE of Xiexing was tiny and isolated, it had a private teacher and a little Confucian school. Deng Xiaoping learned to form his first characters with brush and ink in the charge of this teacher, and attended the Confucian school as well. He must have had a good introduction to calligraphy, for even now in advanced age his handwriting is forceful and distinctive.

Something extraordinary occurred when Deng Xiaoping was just eight years old. On their way home from the village school— so the story goes—a good friend suddenly broke down crying, revealing through tears that his younger sister, his Meimei, lay feverish and seriously ill in bed. His schoolmate, from a poor family, was certain that lacking medical attention she was lost. Little Deng listened to these grave words in silence, then departed quickly. Hardly had he entered his classroom the next morning than he motioned for his friend to come over and secretly pressed five silver dollars into his hand. The eight-year-old had stolen this small fortune, which might have bought 50 pounds of rice, from his father's cashbox.

Deng Wenming noticed the missing cash a few days later and angrily summoned family and servants together. Before he could utter his first threat, the little thief stepped forward and handed the stern family chief a switch. He bore the strokes in silence, tears in his eyes, holding himself straight as "an ink brush." Though his father's anger waned, he was still confused. Now after the fact he posed a few trenchant questions, in reply to which the son haltingly related the story of want and mortal illness in the house of his friend. Deng Wenming interrupted him after only a few sentences, opining drily that he had done right. But "the old man" wished to know why his son had accepted the punishment without explaining or crying out. The boy replied that a thief must at all events be punished, the law requires it. He deserved the whipping, and only a good-for-nothing would cry over it.

Not only Deng Xiaoping's stern father, but also his military protector, the progressive local warlord Yang Sen, made the education of the children of the entire district his concern. Cosmopolitan in outlook, he gave an ear to the Catholic misionaries in Guang'an. As early as 1869 the French Catholic Father Jean Bompas had founded the "Koang-gan-tcheou" parish. Deng Xiaoping's home district evolved from that time forward into an important Catholic center, where until 1938 the French Father Louis Combe and four Chinese priests ministered to the spiritual needs of over 5,000 Chinese Christians.[1]

The father wanted to provide the best conceivable education for his eldest son, and soon sent him to the newly founded middle school in the small district capital eight kilometers away. Deng Xiaoping lived at this school as in a boarding school, making his way back down the narrow path to Xiexing only on weekends.

The Guang'an middle school, built in the European style on a small hill, collaborated closely with the Catholic mission. When the young Deng matriculated there, the French Fathers Émile Viret and Louis Combe were serving the parish. During his school years, the Guang'an parish belonged to the French Catholic mission "Sutchuen Occidental," which occupied the region of the provincial capital, Chengdu, and numbered 45,000 Christian souls.

The Confucian tradition was not dominant in Deng Xiaoping's education, but played a role subordinate to the Christian orientation of the French missionaries and the revolutionary ideas of the founder of the republic, Sun Yatsen. Deng was fortunate not to have been born, like Mao Tsetung, into the world of the nineteenth century. He would have had to sit much longer on the benches of some Confucian school, interpreting a sentence or even just a few characters out of the old books according to a rigidly established, eightfold schema, and learning the elite, stenographic literary language of the upper class.

Deng Xiaoping is a child of change, born on the eve of that short-lived revolution which sundered China's feudal chains. He was just one year old when the "fever" spread through the cities

Deng Xiaoping's middle school in a European building
(west side) in the district capital Guang'an.

and villages of the province: In newspapers and on posters, through word-of-mouth propaganda and business deals, every Szechuanese was called on to contribute to the expansion of the railway system. Progressives of the time compared the river junks, even the Yangtze steamers, to lame water buffalo. In truth, shipping on the Yangtze, Szechuan's main traffic artery, was simply no longer equal to the explosion of trade and the rapid exchange of goods. In order not to be cut off from progress, the province required a modern infrastructure. Recognizing this, the Szechuanese frantically gathered money, lots of money. In the currency of that time, by 1909 forty million ounces of bulk-silver had been accumulated. The largest share had been invested in railroad stocks by wealthy merchants and traders, officials, and Mandarins. As soon as the news leaked out that the entire amount had been lost in shady speculations on the Shanghai stockmarket, an outcry arose throughout the province.

When barely two years later the bankrupt imperial court under foreign pressure announced the nationalization of the railroads, shopkeepers and street merchants refused to pay taxes to the Ch'ing government. From their action a movement arose that spread throughout South China.

Alarmed by the revolt of the people, the Ch'ing court dispatched large contingents of soldiers to remote Szechuan. The most combat-effective contingents were diverted from the province of Hubei with its railway hub, Wuchang. In the absence of a ruling hand of authority, one battalion mutinied on the night of October 10, 1911, and after a night battle occupied the palace of the most powerful governor of South China. As a result of this revolutionary coup, originating in Deng Xiaoping's home province, the last dynasty, long in a state of decay, fell in ruins.

With the fall of the Manchu ruling house, the Szechuanese changed in appearance. The committed cut off their pigtails, their *bianzi,* liberating themselves from a foreign stigma the Manchus had prescribed for all Chinese on pain of death. The uncommitted, though they could not go so far, put up their pigtails with a chopstick.

The republican revolution of 1911 went up in a puff of smoke like a skyrocket. It lacked the impetus needed to evolve into a bourgeois revolution. Chinese youth profited from the fall of the monarchy, Deng Xiaoping among them, for education underwent a reform. Otherwise, things at home stayed pretty much the same. Administration remained in the hands of the military strongmen, who ruled their "kingdoms independent" of the central government as they had from time immemorial, regardless of whether corrupt Mandarins and officials sat in the Yamen (municipal council) in Peking or Chengdu, sucking on opium pipes, rather than opening wide the gates to the modern age.

The youth of Szechuan were known as cosmopolitan, but Szechuan's situation after the short-lived revolution was muddled, because the local military strong-men continued warring on each other, as they had during the time of the Ch'ing monarchy, and with fixed bayonettes forced the millions of starving peasants to work. Youthful, modern-thinking people no longer saw any future here, and oriented themselves toward revolutionaries and cosmopolites. In the wake of the anti-imperialist "May 4th" movement of 1919, it was the fashion among educated youth to go abroad penuriously, aligning themselves with the "work-study" movement.

Not in Szechuan alone, but also in Hunan, Mao Tsetung's home province, young people spoke of the "Qingong Jianxue" movement. As youth leader, the twenty-five-year-old Mao organized the revolutionary youth group "New People's Study Society," a forerunner of the "Qingong Jianxue" movement. To be sure, because he himself was both poor and indispensible, the Hunan peasant's son arranged foreign travel only for others.

In the province of Szechuan, it was an elderly man who served as model for the young people, an educator by the name of Wu Yuzhang. A democrat, he was a follower of Sun Yatsen, who placed himself in opposition to the mounting efforts to restore the monarchy.

In December 1915, China's most powerful military leader, Yuan Shikai, had had himself declared emperor in Peking. Though for historians of China, Yuan Shikai's puppet monarchy is merely an interlude, to the Szechuanese educator and his study program "Qingong Jianxue," it represented a vital threat, for from 1914 on, Wu was being hunted under government warrant. To save his life, he had to escape abroad. It was no coincidence that he went to France, for many Chinese lived in Paris, and relations between the two countries had for some time been developing favorably. There he befriended the two fathers of Franco-Chinese cooperation, Li Yuying and Cai Yuanpei. Together with the ethics professor Cai, in 1912 the philanthropist Li had founded the "Société chinoise d'éducation rationelle française." Li and Cai (who had studied in Leipzig and Berlin) functioned as the most popular representatives of the Chinese Republic in Europe.

Prior to the First World War, the term "Qingong Jianxue" still retained its original meaning: work-study. But by the time of Deng Xiaoping's arrival in France in 1920, combining work and study was no longer practicable. The devastating war had altered the "Grande Nation," the economic situation looked bleak in the winter of 1920-21. The situation took so catastrophic a turn that even in China newspapers reported on "Qingong Jianxue." "Of the 1,500 work-study students in France," reported the Shanghai newspaper "Shen Bao" of February 30, 1921, "only some 300 have obtained jobs in factories. The great majority waits for months in vain for employment." Many Chinese, it appeared, had fallen on desperate times.

The Paris police registered the first suicides in Chinatown. One impoverished student, taken to a hospital for emergency surgery, but unable to pay the expenses of treatment, was transferred to the poor house, where he shortly died. A Szechuanese collapsed and died in a bistro. When the proprietor telephoned the Chinese embassy, he met only indifference. No one bothered about the body. Hundreds, dreaming of their daily bowls of rice, went hungry, and were long since beyond any condition in which study was possible.

This notorious penuriousness resulted in the evolution among foreign students of a two-class system. From 1921 on, students in the true sense of the word came only from wealthy families, for room, board, and student fees cost a good 1,000 yuan a year. For so princely a sum, a middle-class merchant in Shanghai or Chengdu would have had to work nearly a year and a half. Not politics, but money became the censor that disallowed even young people from families as well-to-do as Deng Xiaoping's their studies. Material want had an enormous influence on the radicalization and politicizing of the group of "Qingong Jianxue" activists, left financially to their own devices. Likewise, the radicalization of the barely 16-year-old Deng is largely to be ascribed to his frugal, at times miserable, existence as an ill-paid foreign worker in France.

The inhumane situation went so far that the Chinese Communists broadcast the slogan: "Fight for your existence and for the right to study." In a program of action they demanded that over the course of four years every "Qingong Jianxue" activist receive 400 francs per month from the Chinese government. Further, they demanded admission to the anticipated "Université franco-chinoise de Lyon."

The work-study students had placed all their hope in this binational academic institution. Here they thought finally to study, and thereby break out of the mindless daily round of the laborer. Deng, too, wished one day to be able to study in Lyon.

What a disillusionment to read in a statement from the rector, issued only days before the formal opening on September 24, 1921, that the university was open only to students with secondary school diplomas, and that every matriculating student would have to raise money sufficient for his living expenses and submit to an entrance examination.

Although the Communists held a protest demonstration on the grounds of the university, the Chinese administration refused admission to the "Qingong Jianxue" activists. They called in the police, who arrested the 104 demonstrators and deported them to China in October 1921.[2]

The Szechuanese educator Wu Yuzhang could not watch the collapse of the "work-study" movement. Shortly after the death of the self-proclaimed emperor, he returned to China and founded preparatory schools in Chengdu and Chungking for the work-study program in France.

The hundred young Szechuanese who presented themselves in the spring of 1919 in Chungking for a rather unusual examination were still virtually children. Never before had young Chinese been examined here in French, mathematics, and economics, never before in this city had there been a preparatory school for study abroad.

One student was absent when the examination sheets were distributed: fourteen-year-old Deng Xiaoping from the district of Guang'an. He took an individual examination only later and then joined the preparatory class for the "Qingong Jianxue" program as its youngest student. The boyishly diminutive, but precocious, Guang'anese brought with him a good preparation for the "work-study" program in France, for he had already had contact with the French Fathers of the mission. He had also had instruction in the middle school in mathematics, modern Chinese, geography, and physics. Little Deng worked assiduously, and many years later, one of his schoolmates recalled: "Comrade Deng Xiaoping reported somewhat later for the preparatory class. Though energetic, he was taciturn, but he studied very diligently."[3]

It took eighteen months to prepare the students for their stay in France and to teach them elementary language skills. Deng Xiaoping's time in preparation passed quickly with a full schedule and an intense communal life in the boarding school. One problem plagued many of the first class of students, though not Deng: finances. The local chamber of commerce and individual entrepreneurs contributed 100 yuan toward the travel expenses of each work-study candidate. An additional 200 yuan were required, however, and these the young people had to pay out of their own pockets. At his son's departure, father Deng Wenming had provided for him, not lavishly, but comfortably.

In the years 1919 and 1920, Bodard, the French Consul in the provincial capital, carried on an active correspondence with the preparatory schools in Chengdu and Chungking. His consulate had to issue the visas for a total of 378 work-study candidates, including the visa for Deng Xiaoping, who still went by the name Deng Xixian, listing his date of birth on the official form as July 12, 1904.

By the first days of September 1920, things had finally progressed to the point of embarkation. A rusty Yangtze steamer ventured out into the grey-brown eddying current, docking in Wuhan after several days' journey. Deng Xiaoping stood on board with his class. The young people had still only heard tell of the legendary "three gorges." Legends and tales had circulated for ages in the province of the slumbering dragon and of the hidden book of war strategies of the famous chancellor Zhuge Liang (181-234). Now the young pioneers would experience at first hand the mighty waterway coursing furiously through a precipitous mountain wall.

The Yangtze gorges had been passed, the homeland vanished behind a milennia-old barrier. Ahead of the adventurous group of travelers lay the gateway to the West, the exciting port city of Shanghai. Although a walk down the cosmopolitan strand boulevard "Bund" was certainly not comparable to strolling along the urbane Champs-Élysées, nevertheless it signified for the young Szechuanese, saturated with book learning, a first glance into a kaleidoscope of western architecture and European manners.

Such a bewildering world opened itself there to the young boys from the country: the Palace and Cathay Hotels, the massive bell tower known universally simply as "Big Ch'ing," the monumental customs house, the gothically inspired dome of the Commercial Bank. Many splendid buildings in tudor style, lined up like grey tin soldiers. In the shade of the plane trees, light-footed, ragged coolies pulled Europeans wearing white double-breasted suits through the throng in rickshaws. Isolated automobiles forced their way through the sea of people, like the belching steamers in the swarm of dilapidated junks on the Huangpu.

For the group from the rural province of Szechuan, the brief layover in Shanghai became a moment of acclimatization. There was little time for a tour of the city, for passage on the steamer had been booked, and the departure long since arranged by the local representatives of the "Qingong Jianxue" movement. Most Chinese students traveling abroad from Shanghai went to Japan, to Europe, to the United States, and, from 1921 on, also to Socialist Russia.

On September 11, 1920, young Deng boarded the French ocean cruiser "André Lepon" as part of a group of 85 work-study candidates. The Szechuanese group, thrown together with work-study candidates from every conceivable part of the country, went directly below decks. That was where the special "student class" was. Passage cost 100 yuan. The Franco-Chinese societies had negotiated this favorable price with the steamship company. The fare could be that low because the work-study movement had such an enormous draw: In the year 1920 alone ten groups with a hundred Chinese each traveled from Shanghai to France. The year before, there had been just as many.

The modern steamer took barely 40 days to travel the fully 15,500 kilometers from Shanghai to Marseille. Before passing the Suez Canal, it dropped anchor in Hongkong, Saigon, Singapore, and Colombo, capital of Ceylon.

Ship's passage round half the world was in such demand that a second French steamer, the "Porthos," began operating between the two international ports. This ship, with its two mighty smokestacks, looked like the "Titanic" in miniature. The two cruisers offered passengers every imaginable luxury—provided they could pay. The Parisians, Lyonaises, Bretons, and Marseillaises berthed on the upper deck were traveling not as tourists, for pleasure, but were en route between the French concession in Shanghai and their homeland. On the "Porthos," the 22-year-old Zhou Enlai had also traveled to France—even before the 16-year-old Deng.

The fares of the Szechuanese foreign students abroad who sailed out onto the Pacific on the afternoon of September 11 had been paid by the president of the Chungking Chamber of Commerce. They traveled in two groups. The government had assembled the one, providing 400 yuan; the other traveled at its own volition and expense. Deng Xiaoping and one other boy from Guang'an belonged to this one.

Deng was recognizable from afar, for he was by far the smallest in his group. No one thought even remotely of choosing this stripling to be leader of the group of eighty-five. Later Deng Xiaoping was very exaggeratedly characterized as group leader and credited with an above-average organizational talent already in this time period. So wrote the former work-study student Li Huang:

> At the request of Mr. Li Yuying, I traveled [from Paris] to Marseille to pick up Chinese students from the ship for the first time. At that time I met Deng Xiaoping. Fully 200 students had arrived on the steamer, of which about 90 were from Szechuan. Deng Xiaoping was the first to disembark and informed me that there were 90 compatriots from his home province. He told me that he had organized everything, that each group comprised ten people, and that there were nine groups in all. Their baggage was divided into nine piles, so that I could conduct one group after the other ashore and to customs.
>
> With such excellent organization, it was not difficult for me to bring the 90 people ashore in orderly fashion. There, everyone waited with his luggage for the bus that would take us to the train station.[4]

When the "André Lepon" sailed into the harbor at Marseille Chinese faces were visible on the quay; representatives of the Franco-Chinese educational society stood expectantly behind the barrier to receive the excited new arrivals. The program representatives had undertaken the long trip from Paris by train. Since they spoke French fluently and knew the passport formalities precisely, the young Chinese students soon stood with their scanty luggage on French soil. They were taken by bus to their cheap lodgings, and after an initial rest period, the groups set out on a sight-seeing tour of the Mediterranean port city with its dives reminiscent of the orient, and its cathedral in the Romanesque-Provençal style.

The young people from exhausted, impoverished China, which the Europeans after the war knew only as "the sick man of the East," had come to France full of expectations. Already on their tour of Marseille many of their illusions surely burst like soap bubbles. They saw the unemployed blacks, the Spaniards, and Algerians, who wiled away their day with a baguette and a glass of red wine. And their guides, experienced in the ways of France, expressed the view that prospects of study were virtually nil. A person had to be happy if he could earn a living by the work of his hands.

Marseille served as the locus of only their first, fleeting encounter with the West. They proceeded quickly by train to bewildering Paris. Once the train had pulled into the Gare de Lyon, the gawking Chinese had to descend into the tunnel of the métro, for the cheapest way to their destination in the westerly suburb led by subway to the Gare Saint-Lazare. From there, they rode aboveground 13 kilometers further to the station La Garenne-Colombes.

Fifteen minutes on foot through a residential area and the group stood before a two-story, middle-class residence. Here, at number 39, rue de la Pointe, which came out of the Second World War as rue Médéric, was the headquarters of the Franco-Chinese society. From the outside, nothing was visible of the multifarious inner life of the house, which stretched from cellar to attic.

There was a constant coming and going. Some inquired after mail from home, others worked at the printing press or visited the library of the house. Still others gathered for meetings on the top floor. And then there was also a small group of functionaries living there. Even the Communists felt at home in the unassuming villa. It was the seat at the same time of the three most important Franco-Chinese organizations, the "Société d'Éducation Franco-Chinoise" (SEFC), the "Comité Franco-Chinois de Patronage" (CFC), and the "Association Amicale et de Patronage Franco-

View through the gate of the former Chinese Center in
the Parisian suburb La Garenne-Colombes, Rue de
la Pointe No. 39.

Chinoise" (AAFC). One of those who would soon be coming and going in this residence, eventually even living here, was Deng Xiaoping.

On December 18, 1920, he registered with the French alien's registration office. The official on duty entered under the number 140 what he dictated: "Nom: Teng; Prénoms: Hi Hien; Nationalité: Chinois; Naissance: 12 juillet 1904 à Sé-Tchouan (Chine) de Teng-Win-Ming et de Tain-Ché-Teng."[5]

Deng's years in France were to be years of wandering, broken up into brief episodes and month or even only week-long stays in various places. The young Szechuanese never learned the patience to stay put, but, worse, he often had neither work nor financial support from the Franco-Chinese societies.

For lack of funds, the SEFC was forced to carry on its language courses in small towns far from the expensive streets of Paris. So Deng's first way station in France lay in windy Normandy, in the town of Bayeux, 40 kilometers west of Caen. Here he attended a special French course for foreigners, established at a public high school with support from the SEFC. He lasted just three months at his school desk before penury drove him back to the Chinese center at La Garenne-Colombes. His compatriots in the Rue de la Pointe could not offer him much. All they had in the way of employment opportunities was a couple of unskilled jobs. A real apprentice position, or even a program of work-study were total luxuries, the people in charge told him, and for a start handed him an address.

In the city Le Creusot in far-off Burgundy there happened to be work in the armament factory of Schneider-Creusot. For many years now the internationally known enterprise had employed Chinese and other foreign workers. So no curious heads turned when the Chinese, on April 1, 1921, walked into the factory hall. The unschooled young man employed his work time diligently from the first day. He learned filing, turning, drilling, punching—in short, everything a metalworker has to know. But once again, time did not allow him to complete a proper education. Already on April 23 he quit his position.

In and of itself, this three-week stint was no more than an interlude. But seen from the perspective of today, it represents a consequential period of his life: Deng learned here the essential elements of the metalworker's trade, skills he would use in the future during the Cultural Revolution. He also had his first experiences among the French industrial proletariat. Finally, he befriended older, more mature Chinese Communists who played a leading role in France and after 1927 in China.[6]

Just why Deng picked up and left after only three weeks, no one at Schneider-Creusot knows any more. We can assume that from May on he received a temporary monthly stipend of 120 francs through the Franco-Chinese organizations. Until February 1922, he lived in Paris and in the Paris suburb La Garenne-Colombes, working here and there, as a waiter, for example, and as a railway conductor.

The stocky, baby-faced seventeen-year-old knew precisely where he was going as he walked from the main hall of the unadorned, small-town train station. During the ninety-minute trip from the Gare de Lyon in Paris to the town of Montargis he had once more gone over in his mind the instructions of his comrades in the Rue de la Pointe. As a Chinese, he attracted no particular attention here, for Montargis prided itself on its "Chinese" past (established by way of the philanthropist Li Yuying). The young man nevertheless attracted some attention, for at barely 4'11" he was remarkably short even for a Chinese. Eschewing the expensive carriages, he went on foot. His destination lay only five kilometers from the station. At first he followed the Paris-Lyon highway, but soon left it on his left hand heading straight on toward the center of town, turning right toward Chalette just before the canal. He climbed a gentle slope, then had to ask after the town hall. Everyone knew the way, for Chalette comprised just 3,000 souls. At the registration office he put down his name, "Teng Hi Hien," under the number 22 in the town's alien-register. As prescribed, he listed the names of his father and mother and his date of birth. In the column "arrived from" the official noted, "La Garenne-Colombes, 39, rue de la Pointe." As file number of his identification card, he put down 1250 394.

The new arrival must have spent the night in a pension or with friends, for the interview with his new employer was to take place only the following day, February 14, 1922. His job at the Hutchinson rubber goods factory was his second with a large concern after the arms manufacturer Schneider-Creusot. Hutchinson—trademark today of an international concern with 9,000 employees—was a big name already at that time. While today it produces everything from pacifiers to PVC-fittings, in Deng's time the concern had just two big sellers—rubber overshoes and bicycle tubes and tires.

Thanks to an earlier devastating fire in the india rubber warehouse of the "Compagnie Nationale du Caoutchouc Souple Hutchinson Henderson & Cie," the workplace of laborer Deng in the department "Chaussures" was not located inside damp, ancient walls, but in a bright, high-ceilinged hall. The roof over his head rested on trusses designed by the father of modern steel construction, Gustave Eiffel.

Since the young Chinese could not point to any special training, the personnel office assigned him as unskilled labor under the number 4088 to the production of rubbers, and not like so many other Chinese to the division "vélo" or to the area "technique." As one of 4,000 workers, after completing his allotted work, Deng was handed his pay envelope. On the top floor of the extensive hall, which today stores only empty cartons, Poles, Yugoslavians, Russians, Chileans, and, of course, Chinese glued and assembled rubber parts into waterproof overshoes. In mindless piecework, the army of ill-paid foreign workers, among whom the Russians and Chileans were refugees, daily completed 5,000 pairs of overshoes. Every day women and men alike stood ten hours in a row at long tables, repeating over and over again the same manipulations: the soles, the insoles, then drawing the leg over a wooden mold and gluing in the lining. Nimble hands were needed. Perhaps for this very reason personnel had assigned the diminutive Deng to the division "Chaussures."

After work he did not have far to go home. He lived across the street: in front of the factory gate stretched the barracks area Langlée. Deng Xiaoping and many of the 43 Chinese whom management had hired in the spring of 1922 inhabited the "Chinese barracks" where they lived together. The accommodations were also cheap, in any case far cheaper than a pension or a hotel in nearby Montargis, the locus of Deng's nightschool, the Collège de Montargis.

At the school near the church he improved his French and often spent his spare time with friends who lived here in the

Employment card of the rubber overshoe factory of
Hutchinson in Chalette for "Teng Hi Hien" (Deng Xixian). The date of birth, "12 juillet 1904," corresponds
to the Chinese lunar calender. Deng was twice employed
(the first date is crossed out) in the division "Chaussures." "Refuses to work, not to be rehired," reads the
notation of the personnel office.

The factory hall for "Chaussures," designed by Gustave Eiffel; here Deng Xixian worked at the assembly of rubber overshoes.

Chinese work-study students in front of the "Collège de Montargis." Third from the right in the last row is Deng Xiaoping. In the first row, school director Piatier with his family.

"Chinese dormitory." Many among the Parisian Chinese, Zhou Enlai for instance, enjoyed coming out to Montargis on weekends for conversation or a game of tennis.

By November 3, Deng Xiaoping decided once again to change his place of residence. He registered his departure at the town hall, having quit his job at Hutchinson already on October 17. During this time the diminutive Chinese had matured under the hard work and the primitive living conditions, and he dressed with greater self-assurance and presented a more secure appearance. With his passable French, his considerable experience gained in traveling through Normandy and Burgundy, and in living in the metropolis of Paris, he now moved about "like a fish in water." After several months in France, he had developed an enduring preference, persisting into old age, not for the black, unfiltered coffee or the glass of red wine, but for the delicate croissants. In 1974, Deng Xiaoping, having as acting premier addressed the UN Raw Materials Conference in New York, did not take the westward route on his return flight home, but flew east in the direction of Paris. He used his New York *per diem,* not more than 30 yuan, to have a box of a hundred crisp croissants delivered to him on board the airplane at the layover in Paris. "How bourgeois!" the Red Guard would have sneered just five years earlier. Now, with the Cultural Revolution behind him, Deng could return to Peking with his fine French pastry well intact. Generously, he distributed the dainty crescents to the ailing Zhou Enlai and his old comrades in arms from the Paris days.

At the start of the winter of 1922, the peripatetic Szechuanese had first to take the train north to Paris, even though he was heading east in the direction of Dijon. Only by changing trains could he reach his destination. Traveling from the industrial town of Chalette, Deng arrived after a circuitous journey at the village of Châtillon on the upper Seine.

Neither the local metalworks nor the rich agriculture interested him. He had come to broaden his knowledge of French. On the recommendation of the SEFC he paid his tuition and registered at the upper school. The little town with its 4,000 inhabitants was hardly different from Bayeux, his first stopping place in France. Since he had not come to Châtillon-sur-Seine as a pupil, the school administration placed more stringent requirements on him. He attended the Lyceum and sat in a regular class among tall young

Frenchmen. The picturesque Burgundian village offered inexpensive accomodations, and even the school expenses were not too expensive. For this very reason the Franco-Chinese societies had established a relationship with the Lyceum at Châtillon. The peacefulness and provinciality there must have bored Deng, for four months later he again packed his bags.

Deng Xiaoping knew the way from railway station to town hall in his sleep as on February 1, 1923, he registered with the authorities in Chalette for the second time. He had returned to the little industrial town. This time he registered in the alien's register under the number 118. The next morning, he sought out his old plant, and was promptly engaged, though for a limited period only. At personnel, everything went quickly; the card with the dates of his first employment needed only to be corrected; even the division was the same.

Only Deng was not the same. He had grown refractory and rebellious, management would surely have said. If one is to believe his employment card, Deng Xiaoping must soon have been unemployed because he refused the work. His revolt must have been an individual protest action, for nothing is known of a strike or any other workers' action in the division "Chaussures." In any event, after barely five weeks, on March 7, 1923, the management put the lone fighter summarily on the street. With the summary dismissal, naturally he also had to leave the "Chinese barracks" and seek lodging with friends. Most probably he lived during the four months until his final departure from Montargis on June 11 at the Collège des Ortes. A "Chinese dormitory" had existed there since 1914.

Subsequent visits were weekend excursions; Deng never again lived in Montargis or Chalette. Both places must of course have meant a great deal to him or he would not, in August 1985, have sent his paraplegic and favorite son, Deng Pufang, there on a visit.

After his firing and months of unemployment, the revolutionary laborer went underground in Paris. He had re-registered himself with the authorities at Chalette as moving to La Garenne-Colombes, Rue de la Pointe No. 39. Here in the Chinese center, which functioned temporarily also as headquarters for the Communists, Deng Xiaoping was by now a well-known and welcome guest. In the socialist youth movement, the nineteen-year-old numbered among its most active members. He understood uncommonly well how to make himself useful to the comrades five or six years his senior in the leadership. Thanks to his practical skills, his sharp tongue, and the departure of important members of the cadre for Moscow or China, Deng Xiaoping advanced into the hard core of Chinese Communists in France.

FOUR

From Laborer to "Doctor of Duplication"

I N THE FALL of 1920, Deng Xiaoping landed at Marseille. One year later, he would be followed by two young comrades who were soon to play significant roles in the Chinese Communist movement. One was Chen Yannian, the other, Chen Qiaonian. The brothers Chen were sons of a famous father, Chen Duxiu, the first Chinese Marxist. Chen Duxiu knew France well; he had lived there between 1907 and 1910. At home he was known by every progressive intellectual as publisher of the journal "New Youth."

Soon after their arrival, the brothers opened a small left-wing bookshop in Paris which displayed not only their father's writings, but the journals of the French Communists as well. The shop flourished, developing into a meeting place for the left-wing Chinese scene. Around the brothers Chen gathered the avant-garde of the Chinese revolutionaries, including Zhou Enlai and three others of the cadre.[1]

In October 1921, at La Garenne-Colombes, this circle established the "Communist Youth Party of China," which a year later numbered fully 70 members and sympathisers.[2] In the winter of 1922, the Central Committee (CC) of the CCP in Shanghai instructed comrades in Europe to rename their youth party the "Communist Youth League of China in Europe." As though on instructions from afar, they transformed the "Chinese Communist Circle in Europe" into the "Central Organization of the CCP in

Europe," divided into a main cell in Paris, an associate cell in Brussels, and a third cell in Berlin.

Zhou Enlai functioned initially as secretary of the Youth League. The "Central Organization of the CCP in Europe" operated parallel to, or, more precisely, over the League. For the building of this organization, smaller by far and less well-known than the Youth League, Chen Yannian had initially been assigned as executive member.

Once this CP offspring got over its growing pains, Zhou Enlai left the Youth League's leadership to become secretary of the mother organization. In the wake of a reshuffling of personnel following the early departure of several leaders, Deng Xiaoping got his chance: In 1924 he was co-opted into the "Central Organization of the CCP in Europe." Since that year he has been an official member of the largest Communist party in the world.

Already one year earlier, the second Conference of Youth Delegates had elected him to the leadership of the Youth League, to which he had belonged since 1922. Thus, three years after his arrival in France, his actual career as organized Communist began. The Delegates' Conference had elected him executive member-at-large in June 1923. Not yet 19 years old, he found himself together with the League's secretary, Zhou Enlai, and three other members of the cadre in a position of leadership.

The furthest reaching decision of the youth delegates, who had come from Germany, Belgium, and all of France, was the renaming of the journal "Shao Nian Bao," known also as "La Jeunesse," to "Chiguang" (Red Light). On February 1, 1924, after a delay of eight months, the first issue of "Chiguang" appeared. The new biweekly, published jointly by the Central Organization of the CCP and the Youth League, appeared more militant, more topical, more agitatorial. If "Youth" had seen itself as a newsletter for the strategy of the Communist International and the CCP, the goal of "Chiguang" consisted "in the unification of the middle class against the rule of the military strongmen [in China] and in international unification against imperialism."

Deng Xiaoping, youngest and least experienced of all, now belonged to the new editorial board. None other than Zhou Enlai provided the substance of the journal: In 15 editions, he authored 37 articles by himself. Deng Xiaoping operated quietly, patiently, assiduously in the background. With a skilled hand, he engraved

In this pension at No. 17, Rue Godefroy, lived Enlai;
here Deng Xiaoping worked as "Doctor of Duplication."

character after character into the wax stencils he later reproduced on a primitive duplicator. Zhou Enlai's room on the third floor of No. 17 Rue Godefroy served as a makeshift editorial office.

Zhou, the editorial writer, Zhao Shiyan, responsible for legal matters, and Deng Xiaoping, the doer, formed an effective team. The work seemed to suit the nineteen-year-old Deng best. He garnered much praise and rose to be coordinator of propaganda operations. In this new position, he had greater prerogatives. He could commission articles, edit them, or write them himself. He wrote infrequently, however, remaining mostly at his handwork engraving thousands upon thousands of characters into the stencils.

> He drew each stroke beautifully and clearly. He per-
> formed even the duplication so well one might have thought
> each copy printed on a letter-press. In recognition of this
> excellent work, Comrade Deng Xiaoping was dubbed, "Doc-
> tor of Duplication."[3]

The mimeographed issues of "Chiguang" aroused lively interest among the 1,500 "Qingong Jianxue" activists, the students and the foreign workers. Most Chinese were interested in the politics and current events in their homeland. Of course the colony was not a homogeneous group. Fully 30 organizations, unions, and clubs with their own publications struggled for attention. There was marked competition in the Chinese camp.

Revolutionaries agitated on the left of the political spectrum; on the right, it was former Kuomintang members expelled for their opposition to Sun Yatsen's unified front with the Communists. They organized themselves in December 1923 into the Chinese youth party "Qingnian Dang," and published the journal "Voices of the Pioneers." The Communists and the Etatists, as those on the right soon came to be called, avoided each other on the street. A deep-seated animosity eventually grew out of their divergent world views.

The entire issue No. 18 of "Chiguang" was devoted to an ideological settling of accounts with the right. "The Etatists," one article declared, "exploit the anti-Communist slander of several of the rightist elements expelled from the Kuomintang to spread the rumor that following a successful revolution, the Communists installed themselves like magpies in the turtledove's nest. They

Memorial edition on the death of Sun Yatsen of the journal *Chiguang*, for which the stencils were produced by Deng Xiaoping, "Doctor of Duplication."

wished to kill Sun Yatsen and make him a sacrifice to the red flag." The slander was mutual; vilification took the upper hand.

Now even the "Doctor of Duplication" entered the debate. Under his birth name, Deng Xixian, he published in Nos. 18 and 21 the articles, "The Unscrupulous Campaign of Slander of the Counter-Revolutionary Youth Party!" and "The First Lies of the Journal 'Voice of the Pioneers!'"

Deng Xiaoping did not write strictly along party lines, but tried to counter the lies about the situation in China by appeals to the reader's moral sense. "The youth party," he wrote indignantly, "pretends to be the leader of the Chinese living in France and aspires to save China. At their gala on the national day of celebration, wonderful pieces of music were played, fascinating theatrical performances were put on, and everyone danced gaily. To depict this colorful evening of October 10 as a ceremony for the Chinese living in France, however, is sheer hypocrisy when one considers that in the north and south of our homeland wars are being waged. Under such circumstances, how could one stage a ball in the glittering metropolis?"

Deng knew whereof he wrote, for he had attended the colorful evening—not to dance, but to disrupt. Together with a group of comrades, he had forced his way into the festival hall, loudly demanding that the flag of the military Beiyang government be taken down and replaced with that of the revolutionary Canton government of Sun Yatsen. The festival guests refused to make the exchange, whereupon the Communists shouted the slogan "Down with the chained dogs of Beiyang!" and left the hall.

The Etatists had become the chief enemies of the Communists. Verbal scuffles first grew into fistfights and, soon afterwards, even armed clashes. The first serious incident occured at a meeting of the "Joint Union of Patriotic Unification," a coordinating committee of all the Chinese organizations in France. Deng Xiaoping, executive member of the Joint Union, was in fact present at the gathering in February 1924, but escaped injury. "During the meeting the workers' representatives stood up," wrote the Etatist Li Huang, "and vilified Muhua [leader of the Etatists]. Thereupon many people lept from their chairs. A riot ensued; suddenly someone in the crowd threw a chair at Muhua, which the worker-comrade of the Youth Party was just able to intercept. The Hunanese Huang Fu hurled a chair at Zhou Enlai, who in turn screamed at the top of his lungs that the violent measures should be implemented immediately . . . "[4]

From the time of that meeting-hall battle, both the left and the right carried weapons. Not only knives and brass knuckles, but firearms, too, as became evident five months later. The first political murder nearly occurred at a joint meeting of the left and the right-wing KMT factions. In the middle of the dispute, a representative of the right suddenly pulled out a revolver and pointed it at Zhou Enlai. In the nick of time, a Communist rushed at the man from behind, pinning his arms so he was unable to fire. The gun was wrested from the assailant after a brief scuffle.

Several days after this "militant" KMT meeting, Zhou Enlai returned to China. He served a long time in Canton under Chiang Kai-shek at the Whampoa Military Academy before the French secret service ferreted out his partially obliterated traces. Although the great diplomat of the New China was from the outset one of the leading minds of the Communist movement, and had lived from 1922 to 1924 at No. 17 Rue Godefroy, his name appeared for the first time only in January 1925 in the agents' dispatches.[5]

The year 1924 proved to be the year of departures. Many comrades traveled back to China, because Sun Yatsen wanted Communists to work in leading roles in his Kuomintang Party. For those "Qingong Jianxue" activists interested, a belated opportunity for study now presented itself at the "Communist University for Workers of the East" in Moscow, or at military institutes in Moscow, Kiev, and Leningrad.

Following Zhou Enlai's embarkation at Marseille in July, leadership was divided between two comrades. The departure of the first and second generation cadres proved the great opportunity for the ambitious Deng following closely in their rear. In the autumn of 1925 he and the Szechuanese Fu Zhong, seven years his senior, advanced to the positions of supreme authority in the "Central Organization of the CCP in Europe." Comrade Fu functioned as secretary, the twenty-one-year-old Deng as his right hand.

After barely a year's membership in the CCP, Deng now presided over meetings. He had by now become a professional revolutionary, whose living expenses were paid by the organization. Only in the early summer of 1925 did Deng live in La Garenne-Colombes and in the heart of Paris, for in August he moved once more, this time several métro stations further out, to the working-class suburb Billancourt. He now had considerably less free time than in Chalette or in Châtillon, for he had commitments as leading member of the cadre of the CCP as well as responsibilities as executive member of the Youth League. Meanwhile, he still worked within the Kuomintang as Communist "supervisory delegate," although his election was only confirmed on January 1, 1926.[6]

The Chinese Communists had never been particularly interested in the struggle of the French working class, and at best proletarian internationalism allied them to the French Communist Party. They were—in typical Chinese fashion—perennially occupied with their own affairs. Their first major action was designed to compel the opening of the "Université franco-chinoise de Lyon" to work-study students; the second was set off by a tragic event in the far-off homeland.

On May 15, 1925, textile workers in Shanghai walked off their jobs because the factory guards of a Japanese spinning mill had opened fire on strikers. The workers' protest spread. The police of the British concession (extraterritorial colony) wanted to contain the protest—with firearms. The clash escalated into the "May 30 massacre," and only hours later the Chinese colony in Paris knew what had occurred at home.

The Communists called all Chinese living in France to a general meeting. Their journal, "Red Light," published a special edition with the title "Struggle Against the Imperialistic Massacre of the Shanghaiese." At a mass rally on June 7 the assembled members of 28 Chinese organizations At a mass rally on June 7 the assembled members of 28 Chinese organizations agreed to a common "Demonstration Against European Imperialism."

The French authorities consulted for two days whether to approve the application for the planned protest demonstration. Ultimately, they did not approve it, thus relegating the demonstration to the status of illegality. The Chinese were unconcerned and mobilized their adherents and the populace. On June 14, thousands of people gathered at the site of the demonstration, Chinese and French alike. Not wishing a confrontation with the civil authorities, the organizers did not call on the demonstrators to storm the police barricades, but asked them to gather for a further demonstration in front of the Chinese embassy on June 21.

It took place on a summer Sunday. The narrow Rue de Babylone in the elegant Seventh Arrondissement lay as though deserted, when toward 2:30 in the afternoon small groups of Chinese streamed out of the métro station François Xavier and strolled in the direction of the pagoda next to the embassy. Residents remained oblivious to any hint of a riot; the groups still appeared no more than Sunday strollers. Only as taxi after taxi drove up may the suspicions of one or another of the residents have been aroused. Toward 3:00, a great throng of people, in which the diminutive Deng was not to be seen, blocked the majestic entrance gate behind which, in a small park, lay the embassy building. Suddenly slogans like "Hands off China!," "Down with the European oppressors!," and "The Chinese movement is not xenophobic, but social!" rang through the normally peaceful residential street. Someone in the front ranks rang the bell at the gate, and the concierge opened.

While a small vanguard crossed the courtyard, others cut the telephone lines in the concierge's lodge. The leaders must have known their way around, for hardly had they entered the vestibule than they divided into three groups. One made its way through the reception hall, a second reconnoitered the top floor where the families of the embassy staff lived, and a third went through the office of the secretary. Then they cornered Chen Lu in the rear office.

The ambassador was so shocked that he unprotestingly signed the documents presented him by the interlopers. With no will of his own, he put his signature to a note of protest to the French government, addressed to Monsieur Painlevé, demanding the withdrawal of French troops from China.

Following this Sunday action, a veritable storm broke over the Chinatown of Paris. The Prefect of Police raged, politicians inveighed, segments of the press agitated. In large letters under the headline "First Strike," the "Action Française" wrote: "The Parisian Chinese have taken over the embassy in the Rue de Babylone. Are the Elysée's environs next?"

The storm in the press was followed by a veritable wave of arrests and ruthless expulsions. The least occasion resulted in deportation. One worker was deported merely for distributing a "Declaration to the People of France and Europe" in a métro station. In an effort to track down those behind his efforts, his apartment at No. 27 Rue Traversière in Billancourt, in which five months later Deng Xiaoping would live, was ransacked. In a drawer, the secret police found lists of meeting places and addresses of Communist and KMT Chinese. The first deportations followed the storming of the embassy by only three days. A week after the occupation, the authorities had expelled 147 "individuals" by ship or trans-Siberian railway.

Large-scale raids took place in the Rue de la Pointe in La Garenne-Colombes, in the Renault-factory town of Billancourt, and in Parisian restaurants as well as private homes. More than 200 Chinese were interrogated at police headquarters, and editions of the journal "Red Light" were confiscated everywhere. While several important functionaries were caught in the police net, Deng eluded them. With the unexpectedly harsh wave of deportation, the second great militant action came to an abrupt end. The Chinese Communist movement in France had collapsed. Many of those not forcibly transported to their homeland left voluntarily. Only a pitiful rearguard remained. From 1925, the main cell of the CCP in France consisted of only five organized cadres.

A time now began in which the dwindling Chinese community drew the full attention of the French secret police. Meetings no longer took place that were not infiltrated by informers. Their reports went not to some subordinate department, but across the desk of the "Commissaire de Police du Quartier de L'École Militaire" to the "Préfet de Police" personally. In order to learn the names and addresses of Chinese Communists, the French secret service received official assistance from the French police in Shanghai.

Week by week, they maintained surveillance over private residences and places of assembly. The agents discovered that the meeting place of the Communists was a restaurant at No. 5 Place Nationale, close to Deng's place of work, the editorial offices of "Chiguang." A second secret meeting place was in a restaurant in the building at No. 94 Boulevard Auguste Blanqui, only a few steps from Zhou Enlai's former apartment. The Chinese were of course perfectly aware they were being systematically shadowed, and in consequence frequently changed their meeting places and residences. They booked themselves preferably into small, cheap pensions or hotels.

Most of the Chinese workers in France lived in Boulogne-Billancourt, a suburb southwest of Paris. There, they inhabited four residential streets in the immediate neighborhood of the Renault factory. Deng was most familiar with the Rue Traversière, for he lived in the house, now destroyed, at No. 27. From there it was only a few steps to his workplace in the Renault Division No. 76. There he worked for seven weeks as a metalworker. When he wished to attend a meeting of the "Association des Travailleurs franco-chinois," he needed only cross the intersection. The Rue Traversière was this Renault town's Chinatown: at No. 39 the Worker's association was located; at No. 14, according to a police report, was a hotel-restaurant owned by Chinese Communists; and in the houses at Nos. 18 and 27 rooms were let to Chinese workers at Renault.

From the autumn of 1925, the Communist circle comprised only a small radical minority, whose membership had sunk from 300 to fewer than 100 sympathizers. It was easy for the police now to watch every step the comrades took. Because not more than 25 people were present at a meeting in the Café Coopératif in the Rue Charlot, the informer's report of October 25 seemed meager. As a particular detail it was noted that a certain "Teng Hi Hien," age estimated at 23 years, led the meeting.

A second report, dated November 16, described a meeting at No. 23 Rue Boyer at which Deng Xiaoping once more held the chair and by way of conclusion summoned the 47 people assembled there to the "long-term international anti-imperialistic struggle." According to this report, the police did not yet know Deng's exact place of residence. The agent wrote only vaguely, "domicilié à Sèvres ou à St-Cloud." Only in the record of the meeting of January 3, 1926, was Deng's residence known: No. 3 Rue Castéja in Boulogne-Billancourt. The official noted as well that heretofore "Teng Hi Hien" had not transgressed the alien laws.

This well attended meeting was very nearly the final appearance of the twenty-one-year-old Deng in the police register. Only hours after his flight across the border, armed police forced their way into the small residence hotel at No. 3 Rue Castéja. On the upper floor of the two-story house, in guest room No. 5, the beds were still unmade, and on the table and in the bookcase the

Pension at No. 3 Rue Castéja in the Parisian suburb of Billancourt. Here Deng Xiaoping lived in room No. 5 intermittently from August 1925 until his departure for Moscow in January 1926).

officers found leaflets in French and Chinese, agitprop material like "The Chinese Worker," "Sun Yatsen's Testment," Nikolai Bucharin's "ABC of Communism," and various editions of a Bolshevik journal published in Moscow. The "Doctor of Duplication" must have lived here, for the officers found oil-based ink as well as an ink roller and several packages of printing paper. According to the town register, Deng had in fact lived here since August 20, 1925. He had often been observed in the company of his roommates, Fu Zhong and Yang Pingsun.

The brains of the Communist cell had escaped before his arrest because the informers had not done their work cleanly or quickly enough. So it had eluded the whole police apparatus that for the short time from November 6 to December 29—while he had to earn his fare to Moscow at Renault—Deng had changed his abode. That the Renault employee was no longer particularly engaged in his work, but was already spiritually in Moscow, is indicated by personnel's laconic assessment: "acceptable."

The French secret service had not only researched carelessly, but had also reacted too slowly. The hard core of Chinese Communists gathered a few days after New Year at the Gare du Nord, while at the police, final preparations were being made for house searches. On January 7, 1926, the functionaries Fu Zhong, Yang Pingsun, and Deng Xiaoping together boarded the night express for Moscow. Already on the day of their departure, the following communication circulated among the Chinese: "Twenty of our comrades depart Paris today heading toward the Soviet Union. Soon, they will return to China. Comrades! When we see our fighters one after another returning to the front, we should always call to mind the slogan 'Return at the earliest possible moment to China!'"

A good five years' stay in France lay behind the young Szechuanese, who had set out on his travels in the west as a precocious sixteen-year-old full of ideas. He had come to work—but primarily to study; he had, after all, embarked for the west as a "Qingong Jianxue" activist. What he learned, then, were the French language, European manners, something of the nature of the west, and—the ABC of Communism. A still rather diffusely rebellious landowner's son was transformed in France into a pragmatically thinking and acting Communist.

Aptitudes spéciales :

SALAIRE DÉCLARÉ

Année 19	Année 19	Année 19
Année 19	Année 19	Année 19
Année 19	Année 19	Année 19
Année 19	Année 19	Année 19

APPOINTEMENTS						Caisse de Compensation	
Dates	Appointements	Total	Dates	Appointements	Total	Nombre d'Enfants	Allocations

Motif de départ : *Retourne en Chine*

Valeur professionnelle : *A. B.*

Taux horaire :

Autres appos. *Bonnes*

Réintégrations

82409A

Discharge certificate from Renault for Deng Xiaoping.
Cause of separation: Return to China. Assessment of
work performance: acceptable. General behavior: good.

On his arrival at Marseille, Deng had still been a tabula rasa. Had he studied, had he been accepted at Lyon, Deng Xixian would scarcely have become Deng Xiaoping. The awful circumstances in which he lived, the threadbare existence as an alien worker, marked the crucial years of his youth.

FIVE

Among the Bolsheviks

THE CHINESE IN Paris were just reorganizing their remaining forces, when in far-off Canton the awarding of places for students was publicized. At a meeting of the Kuomintang leadership on October 7, 1925, the Comintern representative Mikhail Borodin announced the establishment of a university in Moscow especially for Chinese. The Chinese revolutionaries applauded the Russian enthusiastically for this magnanimous Soviet offer of higher education.

According to Borodin, the university was to be administered by the East Asian Department of the Third International; in fact, it was under the control of the Central Committee (CC) of the Communist Party of the Soviet Union (CPSU). He stressed that it was open to all Chinese. It became in short order, however, a production mill for cadres of the CCP.

The university, the full name of which was the "Sun Yatsen University of the Working Chinese," but which Muscovites knew only as "Universitet trudyashchixsya Kitaya" (UTK), was, though a Soviet establishment, actually financed by the Chinese. Like the "Université franco-chinoise de Lyon," it received monies from the Boxer indemnity which the Ch'ing court in the covenant of September 7, 1901, had ceded to the eleven allied nations.[1]

The UTK was created thanks to the united front between the Russian Communists and the Chinese social revolutionaries. Those who imagined an internationalist alliance of solidarity, however, were soon to be disillusioned. This united front constituted not resolution of conflicts, but rather the yoking together of contradictions among the Russian and the two Chinese camps.

The Kuomintang under Sun Yatsen's leadership hoped to acquire greater Soviet assistance in order to gain strength itself. The Chinese Communists, in turn, exploited the KMT as a catchment basin to enlarge their own party. Although the Kuomintang had taken up the cause of the national revolution, it had not elicited response enough to accomplish it. Still less was it committed to social revolution. The Communists, on the other hand, though they championed the national revolution, sought thereby to proceed as soon as possible to the social revolution.

In consequence of such a complicated coalition, most of the Communist students were organized into the KMT as well as the CCP. The Moscow years of the late president of Taiwan, Chiang Ching-kuo, may be briefly adduced here, for they illuminate the complex nature of the united front among CPSU, KMT, and CCP.

He had registered as a sixteen-year-old in 1925 for the first academic year at the UTK and had taken up his studies only two months before Deng Xiaoping. Ching-kuo was just graduating two years later when his father, Chiang Kai-shek, declared the Communists his archenemies and had tens of thousands of them shot. The young member of the Communist Youth League would atone for his father's atrocities: The Soviets forbade his return to China, then correspondence with his family. Through the intervention of the CCP, he had become the victim of guilt by kinship. He had no option but to pursue additional years of study. One day he publicly challenged the Comintern representative Wang Ming one day, and a short time later his deportation to Siberia was pronounced. On the grounds of frail health, however, the Soviets exiled him to a village close to Moscow. This "re-education" was not severe enough for his compatriots: in January 1933 he was condemned to hard labor in a gold mine in the Siberian Altai mountains. Only in April 1937 did Chiang Ching-kuo return to China, because Stalin supported his father—not Mao's guerrillas—in the anti-Japanese struggle.

In memory of Dr. Sun Yatsen, who had died of liver cancer on March 12, 1925, the Soviets opened the university in November 1925. No less a figure than Leon Trotsky led the inaugural ceremonies, declaring,

> From now on, any Russian, be he a comrade or a citizen,
> who greets a Chinese student with an air of contempt, shrug-
> ging his shoulders, is not entitled to be either a Russian Com-
> munist or a Soviet citizen.[2]

The wild applause showed that Trotsky had touched on a sore point, and even months after this speech, he, not Stalin, was celebrated as the true friend of the Chinese.

Under the czars, the Russians had often pushed the Chinese around as subhuman. Like all Chinese students, Deng Xiaoping soon experienced this residual bigotry in red Moscow. Not just children, but grown-ups, too, addressed them on the street: "Friend, do you need some salt?" The Chinese, with their rudimentary Russian language skills, were confused, thinking their Russian brothers and sisters were concerned for their welfare. But since the same question was always posed, they looked into the matter more closely. A story circulated among the Russians that one hot summer at the time when Leningrad was still called St. Petersburg a Chinese died. His family wished to transport the body to China and bury it there according to ancient custom. So the mortal remains would not spoil during the long train trip, they were cured in salt. Discovering the salted corpse when they opened the casket, the customs officials in Vladivostok could not stop gabbing about the curious manners of the Chinese. The embalming story then spread throughout all of Russia, and from it arose this racial teasing.

Trotsky's interest became the Sun Yatsen University's undoing. Only a year after its opening, the effects of the power struggle between him and the Georgian Stalin extended even to the academic classroom.

Deng Xiaoping had barely acclimatized himself to life in Moscow when in China the new Kuomintang leader Chiang Kai-shek severed the fraying threads still binding the united front of Communists and Nationalists. On March 20, 1926, he initiated his first anti-Communist action, the Zhongshan gunboat incident, prelude to his counter-revolution, which would cost 40,000 Communists[3] their lives.

Chiang Kai-shek's action made such waves at the UTK that one day Stalin and Trotsky showed up together at a KMT meeting and took part in the heated debate over united front politics—naturally from divergent positions. Leon Trotsky was of the opinion that the Chinese Communists had to withdraw from the Kuomintang and evolve independently. Josef Stalin countered that the national question could be resolved only in the context of the proletarian revolution and that, therefore, the Communists had to remain in the KMT. He vehemently advocated strengthening the effectiveness of the Kuomintang through the Communists. Most of those present supported Trotsky in this dispute.

The Trotskyite camp at the UTK became so strong that in 1930 Stalin ordered the closing of the university. Only three institutions of the UTK were excepted: the Research Institute for Chinese Questions, the Translation Office, and the China Press, first opened in 1928.

Still today the UTK is exalted as a Bolshevik Olympus because many celebrities matriculated there. Of some 1,000 graduates, 28 Chinese stand out who entered the history of the Chinese revolution as the "28 Bolsheviks."[4] Under Rector Pavel Mif, this Stalinist group functioned as a monolithic and all-powerful block against so-called "anti-party activities," under which everything remotely associated with Trotskyism or even mere opposition was subsumed.

Only five members of this self-styled proletarian group around Wang Ming, Mao's future opponent, came from working-class families. The majority were scions of the elite, dwindling intelligentsia of South China. Most of them came from the Yangtze river basin, only four from Deng Xiaoping's home province. All 28 had already been CP members before their studies at UTK and after their return became important cadre members of the party and the army on the central or the regional level. But three reached the level of General Secretary of the CCP.[5] Of these 28 Bolsheviks, however, only seven remained long-term CP members. Four rose to the Central Committee, from which they were subsequently removed during the Cultural Revolution. Today, the "last" powerful Bolshevik is General Yang Shangkun. He holds the position of vice chairman of the Central Military Commission. Although Deng never belonged to the "group of 28," Yang Shangkun has long been numbered among his trusted advisors.

If one wanted to amount to anything in the Communist Party, one had to have studied in the Soviet Union. Only Mao could be assured of special treatment—and that only after 1935, for prior

to that the Bolsheviks and the Comintern advisors had been superior political opponents. Still today, many of the struggles over
policy and direction go back to the Moscow years of the comrades
in the leadership, and a pro-Moscow faction still exists in the
superannuated top echelon of the CCP. Far more Chinese went
abroad to the Soviet Union than to France, Germany, or Belgium.

The Sun Yatsen University was a production mill for cadres,
albeit only for Chinese. The "Communist University for Workers
of the East" was open to revolutionaries of other countries. In the
year 1927, representatives from 74 countries were studying at the
"Kommunisticheskiy universitet trudyashchixsya vostoka"
(KUTV). For the revolutionaries from the former Middle Kingdom—also for the travelers to France—the KUTV on Pushkin
Square in Moscow was the precursor of the UTK. Between 1923
and 1924, 1,025 students had registered there, among them the
lean Vietnamese Ho Chi Minh, who, like Deng Xiaoping, had
come from Paris. China's future president, Liu Shaoqi, sent to
Moscow in the winter of 1921 in the first group of eight Chinese,
was also graduated from the KUTV.

Deng Xiaoping's rector, the German social-democrat Karl Radek, came from Lemberg. During the November revolution of
1918, he had fought on the Berlin barricades in Wedding and in
Kreuzberg as the representative of the Russian Communist Party.
After his imprisonment in Germany, he rose in 1919 to the chairmanship of the newly formed Comintern. His second revolutionary excursion to a Germany in turmoil did not end in prison, to
be sure; but Radek stood accused by the German Communists,
instead. They charged him in 1923 with the failures of the SPD-
KPD governments in Saxony and Thuringia. Since Radek, lauded
by the UTK students as a brilliant scientist, let himself be drawn
into the power struggle between Stalin and Trotsky, he was forced
to don his rector's hat in 1927 and abandon his position in the
party. He died in one of Stalin's camps.

KUTV and UTK lived on as the truncations of once mean-
ingful institutions, as emblems of a proletarian internationalism of
a particular sort.

In the winter of 1925, a direct connection ran from the Gare
du Nord in Paris to the capital of the young Soviet republic. The
group of Chinese dressed western style, underway in frosty Jan-

uary to icy Moscow, crossed the French–German border, arriving just one day later in Berlin. They proceeded at once via Warsaw, Minsk, and Smolensk to the city in which revolutionaries were determining the destiny of a giant empire.

The comrades were excited. Here they were to receive what had been denied them in France—the chance to study. The Szechuanese Deng Xiaoping, youngest and smallest of the group by far, could already look back on a remarkable career among the Communists: at 18, leading member of the cadre of the Youth League, at 20, party member, and since his twenty-first birthday, member of the leaders' cadre of the "Central Organization of the CP in Europe." The young man, remarkable for his select clothing, had risen in France from laborer to professional revolutionary.

The group was to stay two years in the Soviet capital, so read the directive of the Central Committee. As a rule, the course of studies at Sun Yatsen University lasted 24 months. For Deng, however, the period of study was compressed to barely eight months; his sojourn in Moscow lasted only from January to August 1926.

The train drove into the Belorussian Station in west-central Moscow. Now the nineteen "travelers to France" stood anew in a strange metropolis. Did they—as they had in Paris—recoil from the gloomy scene, did they stiffen at the terrible cold? In any case, they had not been forgotten. As once before in the mediterranean Marseille, they were expected—and not, this time, as "nobodies," but as comrades. They were driven through the circularly laid out inner city past the Kremlin up to No. 16 Volxonka Boulevard. Here, near the banks of the Moscow, stood Sun Yatsen University. From the main gate, the Cathedral of the Redeemer with its six gilded domes seemed near enough to touch. Today the curious look for the "Xram spassitelya" in vain, for in 1930 the place of worship had to make way for the Lenin Hall.

A parade of leafless trees greeted the newcomers in front of the angular main building. Glancing left, they saw a volleyball field, and beyond that, compatriots warming themselves at curling on the ice. In the summer, the UTK students played basketball there.

The impressive building at the front of the ample grounds comprised about a hundred rooms. The dining hall was on the second floor; the administration, the extensive library, and the classrooms were distributed throughout the other floors.

During Deng's time as a student here, the number of matriculating students increased steadily. By the time of his departure in the summer of 1926, some 500 students had already registered. When a year later as many as 600 fellow students were registered, the administration was compelled to use dormitory rooms in the surrounding buildings.

Although the university was not secret, it was inaccessible to the general public. Anyone wishing to gain admittance had to show his pass to the porter. A news blackout seemed to reign over the UTK. Its academic inner life was only rarely broached in the Moscow newspapers. In the capitalistic west and in China, which, with the exception of the province of Guangdong, was ruled by reactionary warlords, as little as possible was to be known about the production mill for cadres.

The first days of Deng Xiaoping and his "French Chinese" were taken up with sightseeing, tours of the university facilities, and getting to know fellow students, teachers, and the extensive course of studies.

On workdays, from Monday to Saturday, the comrades had countless required courses to attend, among which language instruction was foremost. Every student was required to take the introductory course in Russian and an elective course in English, French, or German. Because Deng stood out with his knowledge of French, the administration soon appointed him French interpreter in his own as well as other classes. Most of the teachers spoke only Russian, so their instruction and the questions of the students had to be translated by an interpreter. This of course was exhausting and time-consuming.

The Russian course was divided up into reading "Pravda," cramming grammar, and getting to know Russian revolutionary prose. No, there was neither Gorky nor Tolstoy, the famous Russian literature did not serve as a subject of study.

Six times a week for four hours at a stretch Deng had to attend one of these three courses. Following the Russian course was history, divided into five areas: the history of evolution, the history of the Chinese revolutionary movement (this course was taught by Karl Radek), the history of the Russian revolution, and the eastern as well as the western revolutions. Under the catchword materialism, philosophy was taught.

Explanation of *Das Kapital* stood at the center of political economy. To enhance comprehension, "Karl Marx's Economic Theories" by Karl Kautsky was added as secondary material. In this course, German economists also lectured. A favorite subject, which had originated in America, was economic geography, concerned with the influence of the earth's structure on the origins of society and its evolution. This was taught in English by Communist experts from America and Great Britain.

This, however, did not complete Deng Xiaoping's curriculum. Two further subjects were required of him: Leninism and military science. The first course had its origins in Stalin's lecture "On the Foundations of Leninism" at the Sverdlov University. This course was like a magnet for the young Chinese revolutionaries, for it was taught by the most renowned theoretician of the CPSU. The course in military science was divided into a theoretical and a practical part, in which the budding revolutionaries got acquainted with the implements of modern warfare, machine guns, hand grenades, mortars and the like. This part of the curriculum usually took place in the military academies or with units of the Red Army on the outskirts of Moscow.

This multileveled mountain of curricular material was conceived for two years of study, but could be mastered only if each of the twenty-five students in the twelve academic classes pulled together and stuck to the grind eight hours a day.

The Russians had put the classes together on the basis either of the students' language facility or the level of their political consciousness. The political consciousness of students was quickly assessed: the longer one had been a member of the CCP—not the KMT—the higher his level of Marxist consciousness.

The excessively school-masterly curriculum was arranged from the Soviet viewpoint. No course devoted much attention to the history of the revolutionary league Tong Meng Hui, founded in Tokyo in 1905 by Sun Yatsen, or to the national populist party Kuomintang, or to Sun Yatsen's three populist principles, San Min Zhuyi—the right of self-determination of the Chinese people, social justice, liberal democracy. The students could read the ideas of the university's namesake only in the Russian pamphlet "A Study of Sun Yatsen's Doctrine" by an anonymous writer's collective. In this disquisition, which was free and available everywhere, Sun Yatsen's ideas were presented as remarkable but middleclass, he himself as a progressive, but bourgeois, democrat.

As he had for the course in Chungking preparatory to his journey to France, Deng came late this time, too. The first academic year had already begun in November, while he arrived from Paris only in January. No one minded, though. The young functionary was admitted notwithstanding into the seventh class, the class of the "celebrities." Not only at the UTK, but at the KUTV as well, everyone knew the seventh, the "theory class."[6] And soon everyone was talking about the "Little Cannon," by which they meant the stocky "traveler to France," Deng. Thanks to his hard working nature, he had made himself known at the UTK in just a few weeks.

Deng Xiaoping's class did not shine in lone splendour; it stood in competition with the "Special Class,"[7] which, besides "celebrities," included an already quite old and original character, Mao Tsetung's former teacher, Xu Teli, known by the nickname "Old Grandma." His fellow students admired the zeal with which the fifty-year-old man, already sans many of his teeth, pursued his studies. His strenuous efforts to pronounce Russian correctly despite the gaps in his teeth were legendary.

Because the proletarian Chinese possessed a very low level of education, they had to be taught in special preparatory classes with less demanding instructional material. Their curriculum was divided into Chinese, history, geography, arithmetic, political science, and introductory Russian.

The revolutionary workers were not on that account regarded as second-class students. The administration consistently assigned them important functions. Thus, for example, one worker functioned as elected leader of the student commune, and another supervised activities in the dining hall. "Commune" meant a self-governing student body, which issued a weekly bulletin and conducted a "comrades' court." This disciplinary institution dealt with public cases, wife-beating for example. The fundamentally democratic institution empowered the student body to confirm or overrule its verdicts by ballot. In the case of the battered wife, the guilty husband was expelled and sent back to China.

"I was always very happy if I could manage to buy a croissant and a glass of milk," Deng once told General Yang Shangkun referring to his time in France. How different his days in Moscow, where he ate almost lavishly. There were certainly obstacles to obtaining meat or fish for native Russians. Not for the UTK students, however. The pioneers of the first academic year were literally pampered with chicken, duck, and fish. In addition to the three hot meals usual in China, they were offered two further snacks a day. Not till two months after Deng's arrival did the administration curtail these extravagant provisions, for the Soviet government now stepped up its exportation of flour, meat, fish, and butter to overcome its foreign exchange deficit.

Deng Xiaoping could have come from Paris in rags—one day after his arrival at most he would have been dressed in new clothes, and that free of charge. Only hats and ties had to be purchased optionally by fashion-conscious comrades. From overcoat down to fur-lined snow boots for winter and leather sandals for summer, from tooth-paste to shoe polish, everything was provided. Student dress was not out of the norm here, for men's fashion in the Soviet capital was still of a western cut. Not many students wore high-buttoned "Lenin jackets," and only a handful of dandies dared appear in class in the purple Ukranian shirts that buttoned to the left. The delicate Chinese women had a harder time of it. They had to make do with mannish trousers.

Not only in clothing and food was the best provided; housing and cultural events were offered unstintingly too. The "Little Cannon" was often to be found at the club, where bridge or chess, rummy or halma were played, and where there were newspapers and a bar. The administration was constantly distributing free tickets for cultural evening performances. Riding, dancing, and playing ball were optional at the students' expense. There was even a photography club at the UTK with a well-equipped dark-room. Each student received a suitable allowance of pocket money. If he was frugal, he could always divert some to his family at home.

Since the 21-year-old Deng still numbered among the 340 "pioneers," he was assigned sleeping quarters on the fourth floor of the main building. His successors had to be housed in four neighboring buildings because more classrooms were constantly required. Women were housed in the elegant residence of a dispossessed nobleman in Petrovka Street.

Gripes about the accommodations were heard only when married students came to the UTK, for the moral preconceptions of the Bolsheviks were strict, and absolute segregation of the sexes was the rule. When the dissatisfaction of the young couples was no longer to be ignored, a Chinese proposed that the administration establish a "separate rendezvous room" for married couples. The administration accepted the proposal as a temporary solution; not until 1928 did married students receive their own dormitory rooms. The birthrate of "little revolutionaries" rose so considerably that one day Rector Radek observed cheerfully, "This problem is easily solved. We can set up nurseries, and then even a kindergarten."

That the Soviets presented the UTK Chinese their best, their most hospitable side was calculated. They knew that taking good care of the revolutionary intelligentsia would repay its costs many times over in the future. Stalin and the Comintern comrades thought in the long term. For one thing, the CPSU wished to tie China's revolutionaries to itself. For another, they sought out influential allies at every level in this vast, seething agricultural land.

In 1916, the epoch of the military governors had begun in China. After the death of the self-proclaimed Emperor Yuan Shi-kai, the former Ch'ing empire became entangled in a battle of warlord against warlord. Foreign powers such as Japan, France, and Great Britain occupied their "zones of influence" and heated up the power struggle of the militant provincial governors. The former Middle Kingdom functioned until 1928 as a patchwork carpet on which regional adversaries thrashed about. For this reason, chroniclers call the years from 1916 to 1928 the time of the warlords.

Wishing to win over General Feng Yuxiang, a Christian, as an ally, Stalin invited him to Moscow. The "Christian General" was very interested in Stalin's military assistance. He departed China about two months after Deng's arrival in Moscow. The influential warlord was accompanied by his wife, the future Minister of Health of the Peoples' Republic of China, and a small entourage. As he stepped from the train in Moscow on May 9, 1926, the Soviets received him as a high-ranking guest of state.

During his days in Moscow, General Feng lived at the Hotel "Europa." He was often visited there by his future subordinate, Deng Xiaoping, and other Communist UTK students. As an "honorary student," he could come and go at Sun Yatsen University as he pleased. In just a few weeks, the chubby, gregarious Chinese had become the toast of Moscow. Invitations arrived daily, and he met with luminaries such as Mikhail Ivanovich Kalinin, the nominal Soviet head of state, Leon Trotsky, and Lenin's wife, Krupskaya. Although he never met with Stalin, he enjoyed his full support. While the party leader had initially promised him military equipment sufficient for 50,000 troops, he later increased that pledge eightfold.

After four months, on August 17, the General boarded the Trans-Siberian Railway headed east. His entourage had increased: on instructions from the CC of the CCP, three well-known Chinese functionaries, 98 Soviet advisors, and . . . the "Little Cannon." After an absence of six years and five days, Deng Xiaoping returned via Mongolia to his homeland.

When Deng had steamed out onto the Pacific Ocean in September 1920, China had resembled a troubled ocean. Now, as he returned six years later, it was a storm-tossed sea. Imperialistic exploitation, warlord terror, inflation, pillage, and regular warfare had deluged the country for years.

Even the Kuomintang, several weeks before his return, had involved itself in the provincial wars of the military cliques. In July 1926, "Beifa," the northern campaign, had begun. Chang Kai-shek, in alliance with several military strongmen from the south, had set out from the centrally situated city of Nanjing against the northern warlords.

His National Revolutionary Army had already taken up the march when the "Christian General" accompanied by the "Little Cannon" arrived at his headquarters of Wuyuan in Inner Mongolia. Impatiently, Chiang Kai-shek awaited the new, powerful KMT member, for the actual campaign in the north could begin only after Feng Yuxiang promised to add his two hundred thousand troops to the KMT army of less than half that strength. Without his army, the two most powerful warlords of the north would have had an easy time of it, for they commanded armies comprising seven hundred thousand troops.

Having made the pledge, the "Christian General" was commander-in-chief of the United National Army, while Chiang Kai-shek commanded the National Revolutionary Army. The Communists fought side by side as allies. While some few Communists quite openly voiced their point of view, fully a hundred of their number infiltrated Feng's army and administration to operate there surreptitiously. Deng Xiaoping had already befriended the pro-Communist General in Moscow and had no need to conceal his orientation. After their arrival at his remote headquarters, Feng promoted the widely traveled young cadre member to the rank of corps commander.

Practically talented as he was, Deng assisted the 98 accompanying Soviet advisors in their restructuring of Feng's powerful army along the lines of the Red Army. Parallel to the military command, the Russians also created a political command: Each corps was given a second chief, a politcommissar. This commissar's responsibility was the political education of the troops. The basic principle here was that if the Communist Party commanded the gunbarrels, it ranked ultimately above the military commander. In practice, of course, the military commander usually had the say. Since this principle proved in emergencies to generate conflict, Stalin nullified it later during the battle of Stalingrad.

The Chinese Communists adopted this principle for their troops, and retain it to the present day. No one in China knows better than Deng Xiaoping all that is implied in the term "politcommissar." Thanks to Feng's personal influence, for the first time in his life—he was just 22 years old—he received the position of politcommissar, a function he was to exercise at varying levels, with only short interruptions, for the next 23 years. General Feng appointed him politcommissar of his Seventh Corps.

Beifa, the northern campaign, was carried out successfully. It looked as though China could be unified by a progressive coalition in the spirit of Sun Yatsen. Xi'an, the ancient imperial city in the province of Shaanxi, fell as early as November 28, 1926. The Communists could rejoice. There were now two centers to the revolution, Canton in the south, and Xi'an in the north. Since Feng Yuxian had departed Moscow armed with new ideas, soon after the seizure of Xi'an he founded the Sun Yatsen Military Academy. The Whampoa Military Academy now had a competitor 2,000 kilometers to the north. To be sure, the northern academy did not employ any "celebrities" like Zhou Enlai or Nie Rongzhen as instructors, but primarily young Communists like Deng Xiaoping.

The diminutive politcommissar was responsible for planning

the curriculum. But the full range of his activites was far broader. He went into classrooms himself and taught that unfair covenants had to be annulled, and that the revolutionary soldier had nothing in common with the uncouth, despised mercenaries of a warlord's army. Often, Deng Xiaoping left the campus of Sanyuan, 40 kilometers north of Xi'an, to teach workers and peasants on the spot.

The northern campaign was in full swing when Sun Yatsen's brother-in-law, Chiang Kai-shek, was preparing for a coup. He exploited his prominent position as commander-in-chief of the National Revolutionary Army to rescind the campaign coalition. Worse, with lightning speed he turned his bayonettes on the heretofore allied and unsuspecting Communists.

With Chiang Kai-shek's anti-Communist "Shanghai Massacre" of April 12, the year 1927 brought the turning point in the political development of China: the first Nationalist-Communist civil war between the CCP and the KMT.

With his strict leadership of party, army, and government, the Communist-hunter so impressed the west and Japan that they recognized his Nanjing regime as the legitimate government of China. Even Deng's pro-Communist superior showed himself impressed—so very impressed that he went over to Chiang Kai-shek.

Now suddenly Feng Yuxiang thought he recognized the weakness of the Communists. He knew the greater financial provision the right-wing KMT faction in Nanjing had made him was better than that of the left in the city of Hankou, today the largest municipal district of Wuhan. And in general it occurred to him that he actually only wanted to support Stalin and his Chinese Bolsheviks until he could call "the heart of China," the province of Hunan, his own. On July 8, 1927, the man once honored in Moscow gave his Communist confederates their walking papers—the "Little Cannon" naturally included.

Ignominiously sacked, the politcommissar rode the train from Xi'an to Hankou where he settled under the protection of the left-wing KMT municipal government. He had to hang up his uniform temporarily, for there was only clerical work to be done in this city on the lower reaches of the Yangtze. Nevertheless, he functioned on the immediate periphery of the Central Committee of his party. The scope of his duties was entirely comparable to his Paris activities as "Doctor of Duplication."

Soon after his arrival, though, things got too hot for the comrades in the Yangtze city. Here, too, the spectre of anti–Communism was abroad. The left-wing KMT municipal government wished to remain free of Communists because it was rapidly coming under pressure from the much more powerful right-wing Chiang Kai-shek faction.

Now the Communists, always open to alliance, were suddenly homeless. They could only still visit Hankou in the greatest secrecy. As they recognized their isolation, they reached hastily for their weapons. Well before all 120,000 residents of Nanchang, capital of the southeastern province of Jiangxi, were awake on the morning of August 1, 1927, the CCP had initiated a revolt.

Now, the Chinese also had their "dress rehearsal," as Lenin had characterized the Russian revolution of 1905 as a preparation for the October Revolution. The insurrectionists had to abandon the city, however, after just three days. Nevertheless, the occupation of Nanchang represents not only the beginning of armed struggle between the CCP and the KMT, but also the first meeting between the most important Communist military commanders and those with whom Deng Xiaoping would share many tears and much joy in the years to come: Chen Yi, He Long, Lin Piao, Liu Bocheng, Nie Rongzhen, Zhou Enlai, and Zhu De.

A week later, 300 kilometers to the north of the site of the ill-fated city revolt, 20 high-level cadre members gathered for a so-called "session of criticism and self-criticism." They had to enter their meeting place at the house of a Russian in Hankou secretly, for in the meantime the city had once more become "white" territory. Since the abortive Nanchang revolt, conspiring together had been absolutely forbidden Deng and his comrades of the CC.

Among the assembled "flat noses," one "long nose" stood out. This was the twenty-nine-year-old Georgian V. V. (Besso) Lominadze, who had just arrived as the new Comintern liaison. Deng took the minutes of the organizational meeting. Present were Mao Tsetung and four other CP leaders.[8]

August 7, 1927, would be a memorable date for Deng. On this summer's day in the blast furnace Hankou had become, he encountered for the first time his future friend and subsequent opponent, Mao Tsetung. Deng, the keeper of the minutes, had to record how the CP General Secretary, Chen Duxiu, was attacked from all sides as a right-wing opportunist and KMT collaborationist. One of his final notations in the minutes declared that the General Secretary had been unseated. At this August meeting in Hankou, the widely traveled cadre learned his first lesson in intra-party doctrinal struggle.

It was not actually China's first Marxist, but rather Stalin, directing things from Moscow, who had earned criticism, for the core of his doctrine was an absolute belief in the revolutionary mission of the small Chinese working class, coupled with a deep mistrust of China's vast peasantry. From this orthodoxy, the Russian Communists representing the Chinese had derived an action alliance with the nationalistic bourgeoisie, represented organizationally in the KMT. In Stalin's conception, this united front would be dissolved only when industrial capitalism had matured in China. Although the character of the Kuomintang had been fundamentally altered with Chiang Kai-shek's accession to power, Stalin persevered in this alliance, and his influential Comintern advisors saw to it also that his politics got a hearing in China.[9] After Chen's unseating, the Communist Party was factionally split. The "Red Bandit," Mao, voluntarily holed up in the Jinggang Mountains in the southern province of Jiangxi, while the Bolsheviks went underground in Shanghai. Deng Xiaoping joined the Bolsheviks and followed the CC to Shanghai. He would remain there till early summer 1929.

In his hideout he pored over records, prepared resolutions, transmitted directives, and concerned himself with the party records of the Central Committee. It would be entirely incorrect to assess the little man simply as a subaltern desk-top cadre worker. On the 6th Party Congress, which owing to the "white terror" of the KMT had to be held in Moscow at the end of June 1928, the delegates elected him *in absentia* deputy leader of the Secretariat of the CC. His office was not yet especially significant, on the other hand, for his new duties were exclusively administrative.

Deng functioned as planning and organizing right-hand to the new General Secretary, Xiang Zhongfa, whom they might better have called General Administrator. The former ferryman, like Deng Xiaoping a graduate of UTK, was no more than a token proletarian, figurehead of the imposed line of Bolshevisation. Li Lisan, "traveler to France" and son of a teacher, ruled as *éminence grise* of the party.

As in all his previous positions, here, too, Deng Xiaoping

soon became someone spoken of approvingly. Because of his un-obtrusive manner and, above all, his accent-free Shanghai dialect, which this Szechuanese had mastered after only a few months, he proved the ideal contact man for the illegal struggle in the dangerous metropolis controlled by the KMT.

The winter rains had just set in when the 23-year-old Deng Xiaoping renounced his bachelor's existence and married comrade Zhang Qianyuan. Zhang resigned her post as secretary of the CCP District Committee of Huichang in the southeast of Jiangxi, and joined him in Shanghai in the French concession on the Avenue Edward VII. To this day, we know nothing further about Zhang Qianyuan. Her younger sister, on the other hand, became well known. She was very active politically during the years of the founding of the New China and before the Cultural Revolution rose all the way to membership on the Standing Committee of the All-Chinese Women's League. Simultaneously, she acted as delegate in the Communist government, the National People's Congress (NPC).

Deng's first marriage ended tragically after only eighteen months. Zhang Qianyuan died following a miscarriage. The 24-year-old was now a childless widower. Certainly this fateful blow had a profound effect on his committed, even dogged, approach to his new, his first great party mission.

SIX

A Tragic Mission

FROM 1927 ON, the party had access neither to military power nor to secure areas of retreat, the Party Congress in Moscow had decided to establish peasant councils in the countryside, to dispossess landowners and wealthy farmers, and to distribute acreage among the tenant farmers. The Communists sought by these measures to create a revolutionary buffer zone in the flat lands. Anticipating this strategy, Mao had established the area of "his" military base of operations in the tortuous Jinggang Mountains of the province of Jiangxi.

The Central Committee in Shanghai considered the 1,800 kilometer distant southern border province of Guangxi—today, the autonomous region Guangxi-Zhuang—as exactly ideal for the establishment of a "Su Weiai." "Do you know the Su Weiai?" was a question frequently asked by marauding KMT soldiers of peasants in the field when they were out chasing Communists. The intimidated peasants would shake their heads. And how could they know the "comrades" Su Weiai, since "Su Weiai" referred to an area, a red soviet area.

Many factors argued for a red base area of operations in the province on the Indo-Chinese border. First of all, the indigenous people of the Zhuang constituted a huge, rebellious human potential. This well-known Thai minority—today numbering 12 million people—had been buffeted and driven out for hundreds of years by the Chinese. Once, the Zhuang, together with other tribes, had inhabited large areas of South China, but were continually being pushed further south into the foothills of the Himalayas. The Zhuang in the fertile valleys of the rivers You and Zuo were regarded as exceptionally courageous and rebellious. Their leader, Wei Baqun, was feared as a rebel beyond the borders of the province. The Communists could build on him and his primitively equipped fighting force, as well as on their comrades who had taken refuge here after the suppression of the Canton rebellion of 1927. The second factor was an abortive palace revolt against Chiang Kai-shek by two local military strongmen who had been put into power by a provincial governor well disposed toward the Communists.

Both these factors helped the office workers of the Central Committee to his first independent party assignment of greater significance: Deng Xiaoping was to establish two new "Su Weiai" in the narrow valleys of the Zuo and You rivers.

Surreptitious agitation, shaking off spies, the use of dummy addresses—Deng Xiaoping had learned all these tricks of an underground fighter. But compared with his conspiratorial work in Shanghai, his activities in Paris were no more than a game of hide-and-seek. The battle in the Shanghai underground around the time of the world economic crisis was no less dangerous than the revolutionary struggle in Czarist Russia. Pass checks, surveillance, round-ups—Deng had constantly to reckon with the possibility of his exposure.

It proved to be tremendously dangerous for a cadre worker like him to abandon the protective maze of the Shanghai streets. Just how was he to get to Guangxi? By train, through "white" territory to Canton? And from there, by junk upriver to Nanning? Very risky! And what then? Deng Xiaoping knew how to take care of himself. He looked up an old friend from his Paris days. He got decisive advice from Ho Chi Minh, who was likewise living in the Shanghai underground. The Viet Namese Communist advised the sea-route, and gave him the address of a contact in Hongkong. Now Deng could depart; disguised as a businessman, on the strand promenade "Bund" he boarded a steamer which took him to the Crown Colony.

From British ruled Kowloon, the Viet Namese underground conveyed him further along the sea-route, for a river journey via Canton and Wuzhou to Nanning was, for known Communists, inadvisable. Only the detour via Indochina remained open to the party envoy. Deng embarked for Haiphong on the Gulf of Tonkin.

Not least thanks to his facility in French, he made his way easily by train to Hanoi. Now it was only a scant 200 kilometers to the Chinese border, which he crossed at Pingxiang; unrecognized, he reached the bustling border city Longzhou. From here he could travel downstream on a passenger junk to Nanning.

After preliminary reconnaissance in the provincial capital, he allowed his rear guard to follow.[1] Operating subversively, the cadre assigned him soon succeeded in infiltrating the leadership of the Nanning police authority. At first, the embryonic "Su Weiai" met at the police station. When this location became too dangerous, the Communists rented a small shop at No. 96 Zhongshan North Street. Only the initiated knew that in the shop that rented and repaired gas lamps, Politcommissar Deng received directives from Shanghai which he transmitted to the liaison cadres in the two river valleys.

Thanks to the family ties of a comrade by the name of Yu Zuoyu—the younger brother of the liberal provincial governor—the Communists were able to infiltrate the governmental apparatus of the province unhindered. After a month, they had positioned 300 surreptitiously operating cadre workers in the military organization and had taken over officer training.

Three months after Deng's arrival, the situation changed strikingly. The governor and his closest advisor suddenly veered sharply left into the arms of the powerless Hankou wing of the KMT and declared war on China's most powerful man. This surprise attack was not at all in Deng's interest, for it caught him and his men in the midst of preparations for a revolutionary insurrection. The hot-headed, isolated action against Chiang Kaishek foundered, however. The governor was forced to flee into the Shanghai underground, while his advisor joined the Communists.

The suppression of Chiang's rash opponents appeared to Deng, functioning once more as politcommissar, to be the proper moment to strike. In all haste, he commanded that the Nanning garrison be plundered. He ordered that defecting soldiers be enlisted and that the contents of the city armory—6,000 rifles, mortars, machine-guns, radio sets, and quantities of ammunition—be loaded onto river junks.

While Commander Zhang Yunyi marched upriver with the

deserters of two brigades along the banks of the You Jiang, the right-hand river, Politcommissar Deng escorted the arsenal and equipment on one of the requisitioned junks. In October 1929, the military leaders and their political superiors met as prearranged on the upper reaches of the right-hand river in the small town of Bose.

Simultaneously, the Communist brother of the former governor had departed the provincial capital and marched upstream with the Fifth Red Army Corps along the left-hand river, the Zuo Jiang, toward Longzhou.

Arrived in Bose, Deng took up quarters in a cottage outside the small town of ten thousand inhabitants. In order not to arouse excessive curiosity, he took lodgings in the building of the Cantonese Compatriots Association.

Today, Bose is a well-known name, for the place was once a bridgehead in the provincial triangle Guangxi, Yunnan, and Guizhou. For hundreds of years, a trade route had led through the picturesque town perched on a mountainside connecting Canton with Yunnan's capital, Kunming, and the countries of Laos and Burma. Whoever controlled this town on the upper reaches of the right-hand river ruled the entire western part of Guangxi, which, with its 220,400 square kilometers, is only a little smaller than Romania.

Politcommissar Deng and his commander, Zhang Yunyi, were thinking in these terms when they selected Bose as the site for their uprising. At the beginning of November a courier briefed the CC in distant Shanghai on Deng's plans. The answer was not long in coming: Yes, the place was appropriate, and the moment propitious, since the KMT leadership was embroiled in internal power struggles and, hence, paralysed.

With amazing self-assurance, the inexperienced politcommissar together with his commander organized the troops on the left-hand river into the Eighth Red Army Corps and those on the right-hand river into the Seventh Red Army Corps. Now the rebellion against the enemy garrisons along the river banks and against the landowners could begin. Deng Xiaoping allowed himself one more particular and pointed inspiration. He chose December 11 as the day of the uprising: On this date two years earlier the uprising of the Cantonese workers had foundered.

The chief of staff recalled,

Early on the morning of December 11 it was cold, and the clouds hung low; it was drizzling. We called our soldiers and the populace to an assembly before eight o'clock in the market square. The demonstration began; the flag with hammer and sickle was hoisted. After Deng Xiaoping had spoken, Zhang Yunyi made a short speech. My task was to announce the establishment of the Seventh Corps of the Red Workers' and Peasants' Army, and then to call up the responsible leaders in order.[2]

Now the real work began, namely "the downfall of the Kuomintang, liquidation of corrupt officials and despotic landowners, as well as creation of workers', peasants', and soldiers' councils." After the peacefully concluded demonstration, revolutionary Greyshirts plastered the rather brief, more or less accurate text of the two speeches prominently on the building walls in Bose and on the very same day 50 kilometers upstream in the city of Pingma. The proclamation was signed by a certain Deng Bin and Zhang Yunyi. Zhang Yunyi we know . . . but who was Deng Bin? A new cadre worker? Deng Bin was no one else but Politcommissar Deng Xiaoping.

The education of the peasants and the organization of the fighting forces were Deng's next assignments for the Bose Soviet. He subdivided the Seventh Corps into three divisions, initially of five thousand, later of thirty thousand soldiers. He set up the headquarters of the municipal fighting force in his lodgings. He transferred command of the Third Division to the Zhuang leader Wei Baqun.

Deng operated out of Bose; his central control base was here on the banks of the right-hand river. He visited the valley of the left-hand river only sporadically on tours of inspection.

On February 1, 1930, the comrades established under his leadership the left-hand river soviet and reorganized the three thousand soldiers into the Eighth Red Army Corps. Thereby, the 25-year-old Deng Xiaoping, as political commander, was the chief of an army of eight thousand men all told. In addition, subordinate to him on the right-hand river were the administrations of eleven and on the left-hand river of six soviets.

Though smaller and unstable, the military base on the left-hand river assumed great importance, for there was a French legation in the district capital Longzhou occupied by the Com-

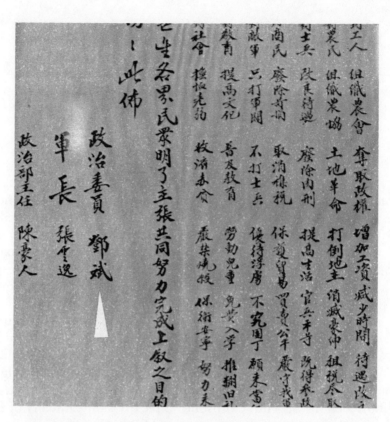

Extract from a wall newspaper of the Red Army: Announcement of the Bose uprising of December 11, 1929, on the Yuo River. The indicated line of text, from top to bottom: Politcommissar Deng Bin (nom de guèrre of Deng Xiaoping).

munists on the day of the soviet's establishment. And here, scarcely 30 kilometers beyond the Indochinese border, Annamese (Viet Namese) rebels turned up almost daily.

On February 9, 1930, the Viet Namese revolutionaries—supported by Chinese comrades—rose up against their French colonial masters. "The Lungchow Soviet," Deng Xiaoping told the American China correspondent Edgar Snow in 1936, "had relations with the Annamese who in 1930 began the workers' and peasants' revolt. French aircraft bombed Lungchow, and we shot one of the planes down." For this, the French avenged themselves months later.

In the river valleys, the revolutionary Greyshirts together with the peasants were bringing in the new harvest as Deng traveled incognito to Shanghai to make his report. After a journey of not quite two months, he arrived just in time for one of those notorious "realignment sessions" of the politburo,[3] at which heads usually rolled.

At this meeting, the informal CP head Li Lisan could develop his thesis of "the ultra-revolutionary situation," without the vehement attack of Zhou Enlai. A truly absurd theory! Li Lisan proceeded from the view that in China, nay, in the whole world, the "revolution is already looking in at the window," that the Chinese Communists needed only attack a few more large cities for the remaining parts of the country to fall like dominoes. So he proposed to direct the spearhead of the national attack against Wuhan. All the Red Corps were to march to the metropolis on the lower reaches of the Yangtze, "liberating" the cities along the way—so ran his instructions. The party leadership subsequently made this suicidal plan known at an internal party meeting. None of the 94 delegates from all the regional soviets—Deng included— had protested against it.

After a brief stay in the coastal metropolis, the delegate from two large soviets once more boarded the ship to Hongkong. Two and a half months later, Deng returned to the right-hand river soviet with the latest instructions in his pocket.

Meanwhile, the counter-revolution had raged. The entire left-hand river soviet had been destroyed, the Eighth Red Corps annihilated by French and KMT troops. In this critical situation, Deng immediately convened his staff and announced the withdrawal of the Seventh Red Corps from the right-hand river soviet, followed by an attack on the second largest city of the province, Liuzhou, then a march into the neighboring province to the east, Guangdong, and assault on Canton. Deng's first party mission was in accordance with the ultra-left line: "Liberation of South China."

The CC directive he had brought with him met with vociferous protest. Deng's staff characterized the left-wing radical armchair strategy as a suicide mission. The popular Zhuang leader implored the group not to sacrifice the remaining right-hand river soviet. While Deng remained silent, the others declared themselves unanimously in favor of a march into the neighboring province to the west, Guizhou. It would be far less dangerous to attempt to establish further soviets there.

After listening a while, Deng conceded only one point to his opponents. He agreed that the march to the west would be less problematic. At the same time, however, he argued that a march to the east would have far greater revolutionary significance. And that was that, the Politcommissar had the last word. The cadres agreed finally that the Zhuang leader should remain behind with ten thousand men to guard the socialist germ cell in Bose.

But the guard was to survive only six months, and then the dam burst, and the right-hand river turned red with the blood of thousands of brave Zhuang fighters. The counter-revolution was militarily and technically superior. Following the left-hand river soviet, the right-hand river soviet was also annihilated in January 1931. These two base of operations areas went down as the most short-lived in the history of the revolution.

In the late summer of 1930, twenty thousand men under the command of Deng Xiaoping set out on a doomed mission. The First and Second Brigades moved out from Pingma, today called Tiandong, and Tianyang. The Third began the just under two-thousand kilometer march to the towns of Donglan and Fengshan situated further to the north. At the beginning of October, the nights in this mountainous region were already appreciably cool; the Seventh Corps reunited in Hechi, 400 kilometers north of Bose. Here the leaders established the final structure of the army: the enlargement of the three brigades to three divisions. And they confirmed Deng Bin in his position as politcommissar, Zhang Yunyi as commander, and Li Mingrui as chief of staff.

In 1978 a comrade recalled,

We had abandoned our right-hand river base area and were marching from Hechi and Huaiyuan toward Liuzhou. Along the way we attacked the hamlets of Siba and Chang'an. The fighting was very bitter, but our soldiers held out heroically. Then a reconnaissance patrol observed the enemy advancing with his troops toward the defense of Liuzhou. Our party committee decided under these altered circumstances not to attack Liuzhou, but to turn off at Chang'an toward the province of Hunan. We resolved to join the Central Red Army in Jiangxi under the leadership of Mao Tsetung.[4]

One word from Deng, and the twenty thousand men would have attacked the city of Liuzhou. With its high fighting morale and committed unity, the Seventh Corps would have given the enemy a bloody fight, but Napoleon's dictum would have held true for the revolutionary war of position too: "In matters military, economy determines all." —And the KMT troops possessed modern German and American weapons.

Deng analysed the situation objectively, and realized that the army of the "White Fox" of the Kuomintang was militarily and technically far superior, and that even if they took Liuzhou, after a few days the same scenario would unfold there as had at Nanchang.

If not before, it was clear to him now that his troups could never capture the large cities along their route, not to speak of "liberating" South China, as his leadership had ordered. Deng thus violated party discipline in ordering the bypassing of Liuzhou.

Even eschewing a battle with the "White Fox," however, the hunters became the hunted as they marched on. Every little engagement, every skirmish, required ammunition, but, worse, cost soldiers' lives. Deng's ranks grew thinner and thinner. The Seventh Corps shrank in the course of its flight along the Hunan border to the size of a regiment, and so it only made sense for the Politcommissar to reorganize his troops into the 55th and 58th Regiments.

As this skeleton of an army reached the Lian River in the provincial triangle Guangxi, Hunan, and Guangdong, it was hit by the winter, damp and cold. Mountain passes became snow-packed tracks, and fords were bone-freezing passages. Worse, even, than the frequent surprise attacks of units of the KMT were the mountains, the forests, and the rivers that blocked the way of the two regiments.

In Guangdong, the Lechang—nowadays called Wu Shui—crested to a powerful torrent. Anyone traveling from the south into the province of Jiangxi had to cross its upper reaches at the spot where it emerges from a 2,000 meter high mountain massif. A staff officer wrote,

> The Lechang was deep and raging, the waves were whipped to froth; it was impossible for us to wade across this river. On the steep bank opposite us, we discovered two boats on a sandbank that offered far and wide the only chance of getting over. Politcommissar Deng Bin had climbed to a high vantage to survey the landscape. In consultation with Commander Zhang Yunyi, he decided that the 55th Regiment under his leadership should cross first. The 58th, lead by Zhang Yunyi, would follow with the logistical equipment. Toward three o'clock in the afternoon, Deng crossed with his group and occupied the other riverbank. No sign of enemy troops, far and wide. Toward five o'clock, the greater part of the 58th Regiment was across. Standing by were only the guard company, two infantry companies, and a medical aid group with the field hospital equipment as well as the logistical equipment—around 600 men. Suddenly, shots were fired. As the boat was coming back for us, we realized that enemy troops were approaching us on the Shaoguan Road.[5]

The battle on the opposite shore was so fierce that Zhang Yunyi and the 600 soldiers remaining behind were forced to abandon their position and to cross the Lechang later at other places. Deng's cut-off troop fought its way independently to Jiangxi.

Two months after the costly river crossing, the Communist soldiers were reunited in the town of Chongyi. Tears of joy were quickly followed by tears of grief, for of the twenty thousand fighting men only six thousand survived.

To begin with, the Politcommissar ordered rest for his exhausted soldiers while he, with just a few companions, set out for the hamlet of Jeiba to contact the Red Army of Mao Tsetung and Zhu De, now stationed in the vicinity. On their way back, Deng's reconnaissance patrol suddenly heard the sounds of battle coming from Chongyi, still ten kilometers off. As was soon to become evident, his regiments had been attacked by the enemy from behind.

Deng's duty as an officer was now—no if's, and's, or but's—to rush to the aid of his embattled soldiers. But what did the Politcommissar do? He asked for a piece of paper on which he wrote that he assumed an attack had occurred and that he could no longer endorse a retreat. The troops were to fight their way through without him to Mao in the Jinggang Mountains. He handed the paper to a courier, and set off to notify the Central Committee in far-off Shanghai of his tragic mission.

Deng Bin marched alone over the Miaoxia Pass in the coastal province of Guangdong. In Nanxiong, he caught a passenger junk downriver. As he had so often done, the practised cadre worker disguised himself. He boarded the river steamer to Canton dressed as a businessman. In mid-April, Deng surreptitiously crossed the green border of the British Crown Colony and embarked from there for Shanghai.

What did he wish to accomplish with his report in Shanghai? Did he want to effect abandonment of the deadly Li-Lisan line? If so, he was months too late, for already in September 1930, the 3rd plenary of the 1st CC of the CCP had put an end to the radical left-wing adventurism. As a battle-weary Deng arrived in the port city, the Bolsheviks were already in control. Their supremacy was to last fully four years, and to occasion far worse damage than the Li-Lisan doctrine.

It is of course possible that Deng, on his month-long march, had not learned of the the power shift in the top echelon of the leadership. But what drove him to Shanghai in the middle of the final battle? Why did he leave his demoralized troops in the lurch?

Certainly the Politcommissar had not gone off to Jeiba half-cocked. Before the reconnaissance mission he had transferred political leadership of the troops to Xu Zhuo and had arranged his departure with the party committee. But he made the decision to rush off to Shanghai to make his report unilaterally and spontaneously.

Deng's first big party assignment ended with a serious error which the Red Guard during the Cultural Revolution also discovered and characterized as "desertion." In an article in the newspaper "Information of the Revolutionary Union of Middleschool Students" it was written,

Atop a mountain summit ten kilometers from Chongyi, suddenly hearing the sounds of battle, his hands and legs began to tremble and he grew pale in terror. He drew a piece of paper from his pocket and wrote: "I am just returning from Jeiba and I hear from far off the sounds of fierce fighting. I assume that you have been attacked and are already in retreat. Since it would be impossible to catch up with you, fight your way through without me to the nearby Jinggang Mountains and join up with the Red Army there." To give himself a pretext for his desertion, he added, "I would like to take this opportunity to convey a report about the Seventh Red Corps to the CC." He gave a courier the paper to convey to the troops "it would be impossible to catch up with." He himself turned and took to his heels. Unhesitatingly, he journeyed to the beautiful world of Hongkong.[6]

Two years after the Guangxi mission, a commission reopened the "desertion" affair and asked Deng Xiaoping to submit a statement. He expressed himself in writing and referred oral questions to Xu Zhuo, who at that time worked in the apparatus of the military commission of the CC of the CCP. Shortly thereafter, in total secrecy, the case was closed. Deng Bin's abandonment of his troops resulted in neither reprimand nor further investigation.

Deng Xiaoping's Guangxi mission ended with thousands dead. If his first great party assignment brought him anything, it was a lesson for life. And not just blame and shame, but also the strength to master the demands and the sacrifices the years of war lying ahead would require lay ahead.

SEVEN

Rough Fall, Tough Climb

T HE RESIDENTS OF Shanghai were suffering from muggy summer heat and typhoons when Zhou Enlai's closest associate
departed the city in total secrecy. Communists had scarcely been
able to walk the Shanghai streets since June 1931, when secret
agents of the Kuomintang had arrested the CP General Secretary.
The party leadership had therefore decided to leave the Shanghai
underground gradually and inconspicuously. In August 1931, the
27-year-old Deng Xiaoping left the coastal metropolis headed
southwest.

He had to cover more than 1,200 kilometers by train, on horseback, and on foot through "White" territory. He was forced to
endure many time-consuming detours before reaching the Red
base area he was familiar with in the province of Jiangxi. As on
all his previous travels, this time too he carried precise instructions
in his pocket. The Central Committee had conferred on him the
post of Party Secretary of the district capital Ruijin in southwestern
Jiangxi, just over the border from the famous "tea province,"
Fujian.

The very day he arrived he had to prove his skill as judge and
arbitrator. Fear and anxiety reigned over the 20,000 inhabitants of
this important district capital in the heart of the Jiangxi Soviet,
who had been intimidated by a wave of Communist purges. An
indiscriminate campaign against putatively reactionary elements
raged like an epidemic, and, assuming a momentum of its own,
had spread far beyond the limits of the small inner circle of the
party.

Between 3,000 and 4,000 so-called "anti-Bolsheviks" were under arrest. Only after his arrival did Deng learn that many had already been shot by order of a court martial. To avoid violent strife, he now had to come to grips with questions of life and death, and this time the "enemy" was not external but within his own ranks.

Initially, Deng knew little about the background of these detentions: party members had been arrested on the basis of their declarations in personal files that years earlier—long before the break between CCP and KMT—they had been members of the so-called "AB group," an organization allied with the Kuomintang. Out of the initials "AB," uneducated, fanatical functionaries had construed the stigma "Anti-Bolshevik." Deng investigated the incidents through many meetings with both sides and soon concluded that the party organization had committed fatal errors here. He stepped in forcefully, and the witch-hunt ended.

Thanks to his experiences with the Guangxi mission, he succeeded in pacifying Ruijin in relatively short order. But as early as November 7, he had to vacate his post. Overnight, the town had received a new, prominent status: the "interim" soviet government and the Central Committee had selected Ruijin as "Red Capital." Deng now assisted his comrades, arrived from Shanghai. Because of his knowledge of the local surroundings, he was able to help install the logistical equipment of the Communist Command Center in a restricted zone at the edge of town.

As a former CC co-worker, his duties naturally included assisting highest ranking party functionary, Bo Gu, in quartering the staff. Whether he enjoyed supporting the mouthpiece of the Bolshevik faction was irrelevant: Deng worked now as ever in the role of subordinate functionary, especially since his actual superior, the military expert Zhou Enlai, would arrive from Shanghai only in December.

In the spring of 1932 Deng left the "Red Capital" heading south. The CC had given the former Party Secretary of Ruijin the less important post of a District Secretary of Huichang. It must have been painful, for the district capital, scarcely 75 kilometers from Ruijin, had only five years earlier been under the administration of his late wife. Since he was able quickly to enlarge the party's base in Huichang, he expanded his own sphere of influence in just a few months: the towns of Anyuan and Xunwu were added to the Huichang adminstration. These three areas lay in the combat zone—now in "White," now in "Red" hands—and served as bridgeheads in the south of the province.

In the summer, Deng's professional as well as his personal fortunes flourished. Thanks to Zhou Enlai's endorsement, surprisingly he received the important post of a First Party Secretary of the province of Jiangxi. And his solitary life came to an end with his second marriage: at 28, he wed the beautiful and temperamental Jin Weiying, whom he had met for the first time in Huichang. The cosmopolitan Deng had taken a younger, inexperienced Communist to wife. A Jin—as her friends called her—came from the central coastal province of Zhejiang, and entered the party only in 1929. Her tour of duty as a teacher at the school of the Red Army in Ruijin served as her first "revolutionary" acid test. After a modest wedding, the couple worked in the Provincial Party Committee of Jiangxi. For the newly-weds a harmonious summer was now followed by an autumn filled with excitement, then by a winter of storms, and finally by a fateful spring.

As Provincial Party Secretary, Deng had declared himself publicly and agressively for Mao's "wealthy-peasants-line"—in other words in favor of leniency and against the Bolshevik severity towards the middle-class farmers. Additionally, he had advocated building up regional fighting forces in the districts, rather than concentrating on small units under a central command.

The 30-year-old Szechuanese had drawn bitter, but above all practical lessons from his party assignment in Guangxi. As a still relatively young pragmatist, still prepared to learn, he simply could not do otherwise than recognize Mao's guerrilla and peasant politics as the only correct line. For this reason, it was suddenly he, not Mao, who stood at the center of a Bolshevik attack.

In the April 15, 1933, edition of the newspaper "Red China," a certain Lo Man—also called Li Weihan—voiced his indignation over Deng's political line. He ranted furiously at this former comrade in arms from the Paris days. In the May 6 edition of the CC organ "Combat," Lo Man demanded a "ruthless attack and a brutal struggle" against Deng and all adherents to the Luo-Ming line.[1] The political death of Deng and the Luo-Ming faction would for all intents and purposes shackle the "giant" Mao. Such seems to have been Lo Man's political calculus.

Only a few months before this intra-party press war, Chiang Kai-shek's fourth campaign of encirclement had swept across the

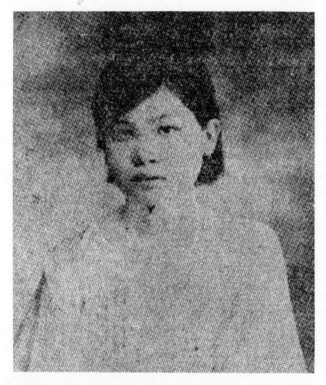

Jin Weiying (A Jin), Deng Xiaoping's second wife.

Red base area of Fujian in full force, compelling the Communists to retreat along the entire line. Comrade Luo Ming, the First Party Secretary of the province, believing defeat imminent, had advocated abandoning the Fujian Soviet and concentrating the decimated forces in Jiangxi. He maintained that fighting morale was poor among the peasants and that a guerrilla war modeled on Mao's strategy was more promising of success than the war of position advocated by Zhou Enlai and the other Bolsheviks.

The Bolsheviks now set upon Luo Ming, this pragmatic and—as would soon be clear—correct thinking comrade. Stirred up, they cried "conspiracy," while among themselves they whispered that Mao was behind it all.[2] They feared the independent "Red Bandit." No one dared challenge him openly and alone. They resorted to back-handed tricks and directed their attacks against Deng and Luo Ming.

Comrade Luo lost his position overnight; Deng's disempowerment was accomplished a step at a time. He had to resign his post as provincial Party Secretary, ceding his seat to his former colleague at Schneider-Creusot, Li Fuchun. Under duress, the "Little Cannon" moved to the propaganda department. Deng's demotion was as it were a finger pointing the fate of Mao Tsetung's third brother, Mao Tsetan, and Mao's old secretary, Gu Bo, who were both dispatched to the political side-lines by the long arm of Moscow through the provincial Party Committee. The purge was a death sentence for Mao Tsetan and the secretary, for, prohibited from taking part in the Long March, they perished in battle against superior units of the KMT.

But for Deng, things did not end simply with a transfer to another post: Lo Man, the Secretary of the CP Organization Office, loyal to Moscow, landed a double blow: he achieved Deng Xiaoping's further degradation by "robbing" him—as the Chinese say—of his wife.

When the stubborn Mao adherent fell, Jin Weiying divorced him in order to marry Lo Man. At first it looked as though she would leave her little ex-husband politically in the dust, for nothing now stood in the way of her own rise. The CC transferred her to the department of her new husband, from which she made the leap into the government of the Jiangxi Soviet. In January 1934, the delegates to the Second National Soviet Congress elected Jin Weiying to the Executive Committee, and to the Central Executive Committee, whereas her ex-husband was not even admitted to the assembly. Jin Weiying had an iron will, and numbered among those few women able to endure the Long March. But then in Yan'an, things turned bitter for her when Lo abandoned her to marry another. Since her health had suffered severely on the march, the party sent her in 1937 for a cure in the Soviet Union. She died there shortly after her arrival.

Lo Man's campaign of personal attack dispatched Deng down below, among the "simple foot soldiers." The man from Szechuan had to endure the ritual of self-criticism. The party demanded that he enumerate his errors in writing and offer an apology. Reluctantly, he criticized his underestimation of the "offensive line"— and that was all. His opponents were not satisfied with this laconic self-criticism though: the presumed conspirator even wound up in a jail cell where he endured starvation.

"Make yourself useful!"—this maxim runs like a red thread through Deng Xiaoping's life: to be of use, in every situation, to his comrades, to the organization. His inexhaustible drive to achieve always set him upright again—even in the year 1933, when he was toppled for the first time.

Deng was back on his feet. Whether his superior Zhou Enlai gave him a hand up is unclear. Mao could hardly have helped Deng, for his hands were tied. Certain it is that Chou's influence would have sufficed to prevent the fall of the friend of his youth from the Paris days. But out of genuine belief in a rigorous course of action, the *éminence grise* of the party had from the outset aligned himself in opposition to the Luo-Ming adherents. Independent of factional struggles within the party, Zhou Enlai throughout his life always rigorously placed politics above friendship. He conceived himself always as a servant to the party, not the advocate of some line.

After his precipitous fall, Deng Xiaoping began his arduous reascent. Released from jail, he proceeded on instructions of the CC to Nancun, a hamlet situated more than 300 kilometers northwest of the Red Capital. His new post was that of inspector. Here he was right at the front, for in the Le'an district, the modernly equipped National Army was harrassing the poorly armed Red Soldiers.

Deng Xiaoping had served barely half a month in Nancun when the party leadership recalled him to Ruijin into the Main

Political Department of the Red Army. There is speculation that the leadership feared Deng might defect to the enemy with all his party secrets. What is more likely is that the party, of greatly diminished cadre strength, simply could not in the long run pass over so dynamic and experienced a functionary as Deng, for the situation of the Jiangxi Soviet was worsening from one day to the next.

Every one in the restricted zone of the "Red Capital," seat of the CC and the high command of the Red Army, knew the little Szechuanese. The leaders—UTK graduates all—knew of course that he had studied at Sun Yatsen University in Moscow and had instructed at Sun Yatsen Military Academy in Xi'an. They therefore asked him to teach at the Military Academy of the Red Army, established in August 1933. The nimble Deng Xiaoping agreed at once and took over the course "Party Organization." Overnight, he had hoisted himself back up among the much older veterans Zhou Enlai, Liu Bocheng, and Dong Biwu, landing exactly where he had stood four months earlier. It was only now that his real rise began, completed during a deadly phase of the civil war.

Deng Xiaoping had been teaching just one month when in October 1933, Generalissimo Chiang Kai-shek, after several vain attempts, assembled a million soldiers, an air force of 200 modern war planes, tank units, and heavy artillery to wipe out the Communists once and for all. As in the old days, he himself commanded this gigantic force, which went down in the Chinese history books as the Fifth Campaign of Encirclement and Eradication. And this time, it looked as though he was succeeding. The Jiangxi Soviet shrank from day to day. In his support, Chiang Kai-shek had imported a "secret weapon" from Germany—Colonel General Hans von Seeckt, born in 1866 in Schleswig, and until 1926 Chief of Army Command of the German Reichswehr. None of the 60 foreign military advisors in China achieved as great a notoriety as this German general. He developed the so-called "blockhouse strategy" with which Chiang Kai-shek hoped to deliver the fatal blow to the Communists.

On Hans von Seeckt's advice, the National Army fought its way relentlessly forward into "Red" territory, securing their advance with dug-out shelters and small log blockhouses erected by construction brigades at every road fork and all arterial roads. In this fashion in the course of several months, a cordon of guard posts was created that threatened to strangle the Jiangxi Soviet. The farmers in the base area could no longer sell their grain and their meat and were cut off from deliveries of salt and cotton. Thanks to "German thoroughness," Chiang Kai-shek's victory crept ever closer.

The Communists countered the "White" blockhouses with "Red" ones; the "White" war of position of the National Army was met by the Red Army with a "Red" war of position. Behind this unimaginative counter-strategy stood likewise a German, who called himself Li De. Only since his identification in the May 27, 1964, "Neues Deutschland" does the world know him by the name he was born with, Otto Braun. Born in 1900 in Ismaning, near Munich, and member of the German CP, Otto Braun, after an adventurous escape from a Berlin prison, went to Moscow and studied at the Frunze Military Academy. After his graduation, Stalin had an Austrian passport given him with which in 1932 he crossed the Russian-Chinese border as an advisor of the Comintern. Deng Xiaoping could not stand this ever pompous military advisor of Bo Gu's with his Prussian military manners.

The disastrous effects of the Communist party-line battles and Chiang Kai-shek's encirclements are shown by the losses of territory of the Red Army: in barely a year, Hans von Seeckt's blockhouse cordon took from the severely weakened revolutionaries meter after meter of "liberated" ground. When Deng Xiaoping arrived in Ruijin in August 1931, even parts of the province of Fujian belonged to the Jiangxi Soviet, which extended over the entire southern portion of the 164,000 square kilometer province of Jiangxi. By October 1934, the Communists were able to move about freely within only several hundred square kilometers. Flight was the only option for the encircled troops. On October 16, 1934, exactly 86,859 fighters of the Red Army—according to muster rolls—crossed the sluggish Yudu River. In just one year, these people covered more than 10,000 kilometers in murderous day-and-night marches. They were constantly harried, if not by the National Army, then by the mercenary army of some warlord.

The Long March (Chang Zheng) began in the bamboo forests of the south and ended after 25,000 li [ca. 8,500 miles] in the loess mountains of northern Shaanxi, after exactly 378 days of hell, which barely 9,000 revolutionaries survived. The history of China's revolution knows just this single epic, whose final line was written only on October 1, 1949, when Mao Tsetung cried to the world: "The Chinese people has arisen!" Deng Xiaoping marched along through this hell, which was for him, as it was for Mao, an ascent out of the abyss into the light.

At the start of the Long March, Deng was in the second rank; his responsibility as sole editor was to bring out the army newspaper "Red Star." In the course of the next twelve agonizing months he would rise to be one of the most important men at Mao's side. At the start, when the troops were crossing the Yudu, all Deng had to do was march. Not until two months later, after their arrival in the city of Zunyi, did his "Red Star" appear for the first time with the militant appeal: "Strengthen Communist Propaganda!" This theme was not an arbitrary one, for an important conference was to take place in Zunyi that would prove to be of paramount importance for Deng's personal fortunes. Even before the column of march had reached Zunyi, the party leadership installed Deng Xiaoping as director of the CC secretariat. At a conference in the district town Liping, 320 kilometers southeast of Zunyi, he represented Zhou Enlai's ailing wife, whose condition was worsening from day to day. She was no longer able to direct the CC secretariat from her litter; hence this office was now transferred to an experienced person, the 31-year-old Deng. Even before his Guangxi mission, after all, he had as deputy director of the secretariat organized records, formulated directives, transmitted instructions, and controlled scheduling of the Central Committee. The official election of Deng as head of the CC secretariat occurred only during the conference in Zunyi. This conference in large measure determined Deng's future political course; above all, however, the future course of the Chinese revolution was determined here. Asked about this, Deng remarked later, "The opportunistic line was corrected at the Zunyi Conference. Comrade Mao, as political leader, brought the party onto the correct path."

What really happened during those days at the beginning of the year 1935 in that obscure spot in the north of the province of Guizhou? On the evening of January 15, the large hall of an elegant mansion filled with people. In no fixed seating order, the leading functionaries of the military and political spheres took their places at a massive mahogony table for a session of the expanded Politburo. An old kerosene lamp gave out sufficient light. If it was cool outside, the atmosphere inside was positively icy, for two factions sat across from each other fighting for their political lives. The randomly furnished room and the absence of any seating order might have conveyed the impression of a spontaneous meeting, but in fact a conspiracy hatched by Mao against the Bolsheviks to push through his guerrilla line was born here.

Mao Tsetung knew that the continuation of his army depended on the outcome of this evening's conference. If he did not succeed in stripping Bo Gu, Otto Braun, and the Bolsheviks of power, the fate of the 30,000 revolutionaries was sealed. Long before Zunyi, already after the first one hundred or two hundred kilometers of the march, Mao, suffering from malaria, had begun enlisting comrades of the "Convalescence Group" for an organized opposition to the CP leader and his German military advisor. With every day of the march that passed, Mao, who was being carried, sometimes lying, sometimes sitting, gathered his followers closer about him. Shortly before Zunyi, he had even won over the Bolshevik Zhang Wentian, the number two in the party hierarchy, to his "litter conspiracy." On the eve of the Politburo session, Mao once more swore his adherents to allegiance. The Politcommissar of the Fifth Army Group recalled:

> I hadn't been in Zunyi a day, when Comrade Mao Tsetung received me in his sleeping quarters. He was suffering from a bad cold and had wrapped his head with a towel like a turban. Though seriously exhausted, he listened patiently as I told him of the dissatisfaction, the complaints, and the mutterings of my troops. Then he laughed and asked if that all meant dissatisfaction with the leadership. When I answered yes, he asked if I couldn't speak of that the next day.[3]

On the first two evenings of the Zunyi Conference, Mao found himself still on the defensive; he occupied himself entirely with giving cues. Then, however, Mao began to break apart the troika of Bo Gu, Zhang Wentian, and Zhou Enlai, and won his return to the Politburo and the Military Commission. His next step was to install his new ally Zhang Wentian in the number one spot in the party hierarchy. He succeeded in this on the second phase of the Long March, without a session of the Politburo's having been held. He was able to accomplish the third step, becoming Chairman of the Military Commission, only in December 1936.

The survival of the Communist Party was in many respects owed to Mao's personal engagement at the Zunyi Conference and the second phase of the Long March. Zhou Enlai wrote in his memoires:

> As we left Zunyi, an enemy division was blocking our way in the village of Daguxinchang. We called a meeting, and decided by a majority to attack them. Mao alone demurred, but he had to acquiesce to the majority.
>
> On the evening before the operation, he was plagued with doubts. He came to me late at night, lantern in hand, and asked me to postpone the order to attack so that he could consider it further. I acceded to his request. In the early morning I called a meeting at which the minds of all those attending were changed. When the others had left, Comrade Mao expressed the view that since decisions were also reached in this way, so large a committee was no longer really needed. A group composed of a couple of people was quite sufficient. Later, we formed a staff of Mao, Wang Jiaxiang, and me.[4]

As so often, Mao was right this time too. An attack would have brought the Red Army heavy losses. Nevertheless, an odor of intrigue clung to the whole affair. Does the end really always justify the means?

Following the Zunyi Conference, Zhou Enlai figured as the most important man in the party; Mao was entirely correct in his alliance. But he was also betting that his new ally was unassuming, that he would never defect to the opinions of others or take seriously even the most absurd objections and counter-proposals, and that lust for power was totally lacking in him.

The Zunyi Conference, held on the evenings of January 15, 16, and 17, 1935, reckons as a cornerstone in the history of the Chinese revolution. And nevertheless—or precisely therefore—until the beginning of the eighties, the strictest secrecy had been maintained regarding it. For more than forty-five years, the party shrouded this meeting, and above all Mao's role in it, in mystery. The Conference at Zunyi was described as the culmination of the power struggle between Mao's line and that of Stalin's Comintern; from Zunyi forward, it was said, Mao "took the leadership of the Chinese revolution in hand." Only the current decline of the Mao cult has allowed the beginnings of a realistic appraisal of the events at Zunyi.

What is fact is that the conference was a collective success for comrades Mao, Zhang Wentian, and Wang Jiaxiang. Mao returned to the Military Commission and the Politburo, and was assigned as assistant to Zhou Enlai, who made the final decisions concerning the military execution of the Long March.[5] The Bolshevik oriented party leader Bo Gu initially retained his position. Only later, without fanfare, did Zhang Wentian replace him. Only Otto Braun, demoted meanwhile to the status of observer, was stripped of power by Mao and his people. During the entire conference, he had occupied a seat next to the door in the second row.

Like Otto Braun, Deng Xiaoping was also sitting in the second row. This fact has been known only in the last few years. Today we can say with certainty that the Zunyi Conference represented a turning point in Deng's life, for only now is it officially acknowledged that he numbered among the participants at all.

In connection with Deng Xiaoping's fall during the Cultural Revolution, his political opponents spread the rumor that he had never participated in the important conference.[6] But from 1979, the truth gradually came to light. For the first time in the history of the New China, the youth journal "Zhongguo Qingnian" published in its November issue the complete list of participants. Deng Xiaoping appears here as director of the CC secretariat. On January 9, 1980, the official news agency "Xinhua" went public with this list of names. Their report contained the interesting addendum: "Those present in an advisory capacity were Deng Xiaoping, Otto Braun, and Wu Xiuquan," Braun's interpreter.

Four years later, on March 4, 1984, the party historians produced a memorandum with additional details. Concerning Deng Xiaoping it said that he had occupied the post of director of the CC secretariat and had been a full-fledged member of the conference, while Otto Braun and General Wu Xiuquan were declared "present in an advisory capacity." Deng Xiaoping was, then, a participant *ex officio,* but his status is not thereby clarified. On the first evening he sat in the corner taking notes. As newly appointed director of the secretariat, he did not take part in the high-powered meeting, but functioned as keeper of the minutes in his capacity as editor of "Red Star." Only on the second or third evening did the group confirm him in the office of Director of the CC secretariat[7] and elect him in addition Deputy Director of the Main Political Department of the Red Army. In the course of this conference, the abruptly deposed Szechuanese had stepped from the second row to take his place among China's future leadership elite as though this were the most natural step in the world.

Early on the morning of January 19, 1935, just under 35,000 old and newly recruited fighters marched out of Zunyi. Deng was now mounted on a horse, since in the meantime he had joined the top command. When the entourage reached the snow-mountains 200 kilometers west of Chengdu in April, the order came that all men of the auxilliary forces had to assume a function in the fighting forces. Hereupon Deng, who had been promoted, moved over to the First Army Group and took over the propaganda department. The barely 4′11″ man yielded the position of Director of the Secretariat to a barely 4′11″ woman, 27-year-old Liu Ying, who would soon thereafter marry the General Secretary of the party, Zhang Wentian.

During the Long March, friendships developed, and animosities grew. Mao and Deng befriended one another. Comrade Tsetung was a person who could never forget. Deng Xiaoping profited thereby: had he not already in Jiangxi remained loyal to the then politically isolated "Red Bandit," and in consequence served time in a jail cell?

Mao enjoyed the company of the little Szechuanese, who reminded him of his slain brother Tsetan. With respect to their jokes that often passed over into sarcasm, and likewise to the seriousness with which they both pursued a common goal, Mao and Deng seemed like twins. The tall man from Hunan liked to lead men and to mold them. At first he gathered mostly peasant lads about him; later, he surrounded himself with educated men like Zhou Enlai, Chen Yi, Lin Piao, and Deng Xiaoping, who not only looked up to him, but could also interrupt him. Towards the end of the March, the youthful Deng always stepped in between the bulky Mao and the lanky Zhou Enlai. These two tolerated the newcomer—in fact, they seemed, the three of them, to understand each other perfectly.

In the year 1935 Mao cemented a still young friendship with his superior Chou. Those who knew the two more closely, however, soon noticed that they were by nature very different from each other. Mao, the crude, totally self-confident son of a peasant, and Chou, the sensitive, almost effeminate scion of wealthy gentry (a family of state officials), had each swerved from their paths to enter the revolutionary ranks from opposite sides. The cool Mao and the affable Chou themselves sensed there were limits to their friendship. So they gladly admitted Deng to their circle of two. Deng Xiaoping became the connecting link each of them needed equally between their two characters. If he more often applied the brakes to Mao, he tended to push Chou. Out of this tripartite relationship, an informal leadership collective was to evolve that substantially influenced the further course of the Chinese revolution.

To the harsh physical exertions of the march, political tensions were added in June 1935. Deng had to look on as Mao, his senior by eleven years, with whom he saw eye to eye, fell into serious conflict with one of the founding members of the CP, Zhang Guotao. Mao wanted to end the Long March in northern Shaanxi. Zhang, however, felt this was too dangerous—northern Shaanxi lay in the middle of an area occupied by Kuomintang troops—and wanted to move further west, to Xinjiang. Following this dispute, on the final 25,000 li, one party had broken into two, both of which claimed sole representative authority. The parting of the ways in the village of Mao'ergai in northern Szechuan figured as the most serious break in party history.

It was a *fait accompli* when on September 2 Politcommissar Mao simply marched off with the commanders loyal to him, Peng Dehuai, Lin Piao, and Ye Jianying, as well as with Zhou Enlai, staff members of the CC apparatus, and the logistical forces. Deng had decided against the Bolsheviks and for the "Red Bandit." He was in Mao's column of march moving north towards the province of Shaanxi.

The high command of this portion of the former main army, which in the meantime had been dubbed the Right Route Army, was held by Peng Dehuai, while the 31-year-old Deng Xiaoping occupied the post of Deputy Politcommissar. His immediate superior was his old friend and countryman Nie Rongzhen, with whom he had worked together already in 1921 at Schneider-Creusot in France. It had never even occurred to this adherent of Mao's to follow Zhang Guotao and his Fourth Front Army. On the other hand, the pivotal military leaders of the Red Army, Zhu De and Liu Bocheng, had broken with Mao. With their 40,000 man Left Route Army, they sought first to establish a Red base area in northern Szechuan. They were later to move to the west after all and, fully a year after Mao, arrive in the new capital Bao'an.

After a hellish flight across eighteen mountain ranges, through twenty-four rivers and twelve provinces, Mao arrived with the four thousand men remaining to him on October 29, 1935, in northern Shaanxi. Stricken with severe typhoid fever, Deng Xiaoping could neither ride nor walk. His life-threatening illness was treated in the district town Wuqi, barely 180 kilometers west of Yan'an. Thanks to strict rest and better treatment, he soon regained his strength. After a halt of several weeks, the force marched on to Wayaobu, today Zichang. By then he was already able to take part in political meetings again.

The villages of Wuqi and Wayaobu figure as the final stations of the Long March. With the elevation of Bao'an to "Red Capital," a new chapter of Chinese revolutionary history began.

EIGHT

Front Years

A BRIEF EXCHANGE of fire on the Marco Polo Bridge in Peking unleashed a huge, death-dealing invasion: On July 7, 1937, Japan attacked northern China with 40 divisions—fully 580,000 men. Actually, the Sino-Japanese war had already begun in 1931 with Japan's invasion of Manchuria. The occupiers now advanced at a furious pace south and west along the central railway line. Peking, Jinan, capital of Shandong province, and Taiyuan, capital of Shanxi, fell in quick succession.

Nationalists and Communists ended their own strife in order to fight the common external enemy. The national contradiction has eclipsed the class contradiction, was Mao Tsetung's analysis of the country's situation. It was only consistent for the Communists, on August 22, 1937, to rename their Red Workers' and Peasants' Army the National Revolutionary Eighth Route Army and place it under the command of China's most powerful leader, Chiang Kai-shek.

About half a year before the beginning of the war, Deng Xiaoping had moved to the new "Red Capital," Yan'an. While the Party Chairman had been issued a spacious apartment with three interconnecting rooms, Deng and Zhou Enlai had to make do with more cramped accommodations.

Yan'an, eight hours by bus north of the provincial capital, Xi'an, quickly evolved into a Mecca for Chinese and foreign revolutionaries. In the broad valley below the "Treasure Pagoda" Bao Ta, peace and quiet reigned at last—or, as the German Anna Wang expressed it,

Yan'an was the epitome of comfort. Compared to the rigors of the Long March, life as it was lived here was luxurious. There was enough to eat, enough to smoke—which was very important for Mao. It was a time of much laughter, a time between the wars.

Anna Wang, the estranged wife of the well-known diplomat Wang Bingnan, still remembers precisely the common mealtimes of those days:

> The atmosphere was unrestrained; the leaders wagered on who could deliver the wittiest remarks. This furnished everyone intellectual entertainment; more than anyone, Mao loved the jokes supremely; he was notorious for his sarcasm, after all.[1]

The laughter in the loess mountains of northern Shaanxi would soon fall silent, for the Japanese were on the advance. Since they had already occupied Taiyuan, less than 500 kilometers away, it was crucial now that deeds quickly follow the Communist-Nationalist alliance.

The Communists organized their troops under the command of the former warlord of Taiyuan. The former KUTV student and well-known youth leader Ren Bishi was named leader of the Main Political Department of the Army, and Deng Xiaoping was named his deputy. The newly created Eighth Route Army was subdivided into three divisions.[2]

All three units were impressively disciplined and well armed. In their grey "Sun Yatsen" jackets, their white leggings and open straw sandals, the ranks, recuperated by now from the Long March and also in part newly recruited, seemed unified and close to the people. Neither insignia of rank nor special uniforms differentiated officers from enlisted men. Even Deng Xiaoping, like any common soldier, wore the high-buttoned cotton jacket of coarse, grey cloth equipped with four pockets, and the leggings, and was shod peasant-fashion in hand-woven sandals. Not even his unadorned visor-cap betrayed his rank. Only one token identified him as someone issuing orders: the wide leather belt around his hips from which hung a heavy pistol holster. The great exception in this egalitarian-seeming army was Mao Tsetung. He preferred a dark uniform with baggy, comfortable pants, and a casual cap without a visor. His dress was more reminiscent of a suit than a uniform.

Deng Xiaoping was not staying in the "Red Capital" when the Sino-Japanese war broke out. Since the end of July, he had been working as a cadre of the Main Political Department in the "Five Terraces Mountains," Wutai Shan, 650 kilometers away in northeastern Shanxi, the neighboring province. From morning to night at the foot of the holy mountain he saw to the political education of the Red soldiers preparing themselves for the great fight.

In the first weeks of September, 1937, Commander in Chief Zhu De ordered the decampment: it was the signal to fan out. Trusting to Mao's guerrilla strategy ("Our strategy is—one against ten; our tactic—ten against one!"), the three divisions scored a series of remarkable victories. Their medium range goal, however, driving the Japanese out of the provincial capital, could be achieved only at great cost to their forces; therefore, they merged the 115th and 129th Divisions and attacked the Japanese frontally. With this first larger offensive, the Communists knocked a thousand Japanese soldiers out of action. Now the road to Taiyuan had been opened, and in fact the Eighth Route Army succeeded on November 9 in taking the provincial capital, 500 kilometers southwest of Peking.

In January 1938, after the Route Army had established a base area in the Taihang mountains and built themselves a good "hunting blind" overlooking the northern Chinese lowland, the Politcommissar of the 129th Division, Zhang Hao, died. Therewith, an important post fell vacant. Who was to fill it? The Military Commission decided after brief consultation on the 33-year-old Deng. The appointment came as a surprise, even to Deng Xiaoping, who thus took a giant step upwards in the military hierarchy.

Meanwhile, the man who never forgot and rarely forgave was functioning as Chairman of the Military Commission. Perhaps that had been decisive: Mao knew he could rely absolutely on his friend Deng, as had been demonstrated during the days in Jiangxi and the Long March. The "One-Eyed Dragon," though—could he be trusted? Mao could not forget that Liu Bocheng, blind in one eye, had once voted with the Bolsheviks and Otto Braun in favor of the "offensive war of position," and had later made pacts with the party-splitter, Zhang Guotao. Mao showed calculation in placing Deng as watchman at the side of his willful General Liu.

From the first day, the two Szechuanese understood each other, although they never became close friends. Deng loved the dry humor of his compatriot and admired his pronounced sense of justice. Liu needed jokes and humorous exaggeration like daily bread, whereas for Deng these were mere garnish. Both resorted often to harsh words, admitting of not the slightest contradiction. When these two stubbornly bumped heads, their fiery Szechuanese tempers would explode into a vigorous quarrel, which flared . . . and then blew over.

Deng, the political strategist, and Liu, the military strategist respected one another because each knew his field so well. Easily riled, the "One-Eyed Dragon" won Deng's complete trust; the man twelve years his senior became his military foster-father. From him, Deng Xiaoping learned the art of combat and survival. In 1943, he would receive the honor of naming Deng's firstborn son. When Deng was still living in his hamlet of Xiexing, Liu Bocheng, son of a wandering minstrel, was already in the service of a Szechuanese warlord. General Liu was, and remained to his death in October 1986, a soldier through and through. For thirteen years—from 1938 until 1951—Liu and Deng would fight side by side, and accomplish such great things that their 129th Division would go down in the history of China as the "Liu-Deng Army."

No sooner had Deng assumed his new position than the 129th Division already abandoned its "hunting blind," descending into the northern Chinese lowland. They succeeded in establishing the base area Pingyuan ("lowland") in the south of Hebei province without serious losses. It was the first time in the anti-Japanese war of resistance that a Chinese unit had ventured so far behind enemy lines, blocking the central Peking-Wuhan-Canton railway line to boot.

Once they had secured their position in Pingyuan, the Liu-Deng Army broke up into small guerrilla units and a regiment that gave the Japanese encumbered with their tanks and artillery no rest. With their "pin-prick" tactic, devised jointly by Liu and Deng, the 6,000-man division succeeded in knocking fully ten thousand Japanese soldiers out of action between January and September of 1938.

Deng received an unusual visit while he was staying in southern Hebei: Evans Carlson,[3] Major in the U. S. Marine Corps, inspected the Communist-Nationalist troop movements in China.

Politcommissar Deng, Liu Bocheng, Zhu De *(from left to right).*

Deng Xiaoping at soldiers' training in Guangxian (Henan Province).

Carlson reported to Politcommissar Deng as Washington's Military Observer and was impressed by his grasp of the world situation. "Tun Shao-pin [by which the American meant Deng Xiaoping] was a short, chunky, and physically tough man with a mind as keen as mustard."

Politcommissar Deng and his commander, Liu Bocheng, both knew how to use their keen minds. The veteran Liu had in addition twenty-seven years of combat experience. Not by chance, then, did the Liu-Deng Army evolve into the most successful unit the Red Army ever possessed. In the summer of 1938, they controlled the entire northern Chinese lowland, also called the Hebei-Shandong-Henan Plain, twice the size of France. The Japanese would never again succeed in breaking off large parts of this liberated territory. Until the war's end in 1945, the "cradle of Chinese civilization" would belong to the Communists.

In the years 1937 to 1940, the 129th Division not only fought victoriously, but also under the direction of its Politcommissar established four Red base areas: in the Taihang and the Taiyue Mountains of the province of Shanxi, identified from time immemorial—in short-hand as it were—by the character Jin; in the northern province Hebei, known as Ji; in the coastal province Shandong, denoted by Lu; and finally in the province of Henan, assigned the ancient character Yu. Collectively, they were called the Shanxi-Hebei-Shandong-Henan Red base area, or more popularly: Jin-Ji-Lu-Yu. To assure their defense, headquarters assigned 30 regiments to each of these base areas, and unified the four military districts into the military region Jin-Ji-Lu-Yu comprising more than one million square kilometers.

The political head of this state within a state was none other than Politcommissar Deng. His word weighed heavily, for he embodied the party, while Liu functioned as its military arm. For the first time, significant power was concentrated in Deng's hands. All political and administrative organs of this area were subordinate to him in his capacity as First Party Secretary of the CC Office of Shanxi-Hebei-Shandong-Henan.

His counsel was sought equally in regard to the establishment of small craft shops such as oil presses, weaving mills, and flour mills, and the procurement of school books for illiterates young and old, as well as in regard to the establishment of a primitively armed peoples' militia. Deng Xiaoping was also in charge of training political cadres for a propaganda squad assigned to popularize the politics of the Communists among the peasantry. The Politcommissar could help theoretically as well as practically—he had, after all, been responsible for building up the right-hand river soviet in the far south ten years before. Already in the first months of the Sino-Japanese war, the Communist slogan "Chinese do not fight Chinese!" had elicited much positive response. It had become evident that the Chinese revered their fatherland as holy and that patriotism lived on from generation to generation. Deng Xiaoping's propaganda troops did not need to fire a barrage of words to incite the population of the countryside against their occupiers. They sabotaged the supplies of the Japanese without the help of the Communists. A wide-spread slogan went: "Mix sand into the requisitioned rice so the dogs bite their teeth out!"

The educational work was impeded, however, by the peasants' age-old hatred of the Chinese military. They trembled at the sight of the Kuomintang soldiers, who swarmed over the villages like locusts, impressing the sturdiest of the young men, often dragging them off in chains. The reputation of the military in China was traditionally lower than that of whores, beggars, and usurers. Scarcely was a soldier's uniform spotted near a village than the peasants fled to the woods. On top of this aversion was the fear of Communists, about whom every landowner spread tales of horrors.

The Chinese Communists recognized the poorer peasantry (the credit for this belongs historically to Mao Tsetung) as the true bearers of the Chinese revolution. This is why parallel to the armed struggle they organized their vigorous effort to win over the impoverished rural population to their program.

So, in accordance with the strategic instructions from Yan'an, to begin with Deng instituted a land reform in every newly established Red base area. With gentle pressure, his agents persuaded the landowners to lower their rents, and to increase the incomes of the destitute tenant farmers. Five years later, this mild handling of the landowners would be replaced by a harsher one.

Every partisan in the Liu-Deng Army had to demonstrate his ability to handle not only a rifle but a hoe as well. The Politcommissar saw to that personally. To spur the worker's zeal and to make the army self-sufficient, a small parcel of land was distributed to every soldier. Even in areas generally occupied by enemy positions, the fighters often stripped off their grey uniforms and worked the fields in peasant garb. They not only cultivated virgin soil, however; they also built schools, and established small craft shops that produced rice bowls, toothbrushes, tooth powder, and even weapons. "Rely on your own strength!" went one of the first slogans adopted by the rural population.

To the millions of impoverished peasants, who formerly might have had to sell their children as a result of a ruined harvest, their new homelands, the liberated zones, seemed like heaven on earth, and Mao Tsetung, the "Red Sun," appeared as their savior. The reverence that lives on today for the "Great Chairman" has its roots in this period, and likewise the high esteem for "Uncle Soldier-of-the-Liberation-of-the-People," Jiefangjun Shushu.

In those years, Deng proved himself an avid pupil of his friend Mao, who in Yan'an had just authored the direction-setting paper "On the New Democracy." Mao theorized; Deng put into practice, or better, related Mao's major principles to the actuality in the base areas under his administration. If Mao wrote of the tripartite division of power on all levels of government, Deng actualized the same division within his administrative units for the representatives of the CCP, the KMT, and the independent parties.

Conversely, Deng's reports on his experiences must have led Mao to new ideas, for he was ensconced in Yan'an while his pragmatic comrade in arms broke virgin soil at the front. Deng Xiaoping's opinion was sought in all matters. He published a series of economic and political articles in the Yan'an journals "Liberation," "The Front," and "The Masses," demonstrating versatility like no other Politcommissar and Party Secretary.

Deng's situation in the late summer of 1939 can be compared perfectly with his situation in the summer of 1933. Now, too, he was experiencing personal as well professional good fortune: after returning to Yan'an as one of the most successful commanders at the front, he married for the third time.

He had known the wiry, petite Pu Zhuo Lin for some time. She had worked since her graduation from the Anti-Japanese University of Yan'an in the Women's Federation of the CP's northern office. Pu Zhuo Lin, who in the seventies dropped her family name Pu and thenceforth used only her Communist Party name Zhuo Lin, was the daughter of the former "Ham King of Yunnan," Pu Caiting. Father Pu had in 1916 given his daughter the name Pu

Qiongying. The wealthy Pu family came from the prosperous south Chinese border province of Yunnan, whose opium was once as sought after as its tea is today. Although the family lived in the rather insignificant district of Xuanwei on the Kunming-Guiyang railway line, the father's smoked and air-dried hams hung in inns and shops throughout the province. During the Sino-Japanese war, canned hams with Pu's picture on the label appeared even in the northern provinces. Even in hard times, the sausage manufacturer's fortunes remained high and he was able to finance excellent educations for his children: her wealthy father sent Qiongying to a boarding school in the provincial capital, Kunming. She proved especially proficient in two subjects—physics and athletics. Since her athletic accomplishments numbered among the top in the province, she even participated in national championship competition.

Midway through the thirties, this eldest daughter, whose political orientation had by then swung to the left, transferred from Kunming to the First Middle School for Girls in Peking. After her final examination in the year 1936, she matriculated in the Department of Physics at the Pedagogical Institute for Women, but the outbreak of the Sino-Japanese war forced her to interrupt her studies. Like many urban revolutionary intellectuals, she made her way in 1937 to Yan'an.

After a simple wedding in August 1939, Deng and Pu Zhuo Lin saddled their horses. Their honeymoon was to last ten days. The young comrade couple—he was 36, she 24—had no objection to company, for "honeymoon" to these two meant something altogether mundane: an exhausting march eastwards to the headquarters of the Liu-Deng Army. Along with the soldiers accompanying Deng, there was also a front-line correspondent from "Xinhua Ribao," Lu Yi, from Shanghai.

On the eve of their departure from Yan'an, the newly wed Politcommissar interrogated the jounalist regarding his qualifications: "How much baggage do you have with you? Do you know how to ride? Are you fit enough to climb mountains? Can you walk in straw sandals, or just leather shoes?" The undertone of irony in Deng's voice was not to be missed. Finally he nodded his approval and announced their departure for Dongyue, location of the Liu-Deng Army headquarters, for six o'clock the next morning.

Zhuo Lin (Pu Qiongying), Deng Xiaoping's third wife.

Wanting to be doubly sure, the Politcommissar asked the city-slicker Lu Yi jokingly just before their departure: "Have you ever been exposed to gunfire? You don't have to come along with me, you know. You can just as well stay at Wei Lihuang's headquarters [a KMT commander allied with the Communists], and post your dispatches from there by telegraph." But the journalist stuck with the group, a motley of soldiers, visiting academics, students, wives and lovers of soldiers at the front, as well as their children.

Deng Xiaoping himself went on foot, having loaded his horse with books and writing paraphernalia. Only women and children—Pu Zhuo Lin among them—rode in the colorful caravan. Even in the absence of enemy harrassment the column advanced only slowly, not more than 25 kilometers per day. Across the Yellow River, they found the countryside empty of people; many fields lay fallow. This situation changed dramatically when they crossed from "White" into "Red" territory. Here, the countryside was alive with people: most peasants had fled into the Red base area.

Before the procession neared the Japanese siege-line, Deng called everyone together. In a pointedly calm tone he announced that in consideration of the women and children and the large quantity of baggage, they would negotiate the enemy positions only under cover of darkness. He reiterated in a serious tone the importance of staying together. His address made clear that he was well informed of the troop strength and the troop movements of the Japanese.

In the year 1986, the retired correspondent Lu Yi recalled:

> Deng Xiaoping acted skillfully and above all swiftly. Decisions fell nimbly from his hand. On the night we had to pass the Japanese blockade, we had actually planned to move out at 21:00 hours. Since we were ready by 19:00 hours, Deng ordered the action to proceed at once.

Behind the Japanese cordon, the populated villages were more frequent. As soon as the procession passed through a hamlet, Deng could be seen in conversation with the peasants. He was gathering information about the circumstances of the tenants and the local landowners, which fell under his duties as Politcommissar.

> At night, we were quartered with the peasants—no, we did not sleep in tents. Deng set night-sentries to guard the

entrance to the village. We slept in general quarters, while he as commander slept with Zhuo Lin in a separate room.[4]

The caravan made its way only slowly to the headquarters of the Liu–Deng Army in the heart of Shanxi province. Often, they had to march camouflaged, for low-flying enemy aircraft went searching for ground troops. But the march went successfully; they were attacked neither from the air nor from ambush.

At the headquarters, Lu Yi met Liu Bocheng for the first time, and on a later inspection tour he got a taste of the "One-Eyed Dragon's" sense of humor. "Today, you must be patient. Today, we will make three visits. First, we'll see an armaments factory," Liu told the correspondent.

> What we entered sometime later was a shed where bayonettes were being made from Japanese railroad rails. After the smithy, we inspected an infirmary and finally a small weaving mill.

Deng and Liu were known as thoughtful commanders. When problems arose, anyone could visit their quarters and be heard informally. The two leaders concerned themselves also with the sick and wounded. In 1986, the German Hans Müller still recalled vividly an infirmary visitor who had rewarded him handsomely:

> It was in the spring of 1940. I lay in the infirmary of the headquarters of the Liu–Deng Army, semiconscious with abdominal typhus, when unexpectedly Politcommissar Deng Xiaoping stepped to my bed and presented me with a whole carton of the fancy "Shanghai" brand cigarettes. Since I smoked about 60 cigarettes a day at that time, I was naturally pleased with this gift.[5]

Hans Müller was not, like Evans Carlson, just passing through, but was a doctor in the Liu–Deng Army. Though he treated many common soldiers and officers, he never treated Deng Xiaoping: "He was simply never sick."

The Sons of Nippon gradually lost ground—if only in the hinterlands. They regarded their positions in the cities and along the railway lines, on the other hand, as invincible. That was a misapprehension they were soon to be disabused of, however. In August 1940, the Communists, no longer satisfied with "pinpricks," altered their tactics. The Army of Deng and Liu Bocheng had advance word of a large-scale Japanese offensive into south-western and northwestern China and rushed now to ready a powerful blow.

From throughout the north, the Communist high command drew together 105 regiments and involved the Japanese in a war of position: 400,000 men offered the Japanese the "Battle of the Hundred Regiments," lasting three months and putting 44,000 enemy soldiers out of action.[6] To be sure, Chairman Mao as well as the Military Commission manifested their displeasure already in the summer of 1940 because those responsible—Liu Bocheng, Deng Xiaoping, and Peng Dehuai—had acted without consulting Central Headquarters in Yan'an and had informed them only after the start of the battle. But with the fall came victory, and Mao sent a congratulatory telegram from Yan'an which said: "The 'Battle of the Hundred Regiments' encourages the people. How about another victory like that?" And Peng Dehuai was decorated by Chiang Kai-shek telegraphically from Chungking.

Like almost all the great events in the history of the revolution, the "Battle of the Hundred Regiments" would also be discredited by the Red Guard during the Cultural Revolution, and Politcommissar Deng personally would be attacked as an enemy of Mao's guerrilla strategy.[7]

After the lost battle, the Japanese agressor reared up like a wounded tiger, raging horribly. The war was to drag on another five years, in the course of which the power bases of the Communists, not the Nationalists, would expand enormously: when the Japanese were forced to surrender their weapons in August 1945, the Communists controlled 19 base areas, home to 95.5 million people.

Deng Xiaoping, who had been in the middle of the tumult of battle, returned uninjured from the lowland to mountainous northern Shaanxi. He, Liu Bocheng, and Peng Dehuai were hailed as heros in Yan'an.

Politcommissar Deng shuttled frequently between the headquarters of his army and Central Headquarters in Yan'an. During the last weeks of the winter of 1942, he stayed in the "Red Capital," for among the party functionaries a "rectification movement" was underway: on February 1, 1942, Mao Tsetung used the occasion of the opening of the Party School there to launch the campaign

The commanders of the 129th Division in Liao Xian
(today Zuoquan Xian, Shanxi Province), April 15, 1940:
(from left to right) Li Da, Deng Xiaoping, Liu Bocheng,
Cai Shufan.

Politcommissar Deng Xiaoping in 1941 in Yan'an.

with his historical speech "The Improvement of the Work Style of the Party." He was not sparing in his sharp attacks against the last remaining Bolsheviks. Without calling the students of Stalin by name, he characterized them as "priests" of universal formulas divorced from reality. He likened their dogma to worthless muck and said, "You can manure a field with dogshit . . . But what can you do with dogmas? Neither manure a field, nor feed dogs; what use are they?" It was principally those who had studied abroad who caught the brunt of his critical barrage. He compared them to a gramophone playing the same record over and over.

Did he also take aim at Deng, traveler to France and Moscow? Apparently not, for Deng was often to be seen during these days of February in Mao's company. To those on the outside, it all looked as if they saw eye to eye. Zhou Enlai's later statement that Deng had very earnestly supported the realignment movement and had been relatively or totally error-free confirms this impression. But Deng Xiaoping lingered in Yan'an only briefly to receive the latest directives from Central Headquarters.

In 1943 his perpetual traveling between the front and Central Headquarters came to an end. Deng was transferred to Yan'an, where he remained through war's end. After only a few months, even the areas of the front most remote from Yan'an knew the name Deng Xiaoping, for the party leadership had promoted the diminutive Szechuanese to Director of the Main Political Administration of the Military Commission. He was now responsible for the political education of the 910,000 Red soldiers and almost one million party members.

The move into the back country brought a measure of peace into his life. In that year, Pu Zhuo Lin gave birth to her first son, Deng Pufang. Only the few initiates knew that Pufang was the Dengs' second child. After her lying in, Zhuo Lin had had to leave the little Lin, born in September 1941 in the district town She Xian, behind in the care of a peasant family and had been able to bring her to Yan'an only two years later. While Deng Lin's name was a combination of her father's and mother's names, the name Pufang, meaning "plain and just," came from Liu Bocheng.

Shortly before the end of the war, Deng took part in the first, and at once the longest, Party Congress of his life. The VIIth Party Congress of the Chinese Communist Party lasted 50 days, from April 23 to June 11, 1945. This party congress was a huge success for Deng Xiaoping. Everyone was prepared for his election to the Central Committee, but not for the promotion of the newcomer by the delegates to seat number 28, precedent even to Ye Jianying, Nie Rongzhen, and Peng Dehuai. This advancement caused a sensation.

Another might also have felt triumphant—Mao, the "Wise Leader" and "Standard-Bearer of the Party." Yes, these were his official epithets since his election to Chairman of the Politburo and the Central Committee early in 1943. At the VIIth Party Congress, Mao celebrated what was probably the greatest success of his life. With his election to Chairman of the CC secretariat, as well as to Chairman of the Military Commission, all political and military power was now concentrated in Mao's hands.

Collective leadership was dead; the cult of personality had been born, as the then relatively obscure labor union functionary Liu Shaoqi explained:

> Chairman Mao is not only the greatest revolutionary and thinker in Chinese history, but also the greatest theoretician and scientist in China. He was not only courageous enough to lead the entire party and all the people in radically changing the world, but also summoned the enormous courage to reform theory.[8]

The congress debated China's future course and concluded with an appeal to Chiang Kai-shek not to annul the Communist-Nationalist united front, for a renewed confrontation of Chinese against Chinese was already in the offing.

The anti-Japanese united front soon proved fragile as a Ming vase. Scarcely had the sons of Nippon fled, when Chinese once more fell upon Chinese. The fraternal warfare was to last three years and to become one of the bloodiest civil wars of the twentieth century. Chiang Kai-shek's 4.3 million man National Army was confident of victory, for since July 1946 the Communists commanded in their "People's Liberation Army" (PLA) only barely half as many soldiers. In addition, the KMT army bristled with modern U. S. weapons such as light and heavy artillery, and they possessed a tank unit and an intact air force.

The PLA possessed only their old armaments, eked out with spoils from the anti-Japanese war. But they had one "miracle weapon"—their solider base among the civilian population.

Already nine months before the outbreak of the civil war in April 1946, the Generalissimo had charged the former Commander in Chief of the Eighth Route Army, Yan Xishan, with the task of annihilating his allies from the Sino-Japanese war. The KMT General from Taiyuan was to innaugurate the civil war against the Communists with his assault.

His "first shot" was aimed at the heart of his opponent, the Liu-Deng Army. He gathered twelve divisions together to attack the fighting force in the provincial triangle Shanxi-Henan-Hebei under the command of the "One-Eyed Dragon" and the "Little Cannon." With a lightning strike he planned to split apart the two base areas established by Deng Xiaoping—Taiyue Shan in the west and Taihang Shan in the east.

In September 1945, the counter-revolutionaries occupied the city of Changzhi on the mid-reaches of the Dan River to force the Liu-Deng Army out of the plain between the two base areas into the trackless mountains. The experienced guerrilla fighters Liu Bocheng and Deng Xiaoping saw through this plan rather quickly. They decided to turn it against its authors. This would succeed, however, only if they could lure the enemy with his superior numbers into a trap.

The two summoned an expanded commanders' meeting in a hamlet barely 40 kilometers north of Changzhi where they proposed their tried and true encirclement and "gunny-sack" strategy. It was the ABCs of guerrilla strategy that underlay the march that now ensued: one brigade attacked the occupied city of Changzhi, while the main force drew a cordon around the city. The enemy was in the trap, now, and could only sit and wait for reinforcements. The Communists had accomplished the encirclement by a careful distribution of troops without committing their whole force, feigning a weaker troop strength than was actually the case. Now the "gunny-sack" tactic had only to work.

As expected, the encircled troops called for reinforcements. Substantial help was sent. Yan Xishan had ordered his deputy to liberate the city with the 22,000-man 7th Army group. That was precisely what Liu and Deng had hoped for. Quietly, they withdrew nearly all the encircling troops and prepared an ambush along the highway—in the form of a "gunny sack" into which the unsuspecting enemy ran headlong as into a cul-de-sac. In the battle of Changzhi, the first of the civil war for the Liu-Deng Army, fully 35,000 Nationalists were killed or wounded. Following this victory, the Liu-Deng Army enjoyed a respite from combat until the summer of 1946.

Politcommissar Deng's prestige rose considerably with the beginning of the civil war, for Central Headquarters in Yan'an directed that his army was to be developed into the strongest combat unit in the entire People's Liberation Army. So it was expanded to twelve divisions with a total of 130,000 soldiers. This powerful force was thereupon assigned a new field of operation and a parallel force: the Liu-Deng Army met up with its partner, Chen Yi and his East China field army in the Chinese central plain Zhongyuan. The two forces coordinated their advance, which was aimed in August 1946 at cutting the vital arteries between the large KMT-occupied cities. The Liu-Deng Army was given the task of controlling the railway corridor between Peking and Tianjin, while its partner was assigned to the central southern connection between Peking and Pukou. Through this strategy, the PLA high command sought to cut off the northern from the southern KMT areas to prevent swift troop movements. To lend political weight to this strategic order, the leadership named the Politcommissar additionally to the post of First Secretary of the Central China Office of the CC. With this dual function, Deng was for the first time given a free hand in a comprehensive mission that would determine the future course of the war.

After a month's preparation, Commander Liu and Politcommissar Deng marched off at the head of their Army eastwards towards the coast. On June 30, 1947, under cover of darkness, they crossed the Yellow River and penetrated the coastal province of Shandong. The Communist offensive had begun.

The force still moved under cover, avoiding the large highways and passing through only hamlets and villages. Less than twelve hours after crossing the Huang He, the high command gathered in a village school to plan the further advance. A young soldier wrote in his notebook:

> On the walls hung military maps with red and blue crosses. After a short time, Commissar Deng Xiaoping appeared, serious and calm as usual. He spoke briefly and precisely to those gathered: "The enemy has concentrated his forces on our flank; we must break through his front lines and carry the war into the KMT areas. . . . The focal points

of enemy attack are for the moment the provinces of Shandong and northern Shaanxi. In Shandong, there are 60 enemy brigades with 450,000 men, and in northern Shaanxi, 15 brigades with 140,000 men. The enemy is using, to borrow Liu Bocheng's term, the so-called 'barbell' strategy. The two weights of the 'barbell' lie in Shandong and northern Shaanxi. The handle is here in our region. Now we have received the assignment from the CC and from Chairman Mao to break through this 'handle.'"[9]

After the Politcommissar, the Commander took the floor and warned about Chiang Kai-shek, who was as strong as ever. There was therefore not much point in liberating one city after another. Liu Bocheng argued instead for a "qualitative leap" to be accomplished by capturing one strategic goal. Making these remarks, he pointed to a map and with his finger tapped the wedge-shaped Dabie Mountains jutting into the northern Chinese lowland, out of whose southern foothills the Yangtze flows towards Nanying. "If we occupy Dabie Shan," he argued, "we will control the Nanying-Wuhan axis. The enemy cannot just accept that, so he will move on us, relieving our brother troops in Shandong and Shaanxi."[10]

In a few words, the clever Liu had outlined the next phase. The march to the south began at the foot of the holy Tai Mountain and led along the imperial canal through the northern Chinese lowland.

This manoeuver irritated Chiang Kai-shek. Was this to be construed as fight or flight? He hastily ordered troops to guard the only east-west traffic artery of northern China, the Liangyungang-Baoji railway line. Transferring these troops forced him somewhat to loosen the noose around the neck of the Communists in the central province of Henan.

Twenty-eight days had passed since the crossing of the Yellow River. The Liu-Deng Army had fought its way slowly forward toward the south. But no high spirits reigned at headquarters, for the army was threatened with encirclement. Chiang Kai-shek's strategy was to encircle the Liu-Deng Army in the trackless region of the headwaters of numerous rivers and to wipe them out in a war of position.

If the two commanders Liu and Deng did not act with lightning speed, their unit would be lost. In contrast to his silence in advance of the "Battle of the Hundred Regiments," Deng informed the high command and immediately received clear instructions: vacate occupied territory, decamp southwards at once, avoid all contact with the enemy, and quick-march to the Dabie Mountains, 500 kilometers away.

To escape certain defeat, the Liu-Deng Army had no choice but to attempt a critically dangerous breakout. As they "set off at a run" on August 7, 1947, marching at a pace of 45 kilometers per day, Chiang Kai-shek was already confident of victory. In fact, it looked for all the world like headlong flight, for the Communists were marching towards an area in which the rivers, swollen by heavy rains, threatened to flood their banks at any moment.

Because of the continual cloud-bursts and enemy air attacks, the Liu-Deng Army was soon able to march only at night. For the Red soldiers, the cry was, clench your teeth and push through! Politcommissar Deng remarked in his dry fashion,

> A commander can do nothing now but go on with utter toughness. Through the sacrifices and the hunger of a small minority, the feeding and security of the large mass is achieved through sheer determination. By our present difficulties, we are purchasing victory and success for the whole nation. We must keep the common interest in view, and ignore these momentary difficulties.[11]

But the greatest difficulties were yet to come.

On the evening of August 17, the totally exhausted soldiers reached a barely 50-kilometer wide area where since Chiang Kai-shek's previous destruction of dams nine years before, the slimy water of the Huang He was standing knee-deep. There was no way to avoid this swamp. Machine-guns, mortars, cannons—everything heavy had to be left behind. During two long days and one short night, the army crept across the grey-brown mire.

The National Army still believed this was a desperate attempt at flight by the Liu-Deng troops. Not before they had crossed the Sha River, barely 300 kilometers from their goal, did Chiang Kai-shek see through the Communist plan. He must have been furious—his worst enemy had escaped once more.

On August 23, the advance guard of the Liu-Deng Army reached the northern bank of the Ru River. One day later—still ahead of the Red force—the KMT units took up positions along the south bank. Despite artillery barrage and air attacks, a small group of Deng's people crossed and overcame the positions of the National Army. The main force built a pontoon bridge upstream across which they reached the south bank without difficulty. Here, a bloody battle for position broke out. Retreat across the river was of course blocked. The guerrillas had to fight their way through the enemy ranks at the cost of great losses and march on toward their final obstacle, the Huai River. The crossing of the Huai He was made on August 26 without exchange of fire. The Communists crossed the river so briskly that the local population thought it a miracle: years later, the peasants still told miraculous stories. One fine day in June—by the moon calender—the Huai He was suddenly frozen so that the Red Army was able to run across to the opposite bank. . . Two days later, the Liu-Deng Army reached the Dabie Mountains in the south of Henan province. The soldiers who had successfully broken out did not have much time to refresh themselves, for they had come to rest virtually on Chiang Kai-shek's doorstep, just 330 kilometers west of his capital, Nanjing. Chiang knew from experience that the Communists would immediately establish a base area, recruit new soldiers, and mobilize the population of the countryside. With 33 brigades quickly drawn together, he engaged the enemy. But the enemy employed his guerrilla tactic, and the battle dragged on. Seeing now that he was beset on several fronts, the Generalissimo was forced to do exactly what the Communists had expected: he reduced the "barbell weights" in Shaanxi and Shandong. Thereby, the pressure of the KMT troops on the base areas there was relieved.

Party Secretary Deng could not concern himself for long with the organization of the Dabie base area. He had to return to the front, for meanwhile the Communists were thrusting towards victory throughout the country. Mao and the high command in Yan'an considered the time had come to force the Generalissimo to the nationally decisive battle. For this, the regionally subdivided party administration had to be amalgamated, and the PLA to be restructured. To control the center of China effectively, the CC broadened its Central China office, and thereby the jurisdiction of Deng's power. The leadership placed Chen Yi as Second Secretary and Deng Zihui as Third Secretary at Deng's side.

Since the field of operations of the Liu-Deng Army lay in the northern Chinese lowland Zhongyuan, it was given the new designation Zhongyuan Field Army and was enlarged by nearly 250,000 soldiers. Now the Communists could venture to confront Chiang Kai-shek's force of three and a half million fighting men.

Dispatching the Liu-Deng Army to the northeast was only one of the many concerted moves undertaken by Mao and the Military Commission in the background. From September, the Communists began encirclimg the cities of northern China. By dint of incredible exertions in a bloody war of position, they succeeded in the battle of Huaihai on January 10, 1949, in defeating the National Army.

In January 1949, the First Secretary of the Main Front Committee could feel jubilant. Deng had been responsible for leading the greatest and most crushing of the three decisive battles. Just how proud he actually was of "his" Huaihai battle would become evident only during the Cultural Revolution. When his second fall from power was imminent in the mid-sixties, Deng invoked his past service:

> If he [Lin Piao, his attacker] had his Manchurian campaign, then I had my Huaihai campaign. Lin fought his way through from the northeast to the south of China; I fought my way through from Nanjing to Chengdu.

Since after the battle Mao had announced the slogan "Carry out the revolution to its conclusion!" the PLA issued Deng's army the order to advance to the northern bank of the Yangtze and wait there. Meanwhile, the CCP delivered an ultimatum to the Vice President of the Nationalist government, Li Zongren—Chiang Kai-shek had already resigned—summoning him to peace talks in Peking. During this time, the guns were silent.

On April 21, twenty-four hours after the KMT delegation had rejected the Communist conditions for peace, one million PLA soldiers on Mao's orders crossed the Yangtze at several places. Deng Xiaoping and Liu Bocheng crossed the sluggish river near Nanjing. At the advance of the overwhelmingly superior Communist force, most of the straggling KMT units took to their heels to save their skins.

The Nationalist government collapsed; the Kuomintang withdrew to Taiwan. Only two days after the river crossing, the Liu-Deng Army entered the "southern capital," Nanjing, and oc-

Main Front Committee of the battle of Huaihai (second from left, Deng Xiaoping, next to him, Liu Bocheng and Chen Yi).

Headquarters of the Second Field Army in October, 1949, on the march towards the southwest. Deng Xiaoping, his deputy Zhang Jiecun, and Liu Bocheng (left to right).

cupied the presidential palace. A short time later, the high-ranking Politcommissar Deng traveled as First Secretary of the East China Office of the CC to Shanghai, 300 kilometers away.

During his best years, the 45-year-old Deng Xiaoping had lived the life of the party. He had achieved greatness along with it and had risen in the two decades just past to be an important party functionary at Mao's side.

On October 1, 1949, in the Square of the Heavenly Peace, the Tiananmen, the First Party Secretary and Delegate of the Second Field Army took part in the ostentatious celebration of the founding of the Peoples' Republic of China. To his duties as important military leader belonged taking part, at the conclusion of the festivities and the luxurious banquets, in direction-setting conferences. Because of his military service he was admitted to the Peoples' Revolutionary Military Council. Deng was elected to the Central Peoples' Governing Council, the future State Council, and received two further representative functions—he advanced to member of the Political Consultative Conference of the Chinese People[12] and its executive committee, the Society for Chinese-Soviet Friendship.

"Carry out the revolution to its conclusion!" Mao had ordered at the beginning of the year. This motto was not out of date even after the establishment of the new socialist state, for the enemy was still just 3,000 kilometers away to the southwest. The party leadership transferred the solution of this problem to the Politcommissar. Thus, Deng traveled to Shanghai with a new and important assignment. There he ordered mobilization, and still in October, the combat proven Liu-Deng Army departed China's secret capital.

NINE

The Great Leap Upward

T HE "WHITE" SOUTHWEST was a gaping wound in the belly of the Red giant. This "wound" encompassed Szechuan and both neighboring provinces to the south, Yunnan and Guizhou, as well as the province which today has been divided up between Szechuan and Tibet, Xikang.

The expansion of the "White" area forced the Liu-Deng Army to fan out, somewhat dispersing their forces. Divided into three columns deployed in fan-shape, they approached the remaining KMT areas. Initially, Politcommissar Deng and his Commander in Chief expected a renewed fraternal war of attrition, for no fewer than 400,000 soldiers of the National Army stood prepared to defend the region. But then things worked out differently. After Deng Xiaoping had assured the commanders of Xikang and Yunnan that if they cooperated, they could retain their territories, the KMT force surrendered without a fight.[1] When Chengdu fell on December 27, 1949, the gigantic empire, with the exception of Tibet, was entirely "Red."

By the end of 1949, even the regional administrative structure of the Communists had been built up: the southwest office of the CC with First Party Secretary Deng Xiaoping, Second Secretary Liu Bocheng, and Third Secretary He Long; the southwest military administrative council with Liu Bocheng as Director and Deng as Deputy Director; the southwest military district under He Long's military and Deng's political command. Important offices. But Deng was given still further positions: as Director of the Finance and Economics Committee he was the financial chief of the southwest, and as Party Secretary, he had responsibility for the administration of the Yangtze city Chungking, in which the CP administration was located.

Coming from Szechuan, Deng needed no "probationary period;" he was able to attack these numerous assignments unhesitatingly. He concentrated entirely on party affairs, the ideological reeducation of the populace, the smoking out of the opium dens wide-spread in Yunnan, the extension to the numerous minorities of equality with the Chinese, and land reform.

The agrarian revolution, which was the foundation of socialist development in China, placed heavy demands on him. For it was necessary to confiscate the fields, the livestock, the draft animals, the plows and other farm equipment from the landowners and wealthy farmers, and to redistribute them fairly among the former tenant farmers and day laborers. As a native, he knew his compatriots, and quickly won their trust.

In April 1950, Deng flew as delegate from the southwest to Peking. There, he garnered much praise from Central Headquarters for his energetic pursuit of land reform and the first party campaign against corruption and waste. He was applauded at the second plenary session of all the military and administrative councils of the country when he spoke in favor of speedier dispossession of the landowners, and a more vigorous cultural and ideological education of the peasants. His great committment to the agrarian revolution resulted not only in short-term success. At the third plenary session in February of the following year, his proposal to establish a collective mutual-aid movement among the villages was greeted as a trail-blazing measure.

As a practical man, Deng knew precisely whereof he spoke to these delegates who had come here from every part of the country. He offered them not theoretical excursuses, but everyday work experiences, and his pragmatism appealed to the high-ranking delegates. Nonetheless, this committment must, for Deng, have been something of a two-edged sword: as the champion of land reform, he was acting contrary to the interests of his own propertied family.

Many members of the Deng clan still lived in his home village. His sister by blood, Xianlie, his step-mother, Xia Bogen, and other siblings, uncles, aunts, and in-laws in the tiny Xiexing had learned of the socialist turnabout only vaguely. Many rumors about horrible acts of vengeance by peasants against their former landlords circulated through the country. Deng was solicitous of his relatives, above all of his youngest brother, the manor's heir, Shuping.

Deng Xiaoping, informed sooner than anyone else in the southwest about coming moves of party headquarters, could act swiftly and at just the right moment. Already in the spring of 1950, before the adoption of the land reform law, he sent for his relatives to join him in Chungking, where he quartered them in the guest house of the military administration. Here, behind high walls, they found protection and were safe from any intrusion.

Deng's protection of his landowner family would be uncovered by the Red Guard during the Cultural Revolution. In 1967, they accused him of having been "Emperor of the Southwest." The radicals reproached him for having brought his relatives, these "cattle demons and serpent gods," to join him in Chungking.[2]

The "Red" administration had operated successfully for barely two years when Liu Bocheng was transferred to Nanjing. There he was to direct the newly established PLA Military Academy as president. As his successor, He Long took his place at Deng Xiaoping's side.

At the beginning of 1952, Mao summoned Deng Xiaoping to Peking. First, suitable living quarters had to be found there for the Dengs. This turned out to be not so simple, since the household had meanwhile burgeoned into a seven-person extended family. Pu Zhuo Lin had brought three more children into the world: in 1947 and 1950, the daughters Nan and Rong, and in 1952, the son Zhifang. Wife and children were to follow later with step-mother Xia Bogen and move into one of those traditional court houses of imperial Peking. Mao had had a former imperial villa on the "South Central Lake," in Zhongnanhai refurbished for Deng and his family. Until 1969, Deng was to live within majestic walls a stone's throw from Mao's courtly house in the western part of the Forbidden City.

A few days after the move to his new home, the Central Peoples' Governing Council, the Chinese cabinet of the founding years, was convened. On August 7, 1952, the members elected the Zhou Enlai to be one of the deputies to the premier, to function simultaneously as foreign minister. The circle had been closed; Deng's new superior was Zhou Enlai. Their collaboration from the Paris and the Shanghai days underwent a renaissance. Promotion to the side of China's most important diplomat made Deng his representative in the Peoples' Governing Council and would soon enable him to step onto the international stage.

But above all, his job was to keep an eye from Peking on the southwest. On January 14, 1953, he would once more be named one of the Deputy Chairmen of the Southwest Administrative Council. He Long directed the Administration on the spot.

Each new position bestowed at once further functions on Deng Xiaoping: in November 1952, the party leadership established a State Planning Commission on the Soviet pattern, which would oversee the first five-year plan. Deng, recognized also as an economic expert, was named to the fifteen-man committee, and on September 18, 1953, he was named Finance Minister, a post he was to occupy just under a year. At the 4th session of the Political Consultative Conference in February 1953, the delegates elected him one of the deputy chairmen, promoting him thereby to direct collaboration with Mao Tsetung, who chaired the People's Front Organization.

All these positions decorated the ever active Szechuanese like medals. But medals are of course just symbols, and symbols carry with them neither real power nor genuine influence. The positions cited above were without exception governmental functions. But what really counted were party functions—and those were assigned by the Chairman personally. Mao promoted his follower from Jiangxi in May 1954 after a successful two-year probationary period in Peking to be the director of the CC Secratriat, a post of intimate contact with the Chairman. But Deng's new party function and his old "sinecures" were worlds apart: in 1935, the party had found itself with 30,000 members, and on the run; in 1952, it numbered nearly ten million members and exercised the power of the state. Besides this, various special departments of the Central Committee were now under Deng's administration.

Deng's promotion grew out of Mao's strategy for expanding his own powerbase. Already on December 15, 1951, the functionaries had learned from an "internal party circular of historical significance" that for several months Mao had been repeatedly attacked. Someone had dared characterize the collective amalgamation of agriculture as "false, dangerous, and utopian agrarian socialism." This someone was Liu Shaoqi, number two in the party hierarchy.

This criticism had caused the Party Chairman to seek defensive aid through Deng, who—as we have seen—was an avid supporter of his policy of collectivization. Reinforced in his position by Deng and also by Zhou Enlai, he instructed the lower levels of the party to set into motion the establishment of so-called "production groups for mutual aid."

As a first step toward collectivization of agriculture, the leadership had decided to combine an average of six farm households into one group. These families were to amalgamate their private fields, support each other mutually in their work, and interchange their draft animals and farm equipment among each other. Since not every peasant owned his own water buffalo and wooden plow, the mutual aid was universally welcomed. But the amalgamation of the fields was a bitter pill to swallow for those who for the first time in their lives had come to own their own little plot of ground. The pill was swallowed, however, often under muttered protest, for faith in the party was exceptionally strong.

Mao, Deng, and Chou ignored all such genuinely felt criticism of the collective movement. By the time the Director of the CC Secretariat had been in office half a year, the Communist Party instituted 35,800 "agricultural production collectives" (APCs). Two years after collectivization had entailed the joining of six households, the numbers were increased to 20 families that now had to collaborate. Each contributed its land, equipment, and draft animals to the collective as a property share. Living quarters and barns, pets and small domestic animals, as well as vegetable gardens remained in private possession.

Even though his father Deng Wenming's farmstead and fields were divided among eleven families, the CC Secretary praised collectivization:

> We must politically educate the prosperous middle-class farmers and the farm families operating privately. In addition, we must institute economic measures to reduce the tendency for spontaneous capitalistic development. We must kindle a great polemic against all prosperous middle-class farmers who have proposed pulling out of the collectives . . . That minority that makes so much noise about their pulling out of

the collectives has to be criticized, and their political influence eliminated. Then they have to be barred from the collectives.

The critic of collectivization, Liu Shaoqi, once the initiator of the personality cult around Mao, by no means wished to turn back the clock. Things were just going too fast for him: only yesterday, it had been the "New Democratic" society; today, it was already the socialist society, and tomorrow even Communism.[3]

For Mao, on the other hand, everything was proceeding much too slowly. At the session of the Politburo on June 15, 1953, he once more criticized his opponents:

> After the success of the democratic revolution, some people stay put in their original positions. They do not understand the change in the nature of the revolution. They continue to advocate their 'New Democracy,' and not the socialistic transformation. In doing so, they are committing errors of right-wing deviationism.

No doubt the Party Chairman at this time still favored gradual conversion to socialism—he mentioned a time-frame of fifteen years—but he demanded an increased tempo. He thought that "moving too fast" meant turning left, while "not moving at all" meant turning to the right. Mao thus employed the trick of accusing Liu Shaoqi to get him to step into the open.

Prior to the origins of this dispute, Mao had summoned his old friend Deng Xiaoping to his side. Since he had the approval also of the Premier, he stuck steadfastly to his course. No longer did any opponent dare openly challenge the troika of Mao, Chou, and Deng. Their critics fell silent, and the collectivization measures were carried out. Seen from today's perspective, Deng Xiaoping and Zhou Enlai were fighting on the wrong—which is to say on Mao's—side. All three overestimated the revolutionary consciousness of the peasants and the support of the party among the rural population. They believed that the invincible will of the millions alone could move mountains; belief in the victory of the revolution was given a higher priority than genuine understanding of the revolution. Deng recognized this fatal error only when it was too late: at the beginning of the sixties, he went over to Liu Shaoqi's camp, and for that was brought down a second time.

Government, party, military, finance, foreign affairs—all these were areas in which the 50-year-old "generalist" Deng had by now gathered experience. In the year 1954, he devoted himself with renewed energy to the work of government, for a great event cast his shadow forward.

The Supreme Soviet in Moscow was godfather to the Chinese Communists when they set about building up their government apparatus and providing their young Peoples' Republic a constitution. To establish a second pillar of power beside the Communist Party, intensive preparation was required. To this purpose, the party leadership established three committees.

The most important, under Mao's chairmanship, was the Constitutional Draft Committee. It was complemented by the Electoral Law Committee, which stood under the leadership of Zhou Enlai, and in which Deng acted as secretary. Finally, there was also the Central Election Committee, led by Liu Shaoqi, which was supposed to oversee elections to the 1st National Peoples' Congress (NPC). Deng Xiaoping alone belonged as a functionary to all three committees. He would receive the assignment of presenting the report on the election program to the NPC.

At the important session of the Congress held between September 15 and 27, 1954, the delegates elected Mao State President and Deng one of the Deputy Premiers of the State Council, superseding the Peoples' Governing Council. Further, they elected him one of the fifteen Deputy Chairmen of the National Defense Council. He was to occupy this post until the Cultural Revolution.

At the Political Consultative Conference, which met at the same time as the NPC, he was put on the standing committee in a leadership function he would retain until April 1959.

The Peoples' Congress adopted the first five-year plan and the constitution. New government organizations were formed and the regional administrations abolished. Since the provinces were now directly under the control of the central government, Deng lost his last office in the southwest. This loss was of course easy for him to bear, for the destination toward which he now was bound lay irrevocably in the shadow of the Imperial Palace. While Deng made a leap upward, someone else took a fall.

In the year 1955, Chairman Mao accused the First Party Secretary of Manchuria, Gao Gang, of being a party schismatic. The name Gao Gang, which Deng Xiaoping had first heard in 1927 when he was an instructor at the Sun Yatsen Military Academy in Xi'an, is associated with the first great internal party power struggle after the founding of the Peoples' Republic in 1949, which ended with expulsions from the party and a suicide—or was it murder?

Of all the countless plenary sessions of the Central Committee, the 4th meeting of the VIIth CC is among the most prominent. Something spectacular occurred between the sixth and tenth of February 1954 in his keynote address at the meeting, Liu Shaoqi touched on the so-called "Gao-Rao pact," by which he meant a plot between two high functionaries. Those gathered listened with interest to the leader of the meeting, but when he demanded punitive measures against the "anti-party elements" Gao Gang and Rao Shushi, they reacted cautiously.

Threatening suicide in the dramatic gesture of reaching for his service revolver, Gao Gang moved sentiment in his favor. The fact, too, that Mao preferred celebrating the spring festival in his homeland to participating in the meeting kept those present indecisive. The meeting was adjourned, and the case turned over to two investigatory committees.

While Zhou Enlai conducted the Gao investigation, Deng, in his capacity as Secretary General, handled the Rao investigation. As was soon to emerge, his future party career apparently hinged on the solution of the Gao-Rao question. At a party conference March 21 to 31, 1955, Deng delivered the "report on the anti-party Gao Gang and Rao Shushi pact." He delved far into the past.

Gao Gang, known also as "Lord of Manchuria," had, after the founding of the Peoples' Republic, been awarded important government posts.[4] His actual power center was not, however, in Peking, but in the industrial city of Shenyang, in the heart of what was formerly Manchuria. He ruled here as First Party Secretary of the northeast office of the CC. From a strictly technical viewpoint, he held the same rank at the beginning of the fifties as Deng, who served as First Secretary of the southwest office. Nonetheless, Gao's position was weightier than Deng's, for the northeast assumed a strategic importance for the whole country in three respects. For one thing, industry was concentrated here; for another, the former Manchuria constituted the staging area for the Korean war; and, finally, it served as a bridge to the neighboring Soviet Union.

The longtime intimate of Stalin Gao Gang exploited his office for self-aggrandizement like no other functionary. As he was reviewing a parade in his stronghold on October 1, 1952, the honor guard was chanting "Long live Gao Gang!," whereas it was customary to shout, "Long live Chairman Mao!" In that same year, Mao summoned him to Peking and named him Deputy National President and Chairman of the National Planning Commission. Gao was flattered. He failed to see through this "promotion" as isolating him from his power base, but intrigued all the more vigorously against Zhou Enlai and Liu Shaoqi. In typical Chinese fashion, he launched his attacks neatly "packaged": the CCP—according to Gao's theory—had evolved out of two parties. One—the more important—was the party of the army and soviets; the other was that of the "White" KMT areas.

Since he was, like Mao, representative of the first type, he was now after the liberation entitled to high party offices. He demanded no meaner position in the government than that of Premier. His presumptuous demands were aimed against Zhou Enlai and Liu Shaoqi, whom he classified as representatives of the second type. Deng related many years later:

> At the end of 1953, Comrade Mao proposed the subdivision of Central Headquarters into a first and a second front. This proposal stirred Gao Gang's enterprising nature uncommonly. . . . Since I was responsible for the southwest, he turned to me. In conversation with me, he expressed the opinion that Liu Shaoqi was still politically immature.
>
> Gao Gang wanted to win me over in order to bring Liu Shaoqi down. I replied that Liu Shaoqi's position in the party was a result of historical evolution. All in all, Comrade Liu was all right, and therefore it was not appropriate to alter his historically evolved position. He spoke also to the economic planner Chen Yun and said that more deputy party chairmen ought to be named. He meant thereby Chen Yun and himself. Now Comrade Chen Yun and I realized the serious problem. We immediately made a report to Comrade Mao Tsetung.

Compared to Gao Gung, Rao Shushi was merely a hanger-on—albeit with an important function. After the founding of the state, he had directed the east China office of the CC in Shanghai, a position held by Deng between April and October 1949. After his transfer to Central Headquarters, Rao developed into a follower of Gao. One can speak of an "anti-party pact," in other words, only after 1952 when Rao came from Shanghai to Peking and was named Chief of the Organizational Division of the Central Committee.

Is it proper to speak of a pact, a "conspiracy" at all, when two high functionaries collaborate to advance their careers? No one but Deng Xiaoping, one-time leader of the Rao investigatory committee, could elucidate that point. But he keeps his counsel; to this day, the report of his investigation is a secret classified document.

Mao, whose position of power was untouched by Gao, at first held himself apart from the party squabble. Because it was directed against his opponent Liu, perhaps? Only a year later, at the National Party Conference of March 1955, did he condemn Gao and Rao.

Only now did all those assembled vote in favor of expelling the two from the party; a short time later, they were in prison. There, Gao Gang is supposed to have committed suicide. Rao Shushi has disappeared, even high party functionaries remaining ignorant of his whereabouts.

From the beginning, Deng Xiaoping had assumed the whole burden of the investigation. After the March Conference, everyone was talking about the capable Director of the CC Secretariat and his organizational talent. In April 1954, without objection from anyone, Deng also assumed Rao Shushi's post as Director of the Organizational Division of the CC. The portals to the party's "Olympus," the Politburo, now stood open to him. At the 5th plenary session of the VIIth Central Committee in April 1955, the CC members elected him and Lin Piao as newcomers to the heretofore paramount leadership committee of the CCP.

The party could not value Deng's resolute handling of the "Gao-Rao affair" too highly, since he had thereby restored peace and order to their ranks. This peace was desperately needed in order finally to enable the organization of a new Party Congress. Eleven years after the VIIth Party Congress, from September 15 to 27, 1956, the VIIIth Party Congress of the CCP took place. It was Deng's duty as Secretary-General to prepare this important event organizationally.

Already on the opening day, the delegates elected him chairman, followed a short time later by his appointment to the highest leadership group of the Communist Party, the newly established Standing Committee of the seventeen member Politburo, to which he had belonged for only four months. His appointment as General Secretary of the CC of the CCP had been the decisive factor in this promotion.

During the years from 1925 to 1936, when the Bolsheviks played the leading role within the party, the post of General Secretary was equivalent to that of Party Chairman. Then, in the wake of the realignment and the concentration of power in Mao Tsetung's hands, this position had been abolished. Now, at this Party Congress, it was reinstituted, albeit with much less authority than before. The six-man Standing Committee, comprising the Party Chairman, his four deputies, and the General Secretary, would henceforth make decisions, while the Secretariat carried them out.

General Secretary Deng functioned as virtually the highest executive officer in the party. The conversion of politics into praxis depended on his skill. The new, influential post not only engaged his practical and organizational talents, but also put him in a position to study in detail the inner life of the ten-million member strong party.

His secretariat stood at the apex of the party apparatus. Under his oversight operated various departments entrusted with individual areas such as agriculture or industry. These departments were supported by a communications network over which the party directives were transmitted to the provincial and district party committees. Most of Deng's direct subordinates were Politburo members or candidate members. To his staff of colleagues belonged men who stand today in the top echelon of party and state: Peng Zhen, Yang Shangkun, Hu Qiaomu. Deng's secretariat soon came to be called the "super-cabinet" of the party.

The great popularity of the General Secretary made itself evident in his reelection to the Politburo. He received the fourth highest electoral result, thus eliciting more votes than both the Deputy Party Chairmen, Zhou Enlai and Zhu De.

The Party Congress of eleven years before had raised Mao to

unrestricted leader of the party and established the Chinese cult of personality. On that occasion, in 1945, Liu Shaoqi had referred to Mao by name over a hundred times in his report. This time, he referred to him only eight times, for this Party Congress was held under the motto "Collective Leadership."

Had Mao already been stripped of power? The reasons for the reevocation of the collective are not to be found within the country itself, but beyond its borders. In February 1956, barely eight months before the VIIIth Party Congress, the two Szechuanese Deng Xiaoping and Zhu De traveled to Moscow to the XXth Party Congress of the CPSU. The Chinese delegation sat in exposed seats as Nikita Khrushchev stepped to the podium. Deng Xiaoping, who had known the energetic comrade with his bald pate already in Peking, scarcely believed his ears when he heard how he spoke about Stalin. While the brother party was still meeting, Deng informed Central Headquarters in Peking of the unexpected attack on the dictator and the cult of personality. Neither Zhu De nor he himself had reckoned on such an assault. What should they do? How react? In Peking, too, good advice was hard to come by.

On the one hand, Mao and the top leaders of the party esteemed Stalin as a great Marxist, even with his faults. On the other hand, the young Peoples' Republic was indebted to its "Big Brother." On his visit in October 1954, Khrushchev had pledged a new line of credit and, at last, the withdrawal of Soviet troops from Port Arthur; in addition, the sibling parties had embarked on numerous joint large-scale projects.

When on his return Deng reported Khrushchev's deposition of Stalin to the Politburo, confusion arose, and the leadership elite split into two camps. One group, in which the deserving military leader Peng Dehuai was prominent, and to which Deng leaned, allied itself unreservedly with Khrushchev's criticism of the cult of personality; the other, which included Mao, did not want to go along with the deposition of Stalin.

The Party Congress of the CPSU was thus the reason that at the VIIIth Party Congress of the CCP the cult of personality and "collective leadership" stood at the center of the debate. The most prominent speaker against the cult of personality was Deng Xiaoping. In his report on the amendment of the party constitution, he said:

How important collective leadership and the struggle against the cult of personality are was clearly demonstrated at the XXth Party Congress. This discovery will exert a powerful influence not only on the CPSU, but also on all the other Communist Parties of the world. It is obvious that decisions made by one person contradict the principles on which a Communist Party is built and necessarily lead to errors.

In this report he establishes in regard to the cult of personality the grounds for striking from the amendment the articles "Mao Tsetung's ideas are the general line of the work of the party" and "studying the ideas of Mao Tsetung is the duty of every party member." Since not only he, but also Liu Shaoqi, Zhou Enlai, and Chen Yun formed a united front against the leader cult, the Party Chairman had to bow to the vote of the majority on this point.

Whether Mao manipulated his wife when ten years later Jiang Qing called Deng's report a "poisonous weed" can only be conjectured. In any case, it has been proved since 1979 that the report on the constitutional amendment of 1956 contributed very decisively to Deng's second fall during the Cultural Revolution.

The striking of the Mao Tsetung ideas from the amendment is in no way to be charged to the initiative of the General Secretary. It is an iron rule of the CCP that such important speeches emanating from a committee—in this case from the Politburo—receive official approval. Deng had only stepped before the plenary as speaker. The question remains: Who conceived the idea of removing the Mao Tsetung ideas from the amendment? To understand the further course of the internal party power struggle, the instigator has to be named.

"At the VIIIth Party Congress," Marshal Peng Dehuai admitted in 1966 during an interrogation bordering on torture, "it was I who proposed striking the Mao Tsetung ideas from the party constitution. Liu Shaoqi accepted my proposal at once. I sought thereby to turn against the cult of personality."

In fact, General Secretary Deng, later defamed as an enemy of Mao, did everything possible to avoid tarnishing Mao's image. Thus, he remarked in his controversial report:

Our party frowns upon the cult of personality. On the eve of the national victory, the proposal of Comrade Mao Tsetung was adopted that birthdays of party leaders would no longer be celebrated, and squares, streets, and enterprises would no longer be named after party leaders. This determination was healthy in counteracting glorification and the cult of personality. . . We can thank the leaders of the party organizations on all levels, and above all the leader of our party, Comrade Mao Tsetung, for our party's victories.

As the delegates, after thirteen days of deliberation, left the Great Peoples' Congress Hall, it was clear that the VIIIth Party Congress would go down in the history of the revolution under the blurred motto "Party Congress of the Collective with Mao Tsetung at Its Head." The abstract criticism of the personality cult, adopted from the outside, and promoted by Deng and others, simply could not take hold. It neither touched the cult around Mao's person, nor lessened his power. All that was new was that a standing committee had been placed at his side. The newly elected General Secretary Deng Xiaoping occupied in this group officially only the sixth place,[5] but his advantage in terms of access to information assured him greater power than that possessed by Zhu De, Chen Yun, or even Zhou Enlai. Deng stood ready to step out of Liu Shaoqi's shadow to Mao's side.

TEN

The Break

EACH MAY, THE weather turns suddenly hot in Peking. After a very short spring, summer breaks in overnight, which is why the flowers sprout only shyly at first. But in the May of the year 1956 everything seemed to bloom more lushly than usual, for Chairman Mao had announced a campaign of democratization, the so-called "Hundred Flowers Movement."

The 62-year-old leader had looked far into the past to envision the future of the young nation. In his favorite books, the ancient Chinese classics, he had discovered the "Movement of the Hundred Flowers" and the "Contest of the Hundred Schools." He wished to emulate these famous academic debates from the time of Confucius.

In his opinion, a multiplicity of divergent views, not merely condoned, but actually required by the party, could only be beneficial to the young socialist democracy. In addition, it would remobilize the silenced intelligentsia in the service of socialistic development. Mao Tsetung aspired sincerely to the "Great Democracy," to show his people and the world: See, Chinese socialism has nothing in common with totalitarianism; it has much in common with democracy.

His friend and longtime follower pricked up his ears. When Deng Xiaoping heard "Great Democracy," he understood anarchy; for the first time in their twenty-four-year partnership therefore he placed himself in opposition to a decision of the Party Chairman. He feared that a "Contest of the Hundred Schools" might spread into a popular movement against the Communist Party. This military and party leader, an organized Communist for thirty-two years, distrusted the masses, that spontaneous, un-organized element. If the party were to let the reins fall, he felt, an undisciplined and uncontrollable confusion would arise. In contrast to Mao, he denied non-party members the right to criticize the party. Errors committed by the CCP were to be corrected on its own initiative. The democratic parties ought not to interfere in the process of criticism and self-criticism, Deng argued in opposition to Mao.

That these objections were not raised on tactical grounds, but partook, and still partake, of the essence of his political thought is substantiated by his remarks from the year 1980: "Our party has committed serious errors in the past, but these errors were corrected by us, ourselves, not by any external force."[1] In his conception, the party constitutes the vanguard; the people, the rear guard. His criticism of the "Hundred Flowers Movement" is based on this dichotomy: democracy, yes, but under the watchful eye of the avant-garde, the party.

In speaking this way, he was responding not only to personal conviction. He dared confront the great Mao also because he knew a powerful lobby stood behind him, first and foremost, Liu Shaoqi, Mao's deputy and longtime opponent. The group around Deng and Liu had in the meantime become so entrenched in the Politburo that at the VIIIth Party Congress of September 1956, they could simply disregard Mao's daring model for the "Great Democracy." Not until five months later, on February 27, 1957, did Mao, supported by Zhou Enlai and propaganda chief Lu Dingyi, venture a second presentation of his concept for democratization—not, this time, as Party Chairman, but as head of state, at a meeting of the Supreme State Conference.

He got no further by this circuitous route, however. Through the assistance of General Secretary Deng, the opposition succeeded in keeping Mao's orally presented demand for plurality of opinion under wraps for three months. His speech, finally published in June, had been so heavily censored by the Politburo that not even between the lines could the reader discover anything more about the possibility of spontaneous demonstrations and freedom of speech.

Mao's speech might have come to light only much later had not the students taken over the streets shortly before its publication. The younger academic generation at China's most renowned universities, Qinghua, Renmin, and Beida, demonstrated for more democratic rights, that is for Mao's "Hundred Flowers Movement." As Deng had feared, the intellectuals fairly gushed with criticism of the party. They bluntly demanded free elections and a democratic order along parliamentary lines.

Plainly alarmed, Deng rushed to the campus of the Qinghua Technical Institute in the north of Peking to call the students to peace and order. He sought initially to placate the angry young people; then he shifted to threats, suggesting that all those criticizing the Communist Party were agents of the bourgeois class. His words were harsh:

> In the course of the socialist revolution, the contradictions between the reactionary rightist elements of the bourgeoisie and the people are the contradictions between the enemy and the people. They are antagonistic, insurmountable contradictions in a life and death struggle.[2]

From the foregoing, he concluded the necessity of a harsh punishment of the so-called "rightist elements."

While Deng defied the two-month long campaign, Mao spun like a weathercock. He gave up his courageous experiment, allying himself with the Deng-Liu group. From July 1, he retouched the facts, and acted as though his "Hundred Flowers Movement" had from the start been an action to flush the reactionaries from their lairs: "You can eradicate the cattle demons and serpent gods only after you have released them; you have to let the poisonous weeds sprout before you can pull them out."[3] How embittered must the tens of thousands of hopeful academics, prepared for debate, have been when they realized Mao's betrayal of his own intentions. How startled must their reaction have been as the united party leadership now—in accord with Deng's threats—perverted the "Great Democracy" to its opposite.

While the nonconformist Mao felt obliged to offer an apologetic self-criticism at the 3rd plenary session of the VIIIth CC on October 9, 1957, the steadfast Deng articulated almost Stalinistically the necessity for the intellectuals to be "proletarianized." He went on, "The leadership of the Chinese Communist Party, the principles of the dictatorship of the proletariat and democratic centralism must never be called into question."[4]

Now the party proceeded, under the intimate collaboration

between General Secretary Deng and Party Chairman Mao, with "rooting out the poisonous weeds." It initiated a nationwide campaign against the "rightists." Woe to those who had criticized the enormous settlements paid the fraternaal Soviet party following the Korean War. Woe to anyone who had opened his mouth too far in an indoctrination group. The slightest criticism of the Soviet Union was branded unceremoniously as anti-socialistic, and anyone who had attacked the party line was stamped anti-Communist.

A veritable witch-hunt spread throughout the country like what had once occurred in the Jiangxi town of Ruijin, with the result that 800,000 party members and nonmembers were classified as rightists between 1957 and 1958, and—as would become apparent only in 1980—2.9 million were denounced as "rightist elements." In the worst case, the consequence was the labor camp; at the least, professional and personal ruin.

The party's sword was directed against Communists as well as democrats; primarily, however, it came whistling down on the heads of the intellectuals. To the public, it appeared that Deng Xiaoping wielded the annihilating blade most mercilessly. With self-assurance twenty-three years later, he acknowledged these strokes he had dealt out that had brought decades-long ruination to hundreds of thousands of lives. At the 5th plenary session of the XIth CC in 1980 he said, "In the struggle of 1957 against the rightists we were activists. I must share the responsibility for the expanded campaign against them, for I functioned as General Secretary."

There is no question that Deng displayed courage in self-critically elucidating his joint responsibility twenty-three years later and carrying out the rehabilitation of over three million falsely accused people. But—and this "but" provides an explanation for China's continually interrupted process of democratization—he could not bring himself to adjudge the whole movement of that time as incorrect.

The rehabilitation he carried out personally did not apply to five leaders of democratic parties, the so-called "five great rightist elements," or to two of the student leaders. In excluding these seven, he persevered in his contention that the campaign had not been incorrect in its essence. "Besides," he commented on January 16, 1980, "I would like briefly to note that the struggle of 1957 against the rightists was necessary and correct. In short: the struggle was not wrong in and of itself; the problem was that it was broadened excessively."

What had this struggle now brought about? If one was to believe the official press releases issued by Deng's CC Secretariat, the party had beaten back the "rabid" attacks of the bourgeoisie. But those who gave credence to Xiao Dao, the unofficial "little channel," got very different and appalling information. People spoke in whispers about loss of faith in the party, about growing fear among the population, and about labor camps—the death-sentence on the installment plan.

In the frigid air of intensifying class warfare, as if by magic the General Secretary suddenly pulled from his pocket Mao's well-known twelve-year program for agriculture and industry, planned years earlier, and once again pleaded for the "Chinese kolkhoz" comprising a hundred farm households joined together. He announced the continuation of transformation of agricultural property relations, even though he was perfectly aware that only a year before there had been peasant revolts against stepped-up collectivization. He seems to have forgotten his own pragmatic call for moderating the tempo of the transformation:

> Even if the mules walk slowly in China, this has its advantages, after all. Cars go fast. But out of control they can be deadly. Our mules are slow, but safe.[5]

No one dared speak out against these collectivization measures. From October 1957 on, the yes-men were in the ascendent in the ranks of the party. Deng made himself prominent as the committed fighter for speeded socialization, while Liu Shaoqi, Chen Yun, and Zhou Enlai maintained a wait-and-see posture. Consequently, the party media featured the General Secretary prominently whenever they could. Thus the party newspaper "Renmin Ribao" published his speech to the 3rd plenary session of the VIIIth CC in full, while Chen Yun's and Zhou Enlai's reports appeared only in abbreviated form.

The highest functionaries had long known of the close friendship between Mao and Deng, the continuance of which arose primarily not out of a common political conception, but out of the force fields of their two characters: Mao, the romantic, liked Deng, the realist, rooted in the soil. In a real way, the two functioned together like Yang and Yin, like sun and shadow.

In November 1957, Mao and Deng flew to Moscow to meet with Khrushchev anew, in harmonious accord as in those days of Yan'an. When it came to experience abroad, Deng was his superior's superior. He had studied in Moscow at Sun Yatsen University, taken part in the important XXth Party Congress of the CPSU, and concerned himself like no other Chinese in recent years with Sino-Soviet relations. Despite all their ideological differences with Khrushchev and his party, Mao and Deng showed themselves profoundly impressed by Soviet economic successes and the successful launch of Sputnik.

After his return from his second and final foreign trip, Mao's ambition seemed boundless. Now he wanted to step up the tempo of socialistic transformation still further. "We have to develop our own socialism," he called out to the 550 million Chinese, "more, faster, better, and more economically sound"—than the Soviet Union? In May 1958, the party leadership announced the so-called "Three Red Banners": general line ("more, faster, better, and more economically sound"), Great Leap Forward (iron smelters), and peoples' communes. By this course, China, the land of socialistic evolution, would catch up economically with the capitalistic industrial giant Great Britain within fifteen years, and even before this achieve the transition to the classless society.

When "Sputnik," the first peoples' commune, with 41,000 members, was established, Deng, too, added his enthusiastic applause, just as when millions set to work to drive up annual steel production from 5.35 million to 10.7 million tons by "baking iron," which was as much as the primitive smelters were capable of.

It was not only Mao and Deng who waved the "banners"; Liu Shaoqi and Zhou Enlai had in the meantime joined the spokesmen of the Great Leap Forward. Chen Yun, who remained silent, was passed over. The leadership appeared united, but the mandated national order lasted no more than seven months.

The General Secretary, for whom praxis had long meant more than theory, paid heed and acted swiftly when the peasant protests could no longer be ignored. Beginning in November 1958, the party gave back to the peasants as private property their houses, land parcels, household equipment including their woks and small domestic animals. The transition to the classless society was deferred further into the future.

At the second session of the VIIIth Party Congress in
May 1958: *(from left to right)* Li Xiannian, Peng Dehuai,
Chen Yi, Mao Tsetung, Deng Xiaoping.

Four years later Deng would speak out against the "Three Red Banners." But not until twenty-two years later would he admit publicly that in the Great Leap Forward, the people's communes, and the general line toward economic development, the party had ignored the laws of reality, and had, with their feverish, overly ambitious way of proceeding, denied the economic exigencies.

Consistent with the revolutionary romanticism unique to him, Mao, the party's advance thinker, had formulated the "banners" as a utopian goal, by no means least of all to demonstrate to Khrushchev and the world that, "in the mid-twentieth century, the center of the world revolution had shifted to China." Deng, his closest comrade in arms, lacked the theoretical wherewithal to extract the real kernel of Mao's thought. Admittedly, the political climate in the country was not exactly favorable to the development of insight, and Marxist-Leninist theory had, since the campaign against the rightists, degenerated into an instrument exclusively of moral pronouncements against the enemies of the party.

After the collapse of his economic program, Mao resigned on December 12, 1958, as State President. Simultaneously, he handed over the daily business of the party leadership to his First Deputy and General Secretary. Mao withdrew behind the imperial walls of Zhongnanhai, shifting the greatest part of the burden of party work onto the shoulders of Liu Shaoqi and Deng Xiaoping, out of whose shared responsibilities grew an easy friendship that was soon to awaken Mao's mistrust and envy.

Neither for the General Secretary nor for his party would the current "Year of the Pig" be a year of fortune. Deng, once so physically fit and athletic, broke his leg during his leisure hours. No, not at soccer or some other rough sport, but at Ping-Pong. The fracture healed slowly, but, for a 55-year-old, completely normally. His personal physicians prescribed activity—swimming and walking. But a year after his accident at table tennis he still walked with a cane at official appearances.

The Party Chairman could no longer bear to remain in seclusion on the shores of the exclusive "Southern Lake." He called the party leaders together to an expanded session of the Politburo in July 1959, at the breezy spa Lushan. Deng, suffering from his broken leg, and, as General Secretary, having his hands full with all his daily duties, had excused himself. Maybe he kicked himself

The Deng family in the year 1958 in Peking: *(from left to right)* daughter Deng Nan, daughter Deng Lin, wife Zhuo Lin, daughter Deng Rong (Maomao), Deng Xiaoping, son Deng Pufang, son Deng Zhifang.

in retrospect; on the other hand he might also have breathed easier for not having been present at the "Summerhouse Mountain," for the Lushan conference would go down as a sorry chapter in the history of the revolution.

At the meeting in the cool mountains above the Yangtze it had originally been planned to put the party politics of the previous years under the microscope and to make corrections to Mao's line. The discussion had not even properly begun when Mao—after a half-hearted self-criticism—attacked his critics with hysterical and heretofore unknown harshness. He positively exploded, shouting that he would take up the guerrilla war again, shaking his fists, and threatening and fulminating. At the center of his attacks was the Defense Minister and meritorious Marshal Peng Dehuai.

For two weeks, the assembled officials were drawn into an uncompromising proceeding against Peng and his "group of enemies of the party."[6] By threatening resignation, Mao forced them all over to his side. Now they condemned Peng Dehuai, who had done only what Deng Xiaoping, since his advent to power in 1978, had instructed, namely, "To seek the truth in the facts."

In his home province, the fertile Hunan, Comrade Peng had seen the effects of the Great Leap Forward first hand: untilled fields, starving and dying peasants, and falsified production statistics. In Lushan he had the chance finally to say openly what others long had known. Mao, though, would "squash" Peng Dehuai as only a dictator can. Fifteen years after Lushan, on November 29, 1974, the highly decorated Marshal Peng Dehuai died, half-paralyzed in consequence of eight years of imprisonment under inhuman circumstances.

The General Secretary had heard only indirectly of this rupture in the Politburo, but he did not hesitate to praise the Great Leap in a "Renmin Ribao" article on the 10th anniversary of the establishment of the state, and to attack the group around Peng Dehuai. On October 2, 1959, Deng wrote:

> Some of the rightist elements in our party wish not to recognize the remarkable achievements of the Great Leap Forward . . . They exaggerate the errors that have occurred during the course of the movement, which the masses have already corrected. They use these errors as a pretext to attack the party line. The movement of 1958 hastened our economic development. But the rightists ignored this and insisted that

the movement manifested catastrophic consequences. The peoples' communes work well, but the rightists ignored this, and attacked this movement as a step backward. They contended that only by abolishing the communes could the living standard of the population be raised. The masses, on the contrary, believe they have made great strides forward . . . The rightist opportunism quite obviously reflects the bourgeoisie's fear of a mass movement in our party.

Deng was writing these doctrinaire lines while the banquet tables still groaned with the delicacies of the anniversary. One year later, however, all festivities of the foundation celebration had to be canceled due to the acute shortage of provisions. Not even matches, toilet paper, or soap were to be bought, and the apportioned grain and oil rations were reminiscent of wartime. With the exception of high rates of growth in steel production and coal extraction, everything looked as if the economy were about to collapse.

Never before in his life had Deng steadfastly shut his eyes to reality. On the contrary, he almost instinctively related his actions to it, and thus always found his way out of dead ends onto a better way. In the year 1960, his skepticism in regard to the Great Leap grew with each written report of the Party Subcommittee, and with each rumor from the "little channel." Hadn't the party gotten fundamentally stuck?

China drifted directly into the "Three Evil Years." The withdrawal of Soviet development aid and several consecutive years of crop failures threw the political economy completely off the rails. Today, we know that between the fall of 1959 and the winter of 1962, nearly 19 million people died of physical overexertion and malnutrition.

Since the General Secretary himself was provisioned with the best of everything inside the "Forbidden City," it must have been intuition that led him to decide to learn the actual situation in the country firsthand. In accordance with ancient habit, he abandoned his "throne" in the spring of 1961 to go down to the grass roots, as the Chinese say. He traveled to the Shunyi district, barely 50 kilometers from Peking. He stayed there for two weeks inspecting conditions in the villages unaccompanied by press or cadre delegation. What he saw must have stopped his breath. Even the farmers of Shunyi, certainly not the poorest of the people, had not seen a morsel of pork in months. Their food and other provisioning had sunk to an appallingly scanty minimum. And then he discovered a second, still graver problem: the corruption of the village party cadres, who took grain from the collective's storage granaries, credited themselves with work points for work not done, and used the collective's property as if they had requisitioned it.

Following his return to the equally languishing capital, an emergency committee was formed to which in addition to Deng, Liu Shaoqi and the two economic functionaries Chen Yun and Li Xiannian also belonged, and which started immediately with "Tiaozheng," bringing the political economy into equilibrium. A few weeks later, Deng's CC Secretariat put forward the so-called "60 articles respecting agriculture." This was a list of concessions to the farmers encompassing 60 points. Even though through them the concept of the peoples' commune was de facto abolished, this list did not constitute any agricultural reform program in the true sense of the word. The cornerstone of the emergency measures was called San Zhi Yi Bao (Three Freedoms) and Baochan Daohu (production quota of the farm household).

The "Three Freedoms" permitted the farmers private ownership of land parcels once more, privately operated secondary industries such as basketry and weaving, and the independent sale of their products on free markets, controlled by neither the state nor the collective. Since the once incorporated farmland now reverted to the tenancy of the individual farm households, the state as landlord received its rent in the form of produce. Each family had to divert a contractually stipulated production quota to the state—Baochan Daohu meant no more than this. With this and other capitalistic measures of liberalization, Deng's agricultural department turned back the clock to end the starvation: property relations in the countryside now corresponded to the state of the half-socialist LPG of 1954. Deng's and Liu's economics revealed many parallels with Lenin's "New Economic Policy" of the twenties.

The apparatus of the General Secretary had functioned quickly and effectively—too quickly, as Mao was soon to explain. Since the Party Chairman's position in Central Headquarters had in the meantime weakened, he had simply been passed over during the implementation of San Zhi Yi Bao and Baochan Daohu. For some time Mao must have sensed the alienation from his old friend, who knocked on the door of his imperial villa less and less frequently, and who was putting heads together more and more frequently with Liu. For two years now, the General Secretary had no longer thought it necessary to see that an accounting of his activities reached his superior.

Mao no longer felt at home in Peking; he saw his support at Central Headquarters rapidly diminishing. Not even the cult surrounding his person, newly kindled in 1959 by Lin Piao and Chen Boda with photographs and sayings, had been able to reverse this trend. The important decisions in the economic sector were made by Deng's "super-cabinet" in conjunction with the requisite ministries and in conferences with Liu Shaoqi, the State President and First Deputy Party Chairman.

Mao departed once more—once more he was drawn southwards. If he thought he would find there a retreat untouched by the concerns of power, he was badly mistaken. When he presided over a Central Labor Conference in Canton in March 1961, the "60 articles" were on the agenda. Scarcely had Mao learned that Deng had already executed a series of decisions than he shouted angrily, "What emperor decreed this?"

In this sudden outburst, Mao—the emperor—betrayed himself. He felt cornered, felt his power slipping through his fingers. This angry exclamation revealed that he saw himself with his 68 years of age in the tradition of the ancient rulers. And in the Middle Kingdom, there was only one Son of Heaven. If a second appeared, the dynasties warred until one subdued the other.

Mao's rage was inappropriate. Deng was acting not for self-aggrandizement, but wished only to save the country from collapse. The thanks he reaped for his patriotic commitment was the fury of the "Red Sun." A break between the two had now become inevitable.

Mao's indignation could not scare Deng off. The future of the socialist system was at stake here, and, therefore, in his eyes, any means were justified:

> At present it is primarily a question of producing more grain. So long as production increases, the private initiative of individuals is permitted. Whether the cat is white or black is irrelevant so long as the mice are caught.

**Deng Xiaoping and Mao Tsetung in the refreshment
room of the Peking Peoples' Congress Hall after the 2nd
session of the IInd National Peoples' Congress in 1960.**

As he had during the "Hundred Flowers Movement," he defied the Party Chairman, and instructed his Secretariat to undertake further emergency measures.

Deng Xiaoping still functioned as the top party official, not, however, as prospective Party Chairman. Any step in this direction would have been sheer presumption—on that point he was perfectly clear. And yet, his acts bespoke the mind of a sovereign and committed leader: "We must adopt the style the people want. What was illegal, we must legalize." No one else uttered such unambiguous statements, neither Zhou Enlai, nor Liu Shaoqi, nor Chen Yun. Instead, they called reticently for a return to a situation in the villages like that at the beginning of the fifties.

Certainly, Deng acted as forcefully as he did also because his economic measures were supported by a majority in the Politburo and its standing committee. In September 1961, his Secretariat announced the "70 articles respecting industrial labor," the most important points of which provided for the institution of piece-work wages, shutting down of unproductive industries, promotion of agro-industrial sectors of the economy, and large investment in the light industry sector and simultaneous curtailing by 15 percent of the outlays for capital goods industries.

Slowly, very slowly, the emergency measures of the so-called Liu-Deng pragmatism would produce successes. In the course of the year 1962, growth rates rose slightly, although the 1956 per-capita grain production in the amount of 307 kilograms would be reached again only in 1975. And in 1979, the apportioned rations of grain, cooking oil, and cotton were still below those of 1957.

The new year started off with a bang. "Opposing Chairman Mao is opposing an individual like any other," his First Deputy contended on January 11, 1962, at a labor meeting of the Central Committee in Peking. Liu Shaoqi, the initiator of the Mao cult of 1945, appeared to be directing the anathema of criticism onto the Party Chairman, while, within the month, Deng attributed the errors of the previous years to the collective leadership.

In his speech of February 6, Deng referred to the circumstance that many comrades had applied themselves too intensely to their daily work, thereby neglecting their party work. He cited faults such as decentralism, ordering people about, arbitrary decisions, and imperious behavior. At the conclusion of this speech,[7] made public twenty-five years later, he warned against schismatic enterprises. All indications were that he did not belong to those critical of Mao.

Meanwhile, the "Red Sun" was waning from one day to the next. Already on January 30, 1962, in front of 7,000 functionaries, Mao had self-critically taken responsibility for the inadequacies and errors of the party on himself. When in May, then, Deng Xiaoping, Liu Shaoqi, Peng Zhen, and those in charge in the Central Committee presented him with a report on the two billion yuan budget deficit, he agreed apologetically to a five-year phase of consolidation.

Why had Deng, in contrast to his partner Liu Shaoqi, held back so much in the question of calling Mao to account? Because he was, in his heart of hearts, a Maoist? Or had his nose put him onto another scent? Perhaps the man of Szechuan sensed already in the spring of 1962 that a profound change was gradually taking place in his former friend and mentor, for in the summer Mao actualized what he had threatened three years earlier on "Summerhouse Mountain"—a renewal of the guerrilla war.

Possibly, General Secretary Deng, as first participant at a conference at the bathing resort Beidaihe, had noticed the gathering storm. Yet, for all his ability to sense changes and shifting allegiances, not even this astute politician could have reckoned on such an audacious about-face. On August 9, the impulsive Mao launched a frontal assault. He attacked Deng and Liu by name, shouting furiously, "You have put the screws on me for a very long time, since 1960, for over two years. Now for once I am going to put a scare into you." With a gesture of disgust, he swept the "60 articles respecting agriculture" from the table, without so much as a word of explanation of the reversal of his attitude.

Barely four weeks after the Beidaihe Conference, Mao rose like the phoenix from its ashes. At the 10th plenary session of the VIIIth CC, he succeeded in reviving the defunct peoples' commune concept, annulling Baochan Daohu and the rehabilitation of Peng Dehuai that had been prepared, and in pushing the class struggle as well as the existence of classes in socialism onto the center of the agenda.

He simply abolished Deng's agricultural department and dismissed the initiator of San Zhi Yi Bao and Baochan Daohu, the Deputy Premier Deng Zihui, whose fall from power overtook him in accordance with the ancient Chinese tactic, "Slaughter the

hen to warn the monkey." The Great Chairman sacrificed a subaltern in order to warn the powerful, that is, Deng and Liu. The
"Red Bandit" was reviving within Mao, who was subsequently
to employ his guerrilla strategy against his own comrades.

Angrily, Deng countered the abrupt about-face of his superior:

> In 1961 the CC Secretariat drew up 70 articles respecting
> industrial labor, which were then specifically confirmed in a
> resolution on the economic problems. At that time, Chairman
> Mao Tsetung was quite satisfied with the 70 articles and ap-
> provingly expressed the view that we would finally have some
> systematic arrangements. Previously, we had worked out 12
> points on agriculture and 60 articles on the peoples' com-
> munes. His speech [self-criticism] to the gathering of 7,000
> participants was also good. But at the conference at Beidaihe,
> he turned about again, and once more introduced the class
> struggle onto the agenda, indeed, in sharper form than
> before.[8]

Out of the break between the two dogmatic South Chinese
grew an antagonism, and out of the tensions in the party leadership
grew a split. On one side stood Mao with his military comander,
Lin Piao, and his political secretary, Chen Boda. The Peoples'
Liberation Army served as their support. In addition, a bombastic
Mao-cult had been newly kindled. On the other side were grouped
Deng, Liu, and Chen Yun. Their surety was the economy. And
where did Zhou Enlai stand? He became a fence-sitter, coming
down now on one side, now on the other.

The lines were drawn ever more rigidly in the Standing Committee. About Deng and Liu, Mao complained, "They treat me
like a dead ancestor." For some time he had been aware that at
conferences, the two sat either on the other side of the table, or
far removed from him. After he had spoken, they applauded and
nodded their agreement, but they did not carry out his instructions.
They sabotaged his acts, turning to the old strategem—"Hide the
dagger with a smile."

In October 1966, recalling the period of the break in their
friendship, Mao complained about the General Secretary:

> Even though Deng Xiaoping is hard of hearing, at meet-
> ings he would always sit far away from me. Not once in the
> six years since 1959 has he made a report of his work to me.

Deng Xiaoping, his wife Zhuo Lin, Zhou Enlai, Li Xiannian and his wife Lin Jiamei *(from left to right)* attending a Ping-Pong game in Peking, March 1961.

At an expanded labor conference of the Central Committee in 1962: *(from left to right)* Zhou Enlai, Chen Yun, Liu Shaoqi, Mao Tsetung, Deng Xiaoping, Peng Zhen.

So far as the work of the CC Secretariat was concerned, he relied entirely on Peng Zhen. Do you think he is a capable colleague? Nie Rongzhen says the guy is lazy.

Later, much later, Deng Xiaoping described his annoyance with Mao at that time. In August 1980 he said:

> I did not like his patriarchal behavior. He acted as a patriarch. He never wanted to know the ideas of the others, no matter how right they could be, he never wanted to hear opinions different from his. He really behaved in an unhealthy, feudal way.

Thirty-five years lay behind them since their first meeting on that stiflingly hot August day in Hankou. From underground fighters, they had become powerful leaders of one of the most important countries in the world. The enormous growth of power in their hands had altered them. The guerrilla fighter Deng had become a statesman who swore by conscientious management and tended towards the bureaucratic; the "Red Bandit" had become a guerrillero of imperial-dictatorial demeanor.

It was not Mao's remarkable experiments—the "Hundred Flowers Movement" and the "Three Red Banners"—that had broken up their twenty-seven-year friendship, but rather his predilection for radical left, even anarchistic, positions, and his unpredictability. It was political, not personal, alienation that had divided Deng and Mao. China's socialistic development drove them apart. Would it some day bring them together again?

ELEVEN

The Dragon Hounds the Bear

"**D**O YOU SEE that little man over there? He is very intelligent and has a great future ahead of him." Mao liked to present his comrades at cocktail parties this way. In this case, his interlocutor already knew the little man standing off to the side.

Khrushchev, who was short, and Deng, shorter still, had already twice before shaken hands—the first time in September 1954, when Khrushchev and the Chairman of the Council of Ministers, Bulganin, along with his Deputy, Mikoyan, were visiting their brother land in the far east. At that time, he had not yet taken much notice of the little man from Szechuan, for Deng was functioning only as one of many Deputy Premiers and as a dignitary in the Sino-Soviet Friendship Society. So far as foreign affairs were concerned, he held himself modestly in the background, giving precedence to the leaders Mao, Zhou Enlai, and Liu Shaoqi. His second encounter with Khrushchev occurred under rather hectic circumstances, during the XXth Party Congress in the spring of 1956 in Moscow.

At the time Mao was giving Khrushchev this opinion of his associate, three years had passed since the first encounter between the Russian and the "little man." Mao and Deng were on terms as good as those in the Yan'an days; the break—chronicled above—lay still far in the future. And it would be some time yet before Khrushchev would get to know the fiery Szechuanese properly.

On the visit to Moscow in November 1957, too, Deng stood in the second rank. Mao drew the entire attention of the Soviets onto himself, for he functioned as leader of the high-level Party and Government delegation, while General Secretary Deng Xiaoping, Defense Minister Peng Dehuai, and Finance Minister Li Xiannian had come along as advisors. In the ideological grappling with the CPSU, Deng still deferred to the Chairman. But on the sidelines he was already preparing himself to jump into the arena to challenge Khrushchev.

The dragon's hounding the bear began early in the winter of 1960; the Chinese Communists felt ideologically and materially betrayed by their Soviet brothers. In mid-November, an indignant General Secretary Deng, armed with a veritable quiver of points of criticism, traveled to Moscow to the Second World Conference of the 81 Communist and Workers' Parties. Not four months earlier, namely, the Soviet Union overnight had canceled 343 contracts and protocols as well as 257 scientific-technical projects, and had recalled 1,390 development advisors from China. In addition, she demanded the immediate cancellation of all debts incurred for economic assistance and weapons purchases during the Korean War. It was not only Deng who proved indignant over this extortion, but also Mao and the traditionally pro-Moscow faction in the CC surrounding Chen Yun. When Khrushchev rashly took this step, he must have known that China's economy stood on the brink of ruin and that millions of people were starving.

No one apprised of these facts was astonished when Deng Xiaoping, in his businesslike but sharp-tongued manner, leveled his accusation against the Soviets. But only a minority of those gathered here from all over the world had an inkling of these internal Chinese problems. Never had they heard public criticism of the powerful CPSU from the mouth of a Chinese, though some had no doubt heard of Khrushchev's criticism of China, voiced in Bucharest.

Deng had contrived his attacks against the party of Lenin cleverly. He had selected a wide-ranging plenary session: here, at the Second Moscow World Conference of Communist Parties, he attacked the CPSU for siding with India in the Sino-Indian border conflict. Deng declared in his speech that never before in history had a socialist country "censured a fraternally allied socialist country, instead of condemning the armed provocation of the reactionaries of a capitalist country." Khrushchev answered this accusation with silence. Only when further border clashes occurred on November 20 did he respond, calling the events "tragic" and "stupid."

The Soviet betrayal of Chinese economic development provoked Deng, still animated by the desire for unity, only to somewhat encoded speech. On the other hand, he found "Khrushchev's praise of Eisenhower and other imperialists" unforgiveable. The hard-boiled, unpolished leader of the CPSU swallowed Deng's harsh words like a bitter pill, remaining otherwise jovial. During the recesses, Nikita Khrushchev acted almost collegial. For the official press photographs, as though among old comrades, he put his arm around the tall Liu Shaoqi and the short Deng, who supported himself on a cane.

The powerful socialist camp learned from the mouth of General Secretary Deng Xiaoping just how fraternal relations stood between Moscow and Peking. By agreement with Mao and the Politburo, he had sown the seeds for a schism in the world Communist movement. In recognition of this "achievement," the Party Chairman was at the airport to meet the homecoming delegation on December 9.

Deng was now in the limelight as the great "anti-revisionist." It was he, too, who stepped to the microphone in Peking in the middle of January 1961, to report to the 9th plenary session of the VIIIth CC about the Moscow meeting. This time, Deng, once more by agreement with Mao and the Politburo, adopted a moderate tone. After his keynote address it was clear that the CCP did not wish to intensify the contradictions and would first await the coming XXIInd Party Congress of the CPSU.

Khrushchev, however, forced the quarrel between the two largest Communist parties in the world, attacking the Chinese brother party in such strong terms that Premier Zhou Enlai walked out of the CPSU Party Congress in protest. This time, Deng Xiaoping observed the events from Peking. To the dismay of the Chinese, at this Party Congress Khrushchev announced the hegemony of his party in the world Communist movement and praised the new party program as further evolution of Marxism-Leninism: "To those who wish to know what Communism is, we can proudly say, 'Read our party program.'" The Chinese regarded this as presumptuous, not to say patronizing, but pleaded nevertheless for national independence and the self-determination of the Communist parties. It was not by chance that Mao had issued the slogan, "Rely on your own power."

Despite all the quarrels, the CCP criticized only a few "revisionist errors" of the CPSU during 1961. The Chinese comrades still admired the gigantic economic development of their northern neighbor. Deng Xiaoping, who attended the IVth Party Congress of the Korean Worker's Party in September in Pyongyang, praised Soviet economic development as "convincing proof of the superiority of the socialistic system." Simultaneously, he distanced himself from the general applicability of the new CPSU program, calling this program's applicability to other Communist states limited. It is remarkable in this context that the Chinese anti-revisionist criticism was directed in full force against Soviet politics, while economic factors were virtually excluded. This dichotomy between economic base and political superstructure appeared over and over again in China's domestic as well as in its foreign policy.

On domestic policy, Deng had in the meantime broken with Party Chairman Mao. In foreign policy, however, they still saw eye to eye. Yes, after Mao, the former UTK student had become the harshest critic of revisionism.

Although after January 1963, the Chinese attacked Nikita Khrushchev publicly and by name, on February 27, they received a businesslike invitation to talks in Moscow. Already on March 7, Deng, in his capacity as General Secretary, informed the Soviet ambassador in Peking that China was "prepared" to engage in talks "on important questions concerning the international Communist movement." In another document, Zhou Enlai informed the Kremlin that the "Little Cannon" was to lead the Chinese Party delegation.

Meanwhile in Peking, preparations for the next round in the fight with the CPSU were in full swing. On instructions of the Politburo, Deng's Secretariat set about drafting a white paper that would later enter the so-called debate over the general line as "Proposal for the General Line of the International Communist Movement."

If one is to believe Mao's political secretary, the proposal, dated June 14, 1963, did not originate with Deng, but with the Great Chairman himself. According to Chen Boda, Mao rejected as erroneous the original white paper drafted by the opponents of his domestic policy. The new version was published as an open letter to the Soviet people in the Party newspaper "Renmin Ribao." The fifty-eight page document, beginning "Dear Comrades," and ending "With Communist greetings," presents the

**Deng Xiaoping between Khrushchev and Koslov in
Moscow, November 1960.**

attempt to renew the unity of the world Communist movement and to end the debate into which in the meantime other brother parties had entered.

Deng was just packing his suitcase when the Soviets expelled five Chinese for distributing the open letter on Soviet soil. Dark storm clouds gathered over Moscow as the General Secretary, accompanied by the mayor of Peking, Peng Zhen, the head of the Secret Service, Kang Sheng, and the last of the "28 Bolsheviks," Yang Shangkun, as well as three other Soviet experts took off from Peking.

The provocations began already at the Moscow airport. The aircraft of the Chinese Air Force had to maintain a holding pattern for several hours because an important British and American delegation was arriving at the same time. Coincidental, perhaps, or intentional? In any case, during the next two weeks Khrushchev would devote his entire attention to the British and Americans, and not to the Chinese.

On July 5, the ideological discussions between the two veteran General Secretaries, Deng Xiaoping and Mikhail Suslov, began. On the very first day, the chief Russian ideologue cast out an attractive offer: if the CCP declared itself ready to cease the public polemic, the CPSU was prepared to dispatch renewed development aid, to broaden bilateral trade, and to enter into negotiations on the disputed areas along the Sino-Soviet border.

Since the minutes of these meetings remain to this day locked in the vaults of the two parties like military secrets, we have to rely on oral information disseminated from the Russian side. According to these sources, the Chinese appeared extremely rigid and arrogant during the entire round of talks. Deng is supposed to have read out his contributions to the discussion, drawn up for the most part in advance in Peking, in Chinese, and to have responded to Suslov's spontaneous interjections with silence. Ideas such as the peaceful path, that is without proletarian revolution, to socialism, Deng is supposed to have dismissed with the brusque remark, "Idle chatter." On the whole, the Russians were impressed by how much the Chinese prided themselves on their "ideological purity."

Of course the Chinese distinguished themselves also by constructive suggestions. Deng proposed an international meeting of all Communist Parties to return to the unity of Lenin's Communist

Internationale. But his Soviet comrades saw just one catch in his proposal: the crafty Szechuanese demanded that the formula for apportioning delegations be determined by party strength and population. Was the uncompromising chief negotiator trying through disingenuous naïveté to infuriate his opposite number, to set a trap for Suslov? As the days went by, the Soviets became more and more embittered by the Chinese intransigence.

While negotiations continued behind closed doors, the propaganda apparatuses of both parties were doing cartwheels outside. On July 14, precisely one month after the publication of the open letter of the Chinese, the Soviets responded in kind with an open letter in which they appealed to "Soviet patriotism" and "the love for freedom of all peoples." Full of indignation, they reproached the preachers of the pure line for daring to attack the "party of the great Lenin, the birthplace of Communism, and the people who were the first in the world to carry out the Communist revolution." At the same time, a giant wave of anti-Chinese protest swept the entire Soviet Union, with factory meetings and demonstrations. Khrushchev personally spear-headed the attack when on July 19, together with Hungarian Premier Kádár, he led a mass rally in Moscow. The Chinese delegation displayed considerable surprise when the Party head suddenly entered the dispute, for just after their arrival, he had sent Deng his regrets.

The Kremlin boss had more important things to do than debate the pure line with the stubborn Chinese. A few doors down, he and Foreign Minister Gromyko had been negotiating an atom-bomb test ban treaty with the special envoy of the American president, A. W. Harriman, and the representative of the British government, Lord Hailsham. This treaty touched Chinese interests also, in that it obliged the signatories to cease atomic weapons tests in the atmosphere, in space, underground, and underwater, and not to transfer atomic weapons to third countries.

In his talks with Suslov, Deng Xiaoping must have characterized this agreement as a "white" conspiracy to deny developing countries access to the new technologies. In accordance with Mao's slogan "Rely on your own power," China would in the following year set off an atom bomb of its own.

Not twenty-four hours after Khrushchev's anti-Chinese rally on Red Square, Suslov and Deng broke off their talks, which had stalled in any case. The communiqué contained the laconic notation: "Deferred to an unspecified time." Yet in the end, the icy controversy did take on a note of friendliness: on the eve of the Chinese delegation's flight home, Khrushchev, to everyone's astonishment, attended a communal banquet. In a surprisingly jovial mood, the Russian, holding his liquor well, exchanged toasts with the Szechuanese, who held his liquor equally well. After nine years of interaction, they were never to see each other again.

Still to this day, Deng Xiaoping's judgement of the Party Boss, deposed soon thereafter, is devastating. In August 1980, he said:

> Khrushchev only did bad things to the Chinese, Stalin instead did something good for us. Shortly after our People's Republic was founded, Stalin helped us sincerely in establishing or modernizing the industrial complexes which would serve as the basis of Chinese economy. Of course, such helps were not offered free, we had to pay for them, but, when Khrushchev came to power, everything changed. Khrushchev tore up all the agreements between China and the Soviet Union, all the contracts that had been signed during Stalin's time. Hundreds of contracts.

As the General Secretary and his negotiating team took off from the Moscow airport on July 20, 1963, one might have had the impression he was leaving enemy territory—for security reasons, the delegation had divided itself up between two airplanes. Scarcely had the aircraft of the steadfast "anti-revisionists" taxied to a stop at the Peking airport, when the top echelon of the party leadership rushed onto the runway: Mao Tsetung, Liu Shaoqi, Zhou Enlai, Zhu De, Dong Biwu . . . and Jiang Qing, Mao's ambitious wife. Never had such an extraordinary reception been accorded Deng. The ovation was for the man who had brought about the open schism in world Communism.

From here on, Sino-Soviet relations went rapidly downhill: breaking of relations between the Parties in 1966; two years later, the closing of the Soviet embassy in Peking; then, in 1969, the nadir, the border clashes at the Ussuri River.

If Deng once hounded the Russian Bear, since 1979 he has sought to tame him. On his initiative, the Party theoreticians of the CCP quietly dropped the accusation of revisionism, which Deng had once championed from such a rigidly left-radical viewpoint. He explained on September 2, 1986, that three obstacles block Sino-Soviet relations today: Vietnamese troops in Campuchea, Soviet troops in Afghanistan, and 51 divisions (460,000 men) with SS-20 rockets on the border of the Peoples' Republic of China. The 82-year-old Deng said:

> If Gorbachev takes a firm step towards the removal of the three major obstacles in Sino-Soviet relations, in particular urging Vietnam to end its aggression in Cambodia (Kampuchea) and withdraw its troops from there, I will be ready to meet him.
>
> I have long ago accomplished my historical task of making overseas visits. I have decided not to make any more overseas visits.
>
> But if this obstacle in Sino-Soviet relations is removed, I will be ready to break the rule and go to meet Gorbachev anywhere in the Soviet Union.
>
> I believe that a meeting like this will be of much significance to the improvement of Sino-Soviet relations and the normalisation of Sino-Soviet state relations.

TWELVE

Like a Reed in the Wind

DENG XIAOPING'S QUASI-CAPITALISTIC, resuscitative measures put socialist China back on its feet. The three evil years of starvation were past. Reflecting on the time of the "Three Red Banners," Deng said, "The lesson we were taught was so deadly serious we could never forget it." Convinced that he was on the right course, he now wanted to pursue it and reorganize the economic base. But he was thwarted in this by an embittered Party Chairman, committed to the class struggle.

On Mao's instructions, Deng's Secretariat in May 1963 was to implement "The Ten Points" that constituted the new directives for agriculture. What his about-face at the 10th plenary session in September 1962 had already signaled, this document spelled out unambiguously: class warfare on all fronts against the enemies of socialism.

Let us recall Mao's turnabout: early in 1962, self-criticism of his ultra-left agrarian policy and his approval of a five-year consolidation phase; then in the summer his abrupt "No!" to the Liu-Deng pragmatism. After that disastrous year, things came to silent confrontation between Mao and the General Secretary. After Mao's unprincipled about-face, Deng would have been fully justified at that plenary session in reminding him of the fatal consequences of the Great Leap Forward, but he maintained his silence and did not intervene. At conferences, he usually sat next to Zhou Enlai or his deputy, Peng Zhen, sometimes also next to He Long and Liu Shaoqi, Mao's deputy—in any case, he kept his distance from the Chairman. And once again he remained silent when Mao, disregarding the negative experiences of the peoples' communes, announced "The Ten Points."

It would be false and presumptuous to construe Deng's reticence as cowardice. Certainly at this time he felt a justifiable measure of fear of the unpredictable Party Chairman, and he may simply have failed to perceive what Mao was planning. In the Politburo and its Standing Committee, Mao had become isolated, and had lost his credibility. Publicly, however, his reputation blazed brighter than ever. Lin Piao's vigorous efforts had allowed the "Red Sun" of the east to shine with new heat.

In January 1963, the Party organ "Renmin Ribao" and the Army newspaper "Jiefangjun Bao" changed their formats: in the space where lead items previously had appeared, a daily quotation from Mao now was featured. The crafty Lin Piao would later gather these sayings into the "Little Red Treasury"—better known as the "Mao Bible"—thereby kindling the greatest personality cult of all time. So who dared stand up to Mao, who in the eyes of nearly 600 million Chinese glittered as unlimited ruler of their socialist empire? None of the party functionaries had the stature to risk it openly. Only covert resistance remained open to them.

In September 1964, Deng's CC Secretariat opposed the "Ten Points" so imbued with the class struggle by issuing—without much propaganda fanfare—"The Ten Further Points" as an alternative to Mao's concept. The top boss remained uninformed of this step. During those months, General Secretary Deng was not coming into the office daily; his deputy Peng Zhen, mayor of Peking, fulfilled his routine duties.

Although he endorsed the quiet revision, Deng did not belong to the many advocates of the alternative plan. The critical and pivotal point of the "Further Points" involved the political de-emphasis of the rural party cells. Mao's instructions had been that political work was to rest first of all with the local party organizations, and only secondarily with the peasants. This principle was now reversed: with Liu Shaoqi's collaboration, Deng's Secretariat had newly decreed that one must unite first of all with the majority of the peasants, and only then with the majority of the functionaries. This demand rested on the CC Secretariat's anti-corruption measures of 1962, the so-called "Four Cleanups."[1]

Deng's office had at that time uncovered a deep split between the peasants and the party functionaries, for most of the cadres had degenerated into corrupt timeservers. There were four aspects to their scurrilous practices. They fixed the books of the collectives to their advantage, plundered the stores for their private use, illegally made private use of communal property, and credited themselves with work points for work never done.

When Mao learned of the quietly accomplished revision of his "Ten Points," he reacted indignantly. Not yet three months old, the Secretariat's version was replaced, on January 14, 1965, by the so-called "Twenty-Three Points." Concrete politico-economic and disciplinary measures to combat corruption were replaced with the universal political and ideological class struggle. For the first time, Mao openly set forth the line from which the Cultural Revolution was to evolve with such breathtaking speed.

In Mao's view, the new China stood at a turning point: the socialist transformation of the fifties had been accomplished, but classes and class struggle remained. Now in the mid-sixties, the class enemy was trying to reinstate capitalism step by step, and, indeed, not from without; these initiatives were emanating from within the party itself. "Some of the despots who follow the capitalistic path are onstage; others are standing in the wings," he said. Whom he had in mind is easy to guess.

In private conversation with Edgar Snow five years later, Mao would reveal that several days after this pronouncement he had decided to get rid of his old opponent Liu Shaoqi. A bold undertaking!

Since Deng Xiaoping and the majority of the top party leadership[2] were opposing Mao covertly, he had to proceed sub rosa. As once in the past when he had stood beyond the pale of legality, he would soon have recourse again to his tried and true "Three Step Strategy," familiar to us from the Zunyi Conference.

Deng, who had no inkling of Mao's far-reaching plans for a coup, recalled later:

> After the 10th plenary session of the VIIIth CC, Mao Tsetung once again addressed the class struggle . . . Thereafter, Jiang Qing's directives concerning literature and art and all sorts of peculiar things appeared. In the winter of 1964-65 it was asserted not only that there were despots in the party pursuing the capitalistic path, but also that there were two "independent kingdoms" in Peking.

To judge by these words, Deng felt himself embattled and referred Mao's criticism to himself. He did, after all, govern the one "independent kingdom," the CC Secretariat, and Peng Zhen, the other, the Party Committee of the capital.

Since the "Red Bandit" saw himself encircled by two "Kings" and a group of intellectuals, he secretly made off from Peking. Mao's office refused to furnish information in response to inquiries from Deng's Secretariat. In academic circles, Mao was ridiculed in whispered and allegorical allusions. The most outrageous satires came from the pen of Wu Han, Deputy Mayor of Peking. To be sure, Deng himself never ridiculed his superior; he left that to his friends.

Whereas before his departure from Peking Mao had spoken repeatedly of a revolution against the "bourgeois writers" and "reactionary academic authorities," Deng welcomed the divergent views, ranging from liberal to radical, in academic circles, and complained of the prescribed uniformity of cultural life.

> Today, no one dares write articles any more. The news agency Xinhua receives only two dispatches a day. All one sees on the stage nowadays are soldiers and battles. Is it even possible to produce one hundred percent politically correct films? One thing after another is kept from being performed.[3]

Mao's wife, Jiang Qing, had derived her mission to revolutionize what was happening on the stage, in film, and in music from her modest Shanghai film career in the thirties. Mao allowed his third wife free rein, hoping through her activities in the cultural sector to reconquer his lost position of power in the party.

Deng Xiaoping had never made a secret of his dislike for Jiang Qing. He always avoided her and treated her coldly. Seeking nonetheless to win him over to her plans, she asked the retiring Zhuo Lin to influence her husband. But all attempts were vain. The fundamental discussions she had hoped for between the two of them concerning the revolutionizing of cultural work never materialized. Deng's attitude towards Jiang Qing's pretentious experiments in opera reveals his contempt: "I support wholeheartedly the idea of reforming the Peking Opera. But these productions do not appeal to me; I don't bother to attend them." Today, his statement, "Who knows? Perhaps some day the old works will be performed anew," seems oracular.

Without mentioning Mao's wife and her hangers-on by name, he pronounced a devastating verdict:

> There are people who think only of making a name for themselves by criticizing others. They climb to power over the shoulders of those others. What a person truly represents, they only dimly perceive. Therefore, all they can do is pull on their short pig-tails [their inadequacies].[4]

When Deng criticized a person or a state of affairs, it was never from on high. Whenever possible, he first made himself knowledgeable through practical experience. Thus, his critical attitude toward the revolution in culture and science was the result of his participation in the socialist educational movement.

In the spring of 1964, he was able to experience the confrontation at the famous Peking university Beida between a teacher of the philosophical faculty, Nie Yuanzi, and Rector Luo Ping. While the radical young instructor spoke out in favor of a far-reaching replacement of lectures with independent study, in favor of rather "Red" than "expert," and in favor of a polytechnical curriculum, the Rector committed himself to the so-called "Three Foundations," namely, theory, knowledge, and professional leadership of the academic institutions. Deng had unquestionably to take Luo Ping's side in this controversy. The "Foundations" originated in the "60 articles on higher education" which the CC Secretariat, under his direction, had issued not quite three years before.

At a gathering on March 3, 1964, Deng criticized all students and teachers at Beida who attacked the "Foundations" from the left. At the same time, he ordered recasting the core of the socialist education movement, the so-called "work-group." The strong left-wing student faction had to resign themselves to the reshuffling, for backing the new work-group stood the Party Committee of the University, supported by the powerful Party Committee of the city and by Deng's Secretariat. Two and a half years later the Red Guard would chalk this personnel decision up against him and reproach him for having "encircled the revolutionaries and formed a conspiracy."

Meanwhile around Mao, the noisy opponent of the academics, things had become quiet. Only rarely, and from afar, did he ask to be heard. If one asked the General Secretary, or the "Cultural Revolution Group of Five"[5] installed by the Central Committee, concerning his whereabouts, the response was inevitably that he was taking a cure in the southern garden city of Hangzhou. It never occurred to Deng and his comrades in arms—so deeply were they involved in the socialist education movement—that he might have deceived them.

Feigning senility, Mao consciously pulled the wool over the eyes of the "Kings" of Peking. In reality, he was feeling strong enough to hatch a conspiracy. While his opponents in Peking thought he was in his country house on the western lake, he was staying with his new left-wing friends in Shanghai, 190 kilometers away. From here, he would prepare his comeback. This had to be contrived shrewdly, for the entire party apparatus was in the hands of his opponents.

Mao's first strategic step consisted in his criticism of Wu Han, the Vice-Mayor of Peking. The former university professor had made a name for himself as the author of two historical dramas. When his play "Hai Rui Is Dismissed from Office" was originally performed in 1961, he could not have dreamed it would one day unleash a cultural revolution.

Wu Han and Deng Xiaoping knew each other well and thought highly of each other. They met several times a month in an elegant club reserved for the top echelon and high-ranking party func-tionaries in the Apiary Lane where they played bridge or chatted. Deng valued the liberal historian for his enormous knowledge of Chinese history, primarily of the Ming period. And at that time, Wu Han's plays were being produced. His protagonist, the im-perial official Hai Rui (1514-87), was dismissed by the emperor for openly criticizing him.

The public immediately drew parallels with the present: Mao, the emperor, had dismissed his meritorious Minister of Defense Peng Dehuai. In December 1965, Mao would himself concede, "The Jiajing Emperor dismissed Hai Rui. In 1959, we dismissed Peng Dehuai. Peng Dehuai is Hai Rui."

At first, the Party Chairman ordered only that Wu Han be reprimanded, but none of those in authority paid any attention to him. Deng and Professor Wu continued to meet for bridge. In December 1964, to be sure, Wu Han performed a self-criticism, and everyone believed Mao to be satisfied now. A few days after Wu Han had confessed to errors, Wan Li, a member of the Peking Party Committee, and Deng Xiaoping met to play cards. On this occasion, Comrade Wan expressed the opinion that, "Wu Han won't be another Peng Dehuai." Deng agreed, ignorant of events to come. The General Secretary was groping in the dark. He was completely unaware that Mao was already at work with his cunning Three-Steps strategy. Wu Han, the trump card of the "Kings" of Peking, had to be deposed. To accomplish this, Mao sent his wife on a secret mission to Shanghai. There, two men later to play an important role in the fight against Deng had been working for eight months on a criticism of Wu Han's play. Mao had to revise the critique of the editor Yao Wenyuan and the Shanghai Chief of Propaganda, Zhang Chunqiao, eleven times before the barb finally set.

The Party Chairman remained in the wings, playing the role of prompter. Disingenuously, he asked Deng's deputy, Peng Zhen, in September 1965, whether one was permitted to criticize Wu Han. Unsuspecting, Peng replied that certain errors could assuredly be criticized.

The attack on Wu Han was made from Shanghai on November 10. The finely polished critique appeared under the title "Commentary on the Newly Authored Drama 'Hai Rui Is Dismissed from Office' " in the Shanghai newspaper "Wenhui Bao." The editor of the renowned paper, Yao Wenyuan, reproached the author for grave ideological errors: Wu Han was said to idealize a feudal personality and ignore the prevailing class struggle of the people against the emperor, the bureaucrats, and the landowners. After this delayed theatrical thunder, the actual drama took its course.

While Deng and his family were enjoying the waning autumn in Guiyang and Zunyi, cities of the southern province of Guizhou, winter storms loomed over Peking. Peng Zhen had refused to reprint Yao Wenyuans commentary. The Party Committee of the capital and that of the "secret capital," Shanghai, were on a collision course. Mao now indignantly intervened, inveighing against the "independent kingdom" of Peking, so tightly sealed, "that no needle, no drop of water can penetrate it." Zhou Enlai was successful in mediating this feud of localities.

Peng Zhen relented, and on December 29 the Peking newspaper "Beijing Ribao" and the Army organ "Jiefangjun Bao" printed the complete text of the commentary. One day later, the "Peoples' Daily" followed suit and published Yao Wenyuan's critique on the science page. Concealed behind this decision, supported also by the General Secretary who had by now returned, lay the intention of treating Wu Han's errors as "academic mistakes." The construction of Deng Xiaoping, Liu Shaoqi, and Peng Zhen was that in general the whole dispute concerning the cultural sector—the original Cultural Revolution—was to be understood as a purely academic debate, as a "Contest of the Hundred Schools," as it were. In this spirit, the "Group of Five" composed its "February Theses," which were accepted on February 5, 1966, by Deng and the majority of the Standing Committee as the guiding principles of the Cultural Revolution. But shortly thereafter Deng dissociated himself from the theses, explaining that Peng Zhen had hoodwinked him. "I accepted the report because I had been told that the Chairman had approved."

How could Mao have approved, seeing that he was orchestrating the battle between classes within the party? In addition, he was over a thousand kilometers away from Peking in the Yangtze city Wuhan. "His" Cultural Revolution had long since commenced with a silent coup inside the military. While the left-wing cursed Wu Han as a "dog's head," and the right-wing accused him only of intellectual errors, Mao's new comrades in arms carried out a putsch in the army. Lin Piao, who had, since Peng Dehuai's downfall, made a breath-taking career for himself, retook the bastions of the disempowered Party Chairman.

While everyone was pointing at Wu Han, Luo Ruiqing was deposed in total secrecy. Comrade Luo had served Deng Xiaoping since 1962 as a politically devoted assistant in the CC Secretariat and functioned as his support in the all-powerful Peoples' Liberation Army. As General Secretary of the Military Commission, Luo Ruiqing commanded a position of enormous power, which Lin Piao would first have to eliminate, if he was to win the three-million man PLA for the left-wing camp.

Commander Luo was on an inspection tour in the southern border province of Yunnan when a telegram arrived summoning him to an important meeting in Shanghai. The high-ranking military leader boarded his special plane unassailed by the least doubt. When after a four-hour flight his feet were on solid ground once more, he began to be plagued by an uneasy feeling. His subordinates seemed subdued, and the curtained limousine did not drive him to his customary quarters, the former French Hotel Jinjiang, but to lodgings unfamiliar to him.

On December 8, 1965, he realized that a trap had been set for him. On this winter's day, a political interrogation began under the direction of Lin Piao. Seven days later, Luo stood under house arrest as a "counter-revolutionary," removed from all his offices. The cunning Lin Piao had succeeded through this coup in eliminating Deng's base in the Army. Now, no one could prevent his putting the 38th Army on the march towards Peking.

In order to deceive the Pekingese, the underhanded dealings had to continue. In February 1966, the left wing spread the rumor in true reactionary style that Peng Zhen, Lu Dingyi, and two other functionaries had planned a coup d'état against Mao. Consequently, the "authorities" had placed the PLA garrison in Peking on alert. Deng Xiaoping, who as General Secretary had to deal with the matter, rejected the accusations with the words, "We have investigated the situation. . . Peng Zhen is not in a position to give the army instructions, no more than I am."[6]

But Lin Piao insisted on the veracity of his story—indeed, he contended that Deng himself was involved in the conspiracy. He spoke of a "February Mutiny," whereupon the Red Guard demanded the death penalty for the presumed putschists. Once again, Zhou Enlai stepped onto the scene and stretched his protecting hand over those under attack. Not even the head of the Secret Service, Kang Sheng, believed in a conspiracy, but he thought it useful for the people to believe in one. Finally, Mao admonished the radicals around him to moderation: "Liu Shaoqi and Deng Xiaoping have always worked publicly and not secretively. They are different from Peng Zhen."

Since the right wing had been put on the defensive, the 33,000 men of the 38th Army were able to march into Peking unopposed in March 1966, billing themselves as a "protective force." Deng's military support had been stripped of power! Wu Han had been stripped of power! The first step of Mao's strategy had gone off without a hitch.

Now he proceeded to the second step, neutralizing Deng's deputy, Peng Zhen, and his entourage. Mao said:

> The Propaganda Division of the CC is the palace of the
> princes of hell and must be destroyed . . . I have always held

the view that the provinces are called upon to attack Central Headquarters if the central apparatus pursues its evil practices. If Peng Zhen, the Peking Party Committee, and the Propaganda Division continue to protect evil people, then they and the "Group of Five" must be dissolved.

When Deng heard this declaration of war at the Politburo meeting of March 28, he convened his Secretariat to an emergency session on the ninth of April. From within his trusted circle, he thought once and for all to ferret out the game Mao was playing. Trust—what an illusion! His opponents had long since isolated Deng's Secretariat. To everyone's astonishment, Mao's secretary, Chen Boda, and the head of the Secret Service, Kang Sheng, appeared at the meeting, explaining that as candidates for the Politburo, they had the right to participate. Deng let them have their way, not contradicting them, even though as General Secretary he could have interrupted the two left-wingers when they began attacking his deputy with harsh criticism in Mao's name.

Deng, known for his political instincts, sensed meanwhile what game was being played. In a flash, he went over to the side of the Maoists, joining the dance of the critics. In a few words, he distanced himself from his most able colleagues, and delivered a close family friend up to the radicals.

Peng Zhen had been a frequent visitor in the Deng house. The two wives, Zhuo Lin and Zhang Jieqing, had known each other since the Yan'an days. There, they had worked together in the Women's Federation of the Northern Office of the CCP. What, then, had driven Deng to this lightning change of front? Fear, conviction, and hope! As a flexible politician, Deng recognized quickly the extent of the Maoist Cultural Revolution. He sensed that this was mortal combat. At the same time, he saw himself as a loyal, if critical, follower of his superior. Deng was much too disciplined a party worker to join a conspiracy against the head of the Party. In sacrificing Peng Zhen, he hoped to appease Mao and to contain the extent of his radical enterprise. How mistaken he was!

Now that they knew they had the General Secretary on their side, the left-wingers no longer restrained their demands: unconditional revocation of the "February Theses" and abolition of the "Group of Five." One month after the meeting of the Secretariat, at the meeting of the Politburo in Hangzhou, the "Central Cultural

Revolutionary Group of the CCP"[7] was formed and subordinated to the Standing Committee of the Politburo. Simultaneously, the "May 16th Circular"[8] replaced the "February Theses" as the directional line of the Cultural Revolution. Not only Deng's deputy lost his position, but also the propaganda chief of the Party, Lu Dingyi.

His fear that China might "change her colors," a brilliantly thought-out strategy, and an unscrupulous accomplice enabled Mao in May 1966 to transform "his" Cultural Revolution into China's "Great Proletarian Cultural Revolution."

The great Chairman now readied the third blow, the downfall of his First Deputy and of the General Secretary. The ideological cornerstone of his grab for absolute power was the "May 16th Circular." There it was stated that the capitalistic despots would,

> . . . as soon as conditions are ripe, seize political power, and transform the dictatorship of the proletariat into a dictatorship of the bourgeoisie. We have already seen through some of these people, but not yet all; some of them still enjoy our trust and are being trained as successors, like people of Khrushchev's stamp, for instance, who still nest among us.

Before the resuscitated, 72-year-old Mao laid his cards openly on the table, he appealed to the dissatisfied, because neglected, youth. They came in a transport of enthusiasm, wearing the armbands of the Red Guard. Nine days after the publication of the circular, the first "Dazibao" of the Cultural Revolution appeared at the renowned university Beida. Deng tried everything in his power to keep this wall newspaper directed against the rector from reaching the public. But by then Mao's powerful arm had extended its reach far into the media. From Hangzhou he gave the telegraphic instruction to the news agency "New China" to circulate its radical content throughout the country. As though guided by a magic hand, tens of thousands of schoolchildren and university students streamed onto the streets of the capital after the publication of this text.

Deng did not gird himself against the pressure from the streets; he was overcome with a profound sense of helplessness. Together with Liu Shaoqi, he hurriedly boarded a special plane for Hangzhou. The two party bigwigs pleaded with Mao to return to Peking at once and order a halt to the chaos. But Mao refused; he did not wish to rush into anything; and, in general, Deng and Liu ought to react flexibly to further events. The two had to fly home empty-handed.

Shortly thereafter, Deng convened the Standing Committee and proposed sending the tried and true work groups of party members and nonmembers to the schools and universities. He substantiated his demand with the words, "Since the party structure is no longer intact in the educational institutions, the question presents itself, who can assume the role of the party? The work groups must take over this role." Deng fell back on this proven organizational form from the socialist educational movement, appealing to the youth, "A true leftist cooperates with the party; he has confidence in the work groups in the schools." In the region of Peking, the Party Central Headquarters organized 400 work groups with more than ten thousand cadre workers from the most diverse ministries, factories, and state authorities, and charged them with moderating the students.

Deng now cared only about peace and order and the preservation of the Communist Party. For this reason, he warned against spontaneous, unpredictable actions by the Red Guard, whom he once characterized as "babies" on account of their adolescent age. Were they to be given free rein, they would turn everything upside down, he warned, and forbade demonstrations and the public posting of wall newspapers. When Mao returned to the capital in July after a nine-month absence, he reacted angrily to Deng's directives: "It is un-Marxist for Communists to fear a student movement." Soon afterwards he would characterize the work groups as products of a "bourgeois dictatorship" and of "White terror," and accomplish their abolition.

Mao's return to Central Headquarters coincided with Deng Xiaoping's distancing from Liu Shaoqi, indications of which had appeared already in May 1966. At that time, on May 6, the Shanghai workers had given a triumphal reception to an Albanian delegation. On this occasion, Deng gave a speech[9] notable insofar as it documents a shift in his thinking. If at the VIIIth Party Congress in 1956 he spoke out in support of striking the Mao Tsetung ideas from the party statute, he now praised these ideas as the leading line for the comprehensive work of the party. Liu Shaoqi, on the other hand, had made no turnabout. Addressing their guests from far-off Europe, he had not alluded to these ideas in so much as a word. A further index of the alienation between Liu and Deng is a photograph in which Lin Piao, Zhou Enlai, Deng, and Mao—but not Liu Shaoqi—appear with the Albanian guests in Hangzhou, although we know that Liu Shaoqi, in his capacity as State President, attended this meeting.

Shortly after Mao's return on July 18, the rumor popped up in Peking journalistic circles that Liu Shaoqi planned an emergency session of the Central Committee to send the unpredictable Party Chairman into retirement. Supposedly, the CC members, informed secretly by Peng Zhen and Yang Shangkun, were already on their way when Deng stepped on the scene and in short order redirected the CC meeting into a labor conference presided over by Mao. The Party Chairman now thought the time ripe to inaugurate the top echelon of the CCP to his line. He issued Deng's Secretariat the task of convening the 11th plenary session of the VIIIth CC. Nothing simpler, the veteran General Secretary may at first have thought. Yet the closer the first of August approached, the more difficulties appeared. Shortly before the start of the session he learned that of the 173 members, only 80 would attend. The majority declined out of fear or opposition. Under these circumstances he was going to have to cancel the summit meeting, or at least postpone it. The plenary session did come off, however, because the lacunae had been summarily filled with young rebels.

The level on which the party was functioning at this time is indicated by the course taken by this twelve-day gathering. For a start, Lin Piao offered the legitimately seated CC members a slap in the face; he demanded that all functionaries who opposed Chairman Mao, the "genius of world revolution," be dismissed. Demagogically, he adjured the assembly, "Chairman Mao is farsighted and has thoughts many of which we do not understand. We must carry out his directives decisively, whether we understand them or not." After this carte blanche, Mao personally saw to it that many of the veterans of the Central Committee were expelled. His intention of smashing the Party apparatus, which had grown up over decades and become bureaucratized, with the help of the rebellious youth was signalled by the publication of his Dazibao (wall newspaper) under the headline "Bomb Headquarters."

The victor in this gerrymandered meeting was Lin Piao. The "selected" delegates elevated him to the position of Mao's sole

Detail of the caricature "Parade of the Vagabonds" (also called "Counterrevolutionary Procession"). The wall newspaper appeared in 1967 in Peking during the Cultural Revolution. Shown are high-ranking leaders of the CCP who were criticized by the Red Guard: Deng Xiaoping (General Secretary of the CC of the CCP) is holding a "king" in his right hand and other bridge cards with the inscription "work group" in his left.

deputy. By contrast, Liu Shaoqi was demoted to eighth place in the hierarchy, losing his position as First Deputy. The left-oriented Deng Xiaoping came away with a black eye, as it were. Although he did retain his office as General Secretary, in the expanded Standing Committee[10] he slipped to sixth place. The radicals had displaced him by Tao Zhu, First Party Secretary of Guangdong province.

Lin Piao's twelve-day fracas operated like a stimulant on the Red Guards, who had long since disregarded Deng Xiaoping's prohibitions, and—true to his premonition—turned things topsyturvy. One of the political codes of behavior they issued comprised 23 "commandments," beginning with the demand for physical labor for every citizen and ending with the demand that all books not reflecting the ideas of Mao Tsetung be burned. In their intoxication, they demanded that Peking be renamed Dong Fang Hong, "the East is Red," and that the regulation of traffic signals be changed so that traffic would move on red and stop on green.

How pervasively the pressure to conform spread throughout the country was experienced by Carl Bürger on a flight from Shanghai to Peking. The German businessman reported:

> Each of us had a bowl pressed into his hand, then the field kitchen passed down the rows and each passenger received a portion in his bowl. The stewardesses abused a cadre sitting next to me for failing to eat everything in his bowl. Now, his food would probably have to be thrown out, squandering the wealth of the people. Next the passengers had to sing revolutionary songs. The stewardesses stood by the door to the cockpit beating time with their Mao Bibles. The official behind me must not have sung loudly enough, for he was made to stand and repeat the song solo.[11]

Though oriented to the left, Deng could no longer condone the dictatorial measures of the Red Guard and the violent acts they perpetrated against innocent citizens. At a labor conference of the expanded Politburo on October 16, 1967, he expressed his indignation over the brutal incidents to the "genius" Mao. The radicals seem to have long been awaiting this moment, for Mao-intimate Chen Boda's reply came like a pistol shot:

"Deng is the pioneer of the mistaken path. In the past, everyone was afraid to criticize Deng's mistakes because he believes he knows everything. . . . Deng Xiaoping is very cunning; like an encyclopaedia, he knows everything, and he decides problems quickly, without undertaking investigations and studies. Every time Central Headquarters held a conference, the important thing for him was criticism. Other important matters did not interest him. He never studies the issue and yet he makes decisions. His mistakes are obvious and serious. He never consults the masses, nor is he interested in the mass movements. It would be easier to climb to heaven than to talk with Deng about problems.[12]

Chen Boda could risk such a brazen tone because he now occupied the position ahead of the General Secretary in the Standing Committee and had Mao's backing.

The rise of the left and the fall of the right coincided ever more closely during these heated months of the Cultural Revolution. Deng, reelected just two months earlier as the highest official of the party, stood now on the verge of downfall. Chen Boda's massive criticism proved only a prelude, for Lin Piao now took the stage. He charged Deng, in the absence of any proof, with having taken part in the "February Conspiracy" against Mao.

Deng saw himself pressed from every side. He could no longer expect help from the right since Liu Shaoqi's fall from power. Only one option remained if he was to survive: the ritual self-criticism. From the first minute of the chilly realignment session it was clear to him that he would get nowhere with Mao and his pitiless entourage by so superficial a self-evaluation as he had made after his first sudden fall. So he retreated and spent several days taking stock of himself, and then on October 23 appeared before the group that lay in wait for him with the longest self-criticism of his life:

> I support without reservation not only the instructions of Chairman Mao and of Comrade Lin Piao, but just as unreservedly the speech by Comrade Chen Boda of October 16. At that conference, the political lines of direction and party measures for the Cultural Revolutionary Movement were carefully examined with an eye to eliminating the influence of the false, bourgeois line represented by Comrade Liu Shaoqi and me, and putting the resolution of the IInd plenary session of the

VIIIth CC concerning the Great Proletarian Cultural Revolution into action more effectively still. It is extremely important for this revolution to follow the correct line, worked out by Chairman Mao and embodying the proletariat.

In the meantime, it is clear that this movement like all revolutionary movements brings earlier stages of the class struggle and the struggle over the correct line to a head—the struggle between the correct, proletarian line, represented by the Chairman, and the false, reactionary line, embodying the bourgeoisie. From the beginning of this Cultural Revolution, only Comrade Liu Shaoqi and I among the leading comrades of Central Headquarters as well as within the ranks of the party as a whole have represented the false, bourgeois line.

To fulfill the resolution of the IInd plenary session and to apply the correct line of the Chairman as well as to accomplish the Cultural Revolution victoriously, our errors must be fundamentally criticized. The influence of our false line has to be eradicated. We must assume not only complete responsibility for the errors that cropped up after the IInd plenary session, but also direct responsibility for the failures occasioned by the influence of our false line in every field and in all areas . . .

My pursuit of an incorrect line during the course of the Cultural Revolution does not limit itself, of course, to the use of work groups; this was merely the expression of my inadequacies. The essence of my errors consisted in the injury I inflicted on the mass line of the party, in failing to trust the masses and to support their revolution—on the contrary, in fighting against it. With respect to the class struggle, I did not stand on the side of the revolutionary proletariat. In short, this false line with its grave consequences stood in opposition to the guidelines of Comrade Mao Tsetung . . .

I did not, of course, make these grave errors by chance. They are rooted in my way of thinking and in my work style. It is my failing that I did not even take up the Red Banner of the Mao Tsetung ideas, let alone hold it aloft. From a theoretical point of view, I worked in close proximity to the Chairman. I always had the chance to familiarize myself with his teachings and instructions. But what did I do? I studied the Mao Tsetung ideas—centerpiece of our whole work—worse than anyone, hardly disseminated them, and failed to employ them at all . . .

Since I have proven myself a bad student of the Chairman,

I am no longer fit to have important leadership tasks entrusted to me. By my errors, I have shown myself to be an unregenerate, middle-class bourgeois, a man whose worldview is not yet transformed, who has not yet scaled the heights of socialism.

Ruefully, he conceded three errors: supporting the right wing in 1962, sabotaging Mao's education movement, and dispatching work groups to the schools and universities. With respect to the development of his character, he elaborated:

> Arrogance, self-satisfaction, and the belief in my infallibility had been growing in me for a long time. Only now am I aware of this. Under these circumstances, I was able to discharge my duties only unsatisfactorily. I sought counsel neither from my comrades nor from the masses, and neglected to furnish the Chairman with reports. This was my worst error, for in this I violated party discipline, too. At the end of 1964 he had already criticized me for my "Independent Kingdom" politics. I was shaken by his harsh criticism, to be sure, but at the same time comforted myself with the argument that I was not the man who was misusing his authority . . . Now I sit for the first time before the mirror and behold myself closely; a chill runs down my spine when I do so. Were I to go on working in Central Headquarters with this way of thinking, this work style, and this political viewpoint, it would only hurt the party and the people.

Finally, he praised his opponent to the skies:

> Comrade Lin Piao serves as a model to us all. He has held high the Red Banner of the Mao Tsetung ideas, higher than any of us. He has also trained himself best in the Mao Tsetung ideas and is unsurpassed in putting them into action. . . Defective person that I am, fully convinced I must learn from Comrade Lin Piao, and in his footsteps hold high the Red Banner of the Mao Tsetung ideas, study the works of the Chairman with an eye to praxis, and employ them. This is the only path I can take if I am to correct my errors and still accomplish something of value for the party and the people. Because this self-criticism is my first, it is not sufficiently thoroughgoing. I hope my comrades will criticize me and point out my errors.
>
> Long live the Great Proletarian Cultural Revolution!

Long live the ever-victorious, great Mao Tsetung Ideas!
Long live the Great Teacher, the Great Helmsman, the
Great Commander in Chief, and the Great Leader, Chairman
Mao![13]

Radical self-criticism's stock ran high during the sixties—and
was for the most part worthless. Whether right-wing or left-wing,
everyone kowtowed ideologically to the masses, the party, and
the Great Chairman, vowing to become a new person. The ritual
of the self-criticism was not an invention of the New China, but
originated at a time when the emperor could command obsequious
submission even from Mandarins.

Deng's self-criticism, comprising fully 5,000 written characters, goes beyond the traditional paradigm, however. Its compass
speaks for the enormous party discipline of the 62-year-old Deng
Xiaoping. Never before had he expressed himself so thoroughly
on the subject of his inner nature and his political conception, and
never would he do so again.

Though essentially against his nature to do so, Mao reacted
very quickly to the keynote address. Already on the next day he
complained of Deng's willfullness, not his line or his right-wing
opportunistic errors. Taking an astonishingly unpolitical stance,
apparently only hurt, he explained that though hard of hearing,
Deng always sat so far away from him, and between 1959 and
1965 had submitted no accounting report from his Secretariat. He
criticized him as a "lazy guy," and left it at that!

All in all, Mao played the moderate. Since he did not wish to
deliver his former follower up to the rowdy and flogging Red
Guard, he relented quickly: "It is out of respect that Deng seats
himself so far from me." Zhou Enlai also intervened and appealed
to the cautious gathering:

> We cannot make Liu Shaoqi and Deng Xiaoping respon-
> sible for everything . . . They have their responsibilities, and
> the Central Committee has its responsibilities. The Central
> Committee has not worked well . . . Permit these two to
> pursue the revolution once again. Let them repent their deeds.

But the indecisive Mao was no longer in a position to guide
the further course of the Cultural Revolution, which had evolved
a fatal dynamic of its own. Where once the battle had been of
words, now fists and soon even guns prevailed. Deng's wide-

ranging self-criticism was forgotten, Chou's appeal went unheard; a comprehensive political dismantling now began that would end in exile for Deng, and in a death-cell for Liu Shaoqi. Although the two still appeared for four weeks at the side of the Great Helmsman to review parades of the Red Guard, since the realignment session they had been politically iced.

From the end of October, Deng's CC Secretariat continued to exist on paper only, for the Central Cultural Revolutionary Group had appropriated its assignments. The "campaign of annihilation" against Deng and Liu began in the media: first in the mimeographed sheets of the Red Guard and on wall newspapers in the Danwei and on the streets, then—less maliciously, more in innuendo—in the party press.

Danwei, the unit, is the building block of Chinese society. What the family is in the private sphere, Danwei—whose boundaries are fluid—is in public life: allocation of employment and housing, marriage brokerage and birth records—all these belong to the duties of the unit.

Without calling him by name, the left-wing hack writers branded the contrite little General Secretary with the labels "Second highest despot on the capitalistic path," "China's number two revisionist element," and "Taproot of the reactionary line of the bourgeoisie." His good name was first sullied with the characterization "Capitalist despot" by the Red Guard leader of the university Beida, Nie Yuanzi, on November 8. Seven days later, her accusations against Deng were broadcast by the university radio station. Hearing and reading these accusations, one might get the impression that Deng and Liu were Siamese twins. The attacks were always directed against the "Chinese Khrushchev" Liu and the other despot, that is, Deng.

On December 14, 1966, the top echelon of the party paid its last respects to the mortal remains of Wu Yuzhang, rector of the Peking Peoples' University. He is already familiar to us as the educator Wu, founder of the the "Work-Study" movement in Szechuan, which enabled the precocious Deng to travel to France. General Secretary Deng, wearing a black armband, was among the mourners.

Thirteen days after the solemn ceremony at the Hero's Cemetery Babaoshan—for the time being, Deng's last public appearance—over a hundred thousand citizens of Peking gathered in the windy Workers' Stadium near the diplomatic quarter to criticize Deng and Liu in speeches and speaking choruses. On the same day, Deng's internal party self-criticism was published on wall newspapers. Meanwhile, he was able to move about only in a curtained car within the limits of Zhongnanhai's imperial walls, for an atmosphere of virtual pogrom pervaded the wintry city. On Zhou Enlai's advice, Deng stayed away from the mass rally on January 1, 1967, of over ten thousand students from Peking's technical institutes and universities, because acts of violence were to be expected from the incited throng.

By January 18 it was clear that even Zhongnanhai, the strictly secret headquarters of the party, was subject to the fury of the Red Guard. That cold winter's day, on the highest instructions, they cut Liu's telephone lines. They probably severed the wires to Deng's house as well, to cut him off entirely from the outside world.

Liu and Deng still commanded a following, however, and still officially occupied their posts. They were not as totally isolated, in other words, as it may have appeared in the wake of the previous months' events. When on February 3 Mao received an Albanian party delegation, he had to concede privately, "The critical battle with Liu Shaoqi and Deng Xiaoping has not yet been decided." In the same breath he complained to the foreign comrades of the excesses of the Red Guard, "who were sowing chaos everywhere, flogging people, wounding and killing them."[14]

To lend the ouster of the two "despots" a semblance of legality, Mao convened a session of the Standing Committee for the end of March. This time the outcome of the vote did not need to be manipulated by an "expansion" of the session with new participants, for the Standing Committee had already been increased by four potential Mao supporters to a total of eleven members. Notwithstanding, Mao did not have an easy time of it. He succeeded by a majority of only one vote in removing Liu Shaoqi from all his party offices and ousting Deng as General Secretary. As later leaked out, Lin Piao, Zhou Enlai, Chen Boda, Kang Sheng, and Li Fuchun voted with Mao, while Zhu De, Chen Yun, Tao Zhu voted for Deng and Liu.

After Deng had been ejected from the party leadership, the Red Guard presented a whole range of accusations against him. Aside from the already familiar criticism of individual decisions long in the past, their accusations can be divided into three categories. First, they seized on the following quotations from the fifties to prove that, in their opinion, he had adhered to false theories of "the withering away of the class struggle."

> In the wake of recent events, the situation has changed fundamentally—workers and office employees belong to a workers' collective within the same class. By the same token, poor and wealthy peasants have become members of a common cooperative. Very soon, the distinctions between them will be of historical significance only. The overwhelming majority of our intellectuals has gone over to the camp of the working class . . . Is it correct, then, to divide these groups into two separate camps? Even if we wished to draw such a distinction, we could do so neither appropriately nor exactly.
>
> Our previous task was struggle for the revolution; our next is construction. Contradictions between the classes have substantially been overcome.
>
> With the extinction of the class struggle, the only contradictions remaining are contradictions among individuals. Were we to employ the methods of the class struggle to solve these contradictions we would be committing errors.
>
> Stalin clung to the class struggle, even though it had long since ceased to exist . . . When classes no longer exist, clinging to the class struggle only creates problems. The same case can be applied to China.[15]

So much for the first batch of accusations. In their eyes Deng's positions were "poisonous weeds," diametrically opposed to Mao's call for "development of the class struggle in all directions throughout the country."

The second batch related to his supposedly multifaceted opposition to Party Chairman Mao. His opposition was demonstrated by the following statements:

> Chairman Mao has never said he commits no errors.
>
> Is it possible to be of a different opinion from the Chairman? Certainly that is possible.
>
> Everyone acts subjectively to some extent, even Chairman Mao.
>
> All [the report of the Communist Youth League] talks about is the thought of Mao Tsetung. Where is Marxism-Leninism? It is unnecessary to issue this report.

In this connection they reproached the "second despot taking the capitalistic path" for having stricken from the "Peoples' Newspaper" of July 1, 1966, before it went to press the following sentence: "Comrade Mao Tsetung has an outstanding reputation among the Chinese people and an outstanding reputation among the revolutionary peoples of the world." So much for the second cluster of accusations, which corresponded to Lin Piao's statement that a genius such as Chairman Mao appears in the world only once every few centuries, and in China only once every few milennia.

The third batch of critical points related to Deng's lifestyle. In shrill tones, they attacked his passion for good food, strong liquors, and a "little game." In the eyes of puritanical fanatics, who hated perfume, jewelry, lipstick, fancy restaurants, first-class sections, silk ties, and even chess, his passion for games grew out of a thoroughly decadent nature.

In contrast to Mao, Deng had never made a secret of his love for playing cards. Peasants as well as laborers treasured it, too, for socializing over cards was, and is, the favorite pastime in China—not even the Red Guard's short-lived prohibition could change that.

Now Deng was an excellent card player. He liked not only the popular game of poker, but also rummy and bridge—foreign "poisonous weeds" all, which in the view of the left were subverting the Chinese. He was notorious as an avid player. He is said to have brought out the bridge cards not only daily at home in Zhongnanhai, but often at the legendary Functionaries' Club in Apiary Lane, too, which was frequented also by the "right-wing" greats of the Peking Party Committee, Wan Li, Wu Han, and Peng Zhen. He is supposed to have been often shuffling cards, laying mah-jongg tiles, or knocking billiard balls about until two or three in the morning. Though Deng never played for money, he played avidly for stakes of a sort. When he lost, he crawled under the table like anyone else, as the rules of the game required.

To demonstrate to the public how addicted Deng was to games, the Red Guard publicized an incident heretofore kept secret. Once, in Harbin on an inspection tour of the northeast, the General Secretary was overcome by a hankering to play bridge. Since no adequate partner was to be scared up in this city 1,400 kilometers from Peking, the requisite three partners were flown in by special airplane from the capital. So much for the accusations and the revelations of the rebels.

The Red Guards were not wrong; Deng loved bridge above everything. The world-renowned bridge champion, Chinese-American Yang Xiaoyan, has recently testified to this as well: "At the bridge table," so says the advisor to the Shanghai Bridge Club, "one senses that Deng is a great personality. His playing technique is solid and intelligent, amazingly so for a man his age."[16]

In 1967, exactly one year after the publication of Mao's wall newspaper in which he charged "certain leading comrades in Central Headquarters and in the local party organizations" with violating the spirit of the Cultural Revolution, Deng's overthrow was confirmed. On August 5, while three million Red Guards from all over the country gathered for a rally on the grey, seemingly limitless Tiananmen Square, the last public tribunal against Deng took place amid the jutting corners and angles of the villas of Zhongnanhai. Since the radicals chose to pillory him in the courtyard of his own villa, Zhuo Lin and other family members were drawn into the humiliation along with him. Deng was forced to bend his aged back, stretch his arms behind him, and lower his head to his knees. Bent in this fashion he was to listen to the inflammatory tirades, but he heard nothing—or so it is said—since he had turned off his hearing aid.

On the same day, the Red Guards dragged Liu Shaoqi out to the mob. They tormented the tall, slender, 69-year-old man, beat his hollow cheeks bloody with their "Mao Bibles," and ended by breaking one of his legs. Two years later, on November 12, 1969, "China's Khrushchev," disfigured by torture, would die of pneumonia in the high-security prison of Kaifeng in Henan province.

Deng repented and confessed to being a counterrevolutionary who for years had evaded Mao's control. The mob raged, screaming "Cook the dog's head in boiling oil!" and demanded the diminutive Deng be driven through the streets of Peking wearing a dunce cap. He was denigrated also as "aizi," or dwarf—a grievous insult, for traditionally dwarves are malicious and deceitful, their intestines being longer than those of normal people.

The rattling megaphones of Deng's last tribunal fell silent. At the 12th plenary session of the VIIIth CC from October 13 to 31, 1968, the delegates sanctioned what everyone long had known: the expulsion of Liu Shaoqi from the party and the dismissal of

Deng Xiaoping at the bridge competition "Planning and
Health," organized by the Chinese Bridge Association
and the Chinese Society for Service to Sport on June 24,
1984, in Peking.

Deng Xiaoping from all offices, though he retained simple membership. Liu's and Deng's lives both hung by threads. But Mao severed only one of them. Deng is extremely grateful to him for that:

> All through the Cultural Revolution, Lin Piao and the Gang of Four [the faction surrounding Jiang Qing] wanted to murder me. They didn't do it because Chairman Mao protected me even when I was sent to Jiangxi Province to do manual work.[17]

THIRTEEN

A Family's Fortunes

"**D**RAGON BEGETS DRAGON; phoenix begets phoenix—a hero's son will be a man." The Red Guard supplemented this traditional "genetics" with the addendum: "a reactionary's son becomes a rotten egg." How could Deng Xiaoping, this "dwarf," "dog's head," "cattle demon," and "number two capitalistic despot" have a man for a son? Simply unthinkable, considering he himself descended from a "reactionary."

As a result of the resuscitation of feudal values, not only Deng's sons but his entire clan was sucked into the whirlpool of persecution. His younger brother, Deng Shuping, capitulated and took his own life on March 15, 1967. His brother-in-law Pu Desan, who died in prison at the age of 65, suffered more than any other member of the clan.

When Deng's father-in-law had died in 1950, in accordance with ancient custom, Zhuo Lin's eldest brother, Pu Desan, inherited the meat wholesaling business and the long-established family's lands. Soon thereafter, in the wake of land reform, the heir was dispossessed and condemned to a life sentence of forced labor. Surprisingly, he was permitted in 1962, after a protracted "reeducation," to leave the labor camp a free man. His freedom lasted only till the Cultural Revolution, however. The Red Guard revived the old charge and locked him up again—merely because he had come into the world as the son of the Ham King of Yunnan, that is, as a "rotten egg."

Already during the war years, Deng's third wife, Zhuo Lin, had made the choice for family over politics—actually, only over the high-powered politics of her husband. This decision did not mean that she sought refuge in the role simply of mother—only that she trod the path to emancipation quietly, as a token of which she herself chose her daughter's names, a privilege reserved by ancient custom to the grandfather.

During those usettled war years between 1941 and 1950, redolent with sacrifice, she brought a son and three daughters into the world. With only her husband's uneducated but very capable and affectionate stepmother to help her, she raised the children, Lin, Pufang, Nan, and Rong. With the birth of another boy, Zhifang, all her energies were called upon, for her husband spent his days in the office and his evenings at meetings and assemblies. Deng was a good, but extremely busy, father, who did not have much time for his children until after his second political fall.

Probably the mother made too many sacrifices—for years she was frequently in ill health. As a dutiful Communist, she returned to work when the older children had barely started school. Now it was primarily the grandmother, Xia Bogen, who cared for her grandchildren, and they became self-sufficient from an early age.

Since the winter of 1952, when Deng left his homeland, the extended family had lived in a spacious imperial villa in Zhongnanhai. The children grew up, pampered and protected, in the screened-off, parklike area in the heart of the capital. If they lacked for anything, then it was at most for playmates from other families.

The eldest daughter, Lin, had a childhood full of privations behind her. Born in 1941 during the Sino-Japanese war, she was raised for two years by a nurse and lived an unsettled life until her ninth year. She often had to move with her mother and father, changing just her residence at first, then her schools as well. Her brother Pufang, born two years later than she, experienced much the same.

The second daughter, Nan, and the third daughter, Rong, got to know a more peaceful aspect of the world. They spent their first years of life well taken care of in Chungking. Excitement and change entered their young lives only when the family moved to Peking in 1952, and their little brother Zhifang was born.

Since Miss "Forest," Deng Lin, sang beautifully from an early age, she was soon referred to as the artist in the family. In 1959, she attended the Middle School of the Peking Conservatory, for she wished to become a professionally trained singer. Her high-flying aspirations were shattered, however, by a protracted laryngeal illness. Lin was not to be discouraged, for, in addition to music, she loved painting. Her works in ink proved so good that in 1962 she passed the entrance examination for the Central Institute of Art. There, she studied under the famous traditional brush and ink artist Li Kuchan. Since Lin, the spitting image of her father, saw herself as an artist without political ambitions, she was overtaken by the Cultural Revolution—run over by it, in fact.

The first conflict broke out within the family. With the outbreak of the revolution, Lin's younger sister by nine years, Rong, also called Maomao, showed herself an ardent supporter of the Red Guard. Just sixteen years old, the impulsive, verbal Miss "Maple" brought consternation to the imperial villa.

It seemed Maomao could do anything, for she was the prettiest and liveliest of Deng's daughters. At the outbreak of the Cultural Revolution she attended the Girl's School of the Pedagogical Institute, located near Zhongnanhai. Her schoolmates elected the privileged "sun-child" a Red Guard leader and incited her to criticize the "despots on the capitalistic path." Maomao went looking for trouble at home, advocating to her siblings and parents the concept cited above: "The son of a reactionary becomes a rotten egg." Although by this time even the quiet Lin—like the children of all cadres—wore the armband of the Red Guard, she contradicted her sister so defiantly that one day Maomao turned up at the Art Institute with a gang of rebels and challenged her publicly.

Deng Lin was not at all uninformed, much less was she a fool. At twenty-five, she belonged already to the leadership committee of the Academy. She confronted the noisy radicals rationally, saying their "genetics" was false, for neither Lenin nor Marx were descended from proletarian parents. Lin won this exhibition match, but she would lose the ensuing battle. When she completed her art studies in June 1966 she was unable to find work and had to be supported by her parents.

Although Maomao proved the most radical in the family, she never denounced her father—a frequent occurrence in other cadre families. When Deng was attacked by name, his children were forced to distance themselves from him by a sort of "compulsory exercise" in their Danwei, writing down that through them he was by all means at his disposal attempting to bring the movement in the schools under his control. In addition, they wrote, he issued instructions designed to manipulate their thought, to implement the bourgeois reactionary line, and thereby to undermine the Cultural Revolution.

The father did in fact concern himself with the situation in his children's schools. He inquired especially closely of Pufang and Nan, who studied at the Beida. Once he is even supposed to have invited a work group from the university to visit him at home.

Attempting to place the filial relationship in a general context of obligation, and one appropriate to the current movement, Deng advised his sons and daughters in August 1966:

> If it is a question of a contradiction among the people, family relations can be maintained honorably. If it is a contradiction between the people and an enemy, however, then the relations have to be broken off. In either case, my duty is to provide for the support of the family.[1]

With a sense of foreboding, the father gave "his" Red Guards this directive to carry with them. He was saying, in effect, that were he to be denounced by their colleagues, they would not be left without means.

Like his father before him, Zhifang went in for politics at the tender age of fourteen. Deng's second son followed the footsteps of his radical-left sister, becoming an active Red Guard already during his first years at the Middle School of the Pedagogical Institute.

Nan, born in 1947, was Deng's favorite daughter. He appeared often with her in public. He prized her capable and skillful hand. By the age of ten, it is said, she was already helping her grandmother take care of the household. Like, Maomao, she attended the Girls' School of the Pedagogical Institute, taking up her studies at the Beida in 1964. The introverted Nan, who seemed like a country girl, pursued a scientific course of studies like her mother and her older brother. Pufang was already in his second year of studies in nuclear physics when Nan matriculated in the same field.

Lin was called the artist of the family, Pufang, the academic. No one brought home grades as good as his; no one had such an easy time of exams. Even as a schoolboy he had worn the red neckerchief of the Communist Youth League. In addition to his strenuous studies, he acted as League secretary. Of his fellow students, he was the only applicant to be offered membership in the Communist Party. He is Deng Xiaoping's favorite son.

Pufang, more powerfully built than his father, had been graduated from the Peking Middle School Number Thirteen and had registered in September at the Beida. The Cultural Revolution began in the form of great debates in the schools and universities. A young, politically engaged scientist like Pufang wanted to swim with the stream, not against it. He longed to be actively involved, to have a say in the front ranks: his father's managerial personality awoke in him. At the very beginning of the movement he advanced to deputy leader of the "Cultural Revolutionary Group" of his department, and shortly thereafter of the university as a whole.

His meteoric rise was followed by a sudden crash, for the revolution, taking the turn by now familiar to us, put his father in the pillory. In the wake of the so-called division of classes, the promising Deng Pufang became a "dark" child, as they say in China, the son of a "capitalistic despot." This characterization was henceforth to brand him and many other children of high-ranking cadres. "Dark" children had to vacate their bunks in the student residences and were no longer allotted ration coupons for grain. As if they were foulers of their own nest, they were purged from their Danwei. None dared think of employment, for this was allocated by the unit. The social network the Danwei had offered was transformed into a tangle of trip wires. When, on top of everything, the umbilical cord to the protective family had torn, the innocent children of "reactionary" fathers stood destitute on the fringes of society. So the sons of Peng Zhen and Liu Shaoqi could not even earn a few yuan by giving blood, for they dared not present their student identity cards at the hospital.

In September 1967, instructions came down that Deng's children had to leave Zhongnanhai. Deng himself, Zhuo Lin, and the mother-in-law had to vacate the stately house hurriedly, part from their staff, and move into a tiny building. The class struggle had torn the family unit asunder. Soon it was to shatter Pufang's life.

By September 1968, merely criticizing Pufang as a "rotten egg" no longer satisfied the Red Guard. Incited by the well-known Red Guard leader Nie Yuanzi, an inflamed mob locked the aspiring nuclear physicist into a radioactively contaminated laboratory and barricaded the door. Desperate, Pufang climbed out the fourth-story window and, hanging from the roof gutter, attempted to make his way hand over hand to escape the deadly radiation. His

**Deng Xiaoping's eldest, paraplegic son, Pufang,
August 1984.**

daring escape attempt failed. He plunged twenty-five feet to the ground, sustaining life-threatening injuries to his spine.[2]

Bleeding, his bones broken, he lay on the concrete. What now ensued is scarcely to be matched for inhumanity and brutality. It was a long time before anyone informed the first-aid station of the university clinic. It was an even longer time before anyone in charge there could be located, and it took forever for the cadre finally located to consult with the other cadres. Result: Pufang, whose life hung in the balance, was turned unceremoniously away from the Beida clinic. The frequent brawls and knifings among the students had so numbed and intimidated the doctors and administrators that they came to that irresponsible decision. Some expressed the callous opinion that Pufang himself bore ultimate responsibility for his escape attempt.

The severely injured man was lifted onto a freight bicycle and, wrapped in a blanket, driven off the campus. The cyclist had to wind his way through the narrow, congested streets of the rural suburb of Haidian in order to reach the hospital on the arterial road to the Summer Palace. Here at last they found help. Because of a shortage of bedspace, Pufang spent the first day in the corridor, and was examined by a physician only on the second day. For days on end, he wrestled with death in the Haidian infirmary. The doctors determined that there were vertebral fractures of the spine, but for lack of adequate training could do nothing. Had Pufang received immediate treatment by a specialist, he might not have been paralyzed from the waist down.

He was barely out of danger of death when he was moved to Peking University, three kilometers away, and placed in the hospital there. Here he lay virtually in solitary confinement, when one day the door opened and the worker Wang Fengwu approached him with the words, "Are you Deng Pufang?" Old Wang had not been sent by heaven, but by the Great Helmsman.

In August, Mao had directed the establishment of revolutionary commissions and the dispatching of proletarians to the educational institutions and the ministries to bring an end to the destructive activities of the Red Guard. Wang had left his workplace in the press where foreign language literature, including China's English-language publications, were produced, and had rushed to the Beida in the role of peacemaker.

As this plain man walked for the first time in his life among the places of the mind and of learning, he shuddered, not in awe, but horror. Piles of rubble blocked the road through the campus of the American built university. In the noble buildings around the lake where Edgar Snow's ashes lie buried, windows, doors, and furnishings were smashed. Glass splinters lay on the paths, window frames moaned in the wind, reminiscent of the spirit bells of the ancient pagodas. The spirit of the Cultural Revolution had demanded its tribute.

Since worker Wang was on campus on instructions from Chairman Mao, even the Red Guard showed him respect. One day, a nervous student sought him out with the request that he take some money to his old fellow student Pufang. Since Pufang continued to be treated like a leper, the student did not dare bring the 20 yuan he owed him to the hospital personally. Thus it was as a financial courier that worker Wang made the acquaintance of Deng Xiaoping's son.

In response to his question "Are you Deng Pufang?" in lieu of a reply, came a weak nod of the invalid's head. Wang was puzzled: no medications, nothing to eat on the bedside table, soiled bedding—something was amiss here. He felt his forehead and asked, "Are you feverish?" Again, no reply. Only when he insisted on summoning a doctor did Pufang ask haltingly, "Are you a worker, an old craftsman?" Without knowing the state of Pufang's health, Wang answered, "Yes. And incidentally, you can call on me any time; I live in the southwest building." Pufang overcame his mistrust, and said, "I want to talk to you. I want to know why they have excluded me from the party."

Old Wang was just going to call for a doctor when he discovered two distraught girls in the corridor with tears in their eyes. Maomao and Nan had come to visit their brother, but had not dared enter the sickroom.

Not twenty-four hours later the worker himself came under fire. "Wang, be absolutely clear about Pufang!" he was ordered. He was asked provocatively, "Do you even know who this Pufang is?" Wang nodded. "But of course!" His opponent countered deceitfully, "Pufang is a capable person." Wang had to laugh; he conceded unhesitatingly, "The state needs people like Pufang." This verbal skirmish had suddenly turned serious. Someone else threatened: "If you go on talking like that, we'll send you back to the press." No sooner said than done. The radicals achieved Wang's transfer back to his old work place.

Wang Fengwu, living in 1986 as a retired pensioner near the bamboo park in northeast Peking, never allowed himself to be celebrated or put on a pedestal as a proletarian hero. He belongs to the legions of little people who form the moral backbone of Chinese society. His selfless intervention on behalf of the invalid who had been so knocked about arose out of a natural humanity, not out of devotion to socialism, as the propaganda later tried to make out. Rhapsodic newspaper accounts about him praised his selfless intercession. To visit him in his three-room apartment, you must have the permission of his Danwei, for he is today a secret courier, if a minor one.

Worker Wang did not give in. Despite threats from the Revolutionary Commission of the press where he was employed, he wrote letter after letter in hopes that Pufang might yet receive treatment that would save him. He did succeed in getting the sisters permission at least to visit their helpless and destitute brother regularly. Finally, he was transferred for the first time to a special clinic, the Ji Shui Tan. This hospital near the White Pagoda is affiliated with China's best institute for orthopedic medicine.

But Wang's success was not unmarred. Should he rejoice or weep? Of course he had prevailed, but help had come too late for his protégé; treatment of his spinal injuries had been too long delayed. Of a blossoming, successful man, the chaos of the Cultural Revolution had made a helpless cripple.

Since Deng Pufang's paralysis could no longer be reversed, the doctors transferred him to the home for the handicapped, Qinghe, far out in the northern part of the capital. This state institution originated in the fifties and is one of the largest homes of its kind in the country. Today the complex, comprising five two-story buildings, houses 200 physically handicapped children.

When Deng Pufang was admitted there, Qinghe was in a frightful state; the home was an island of the condemned. Only the insane asylums, prisons, and the labor camps on the Mongolian border surpassed Qinghe in horror. Pufang was put into a room with a dozen people. The invalids thus penned together were caring for a seventy-year-old.

Worker Wang will never forget his first visit there. It was on a Sunday. It had taken him two hours to get to the home on his bicycle. When he opened the door to the room, a bestial stench of excrement and urine made his eyes tear. The soiled bedding had not been changed in months. And amid this chaos, Pufang lay on his bed weaving wastebaskets out of thin wire. The inmates of the institution had to earn pocket money by their own work, for the state supplied only room, board, and nursing. Those who could no longer work and had no relatives were in a pitiful position.

Subsequent visits followed, mostly on Sundays, Wang's day off. Sometimes his family also came along. He would wheel Pufang about in the fresh air in an old pushcart. These strenuous promenades gave the paraplegic a special pleasure. Occasionally, the odd couple stopped in at a luncheonette near the home. Since neither had much money, they often had to settle for Jiaozi (dumplings). The two had long since become friends. In time, the companionable custodian Wang became a substitute father, for Deng Xiaoping, under house arrest in Zhongnanhai, was unable to help his crippled son.

The great reversal in the politics of the CCP came suddenly, not by choice, but in response to external pressures. On March 2, 1969, Chinese and Soviet soldiers engaged in a bloody exchange of fire on Damansky Island (Zhenbao Dao) in the Ussuri river, eliciting huge massing of troops—50 divisions on both sides of the border. As was later known through CIA sources, the Soviets contemplated an invasion supported by a limited nuclear strike.

Since the Chinese expected the "new czars" to launch an attack on their capital, on October 18 Lin Piao ordered the Peoples' Liberation Army onto highest alert. His emergency plan included the evacuation of the top echelon of the party from Peking within twenty-four hours. Liu Shaoqi, held prisoner in his office and gravely ill, was flown lying on a stretcher to Kaifeng; Zhu De, the "Father of the Red Army," to Canton; and Marshal Ye Jianying to Changsha. Of the party's top echelon, only Mao, Zhou Enlai, and Lin Piao remained in nuclearly threatened Peking.

Not only "China's Khrushchev" was considered a security risk, but also his deputy, the "number two capitalistic despot." On highest orders, Deng, Zhuo Lin, and Xia Bogen, together with an armed escort, boarded a special airplane on October 20 which took them to Nanchang, a city located 1,700 kilometers south of Peking.

Another circle had closed. Nanchang is the capital of the province of Jiangxi, and there, in the first "Red Capital," 36 years earlier, Deng had functioned as Party Secretary; there the Bolsheviks had put the screws on him; and there, the Long March had begun. So Deng had flown back to the past—memories of his previous fall must have welled up in him.

The first nights the Dengs were put up in the Zhao Dai Suo, a special guest house for high-ranking cadres. Deng quickly grasped why the leadership had selected Jiangxi for his place of exile. This important province functioned as Lin Piao's bulwark: his subordinate from the 44th Army of the Fourth Field Army, Cheng Shiqing, ruled this "independent kingdom" south of the Yangtze. Already the day after their arrival, some of his men showed up and instructed Deng and the two ladies that they were now to let themselves be "transformed" by the masses. Following this admonition, curtained limousines drove up. The privileged prisoners got in, and were sped westwards out of the city of two million inhabitants. Twenty minutes later, the automobiles rolled across a hard-packed track, pulling to a stop in front of a large, faceless building. As Deng learned from his escort, this was the infantry school of Wang Cheng Gang, belonging to the district Xinjian.

The walled in tract with the school buildings seemed untended—deserted, in fact. Not a soul could be seen; the doors had been torn violently from their hinges, the windows shattered. Here, too, the Red Guards had left their mark.

When the automobiles had pulled out of the entrance drive, the three took their way with their baggage and their guards. In the shade of tall black-green pines, they passed the deserted administration complex and walked up a gently ascending stone path. They still could not see anything of their future home, for an enclosure of holly and a bamboo hedge blocked their view of a neat two-story brick building. For three years they would live together with their guards in this unstuccoed red house behind the laurel trees. Deng and Zhuo Lin occupied the larger bedroom in the upper story; Xia Bogen had the smaller room to herself. A wooden stairway led to a living room reserved for the Dengs. On the first floor they had their kitchen and dining room; beyond this, they were undisturbed by the guards.

The mild autumn went quickly into decline, making way for a cold, damp winter. Hard times now began for the old people, for their apartment was heated by only a small kitchen stove. Since the wood supply in the shed behind the house was quickly used up, Deng, at sixty-five years old, had to take up the ax. He had in general to do all the heavy work, for Zhuo Lin had been ailing from the onset of the cold and damp weather. Her chronic condition, high blood pressure, gave her major problems. She was often plagued by raging headaches which confined her to bed. While Deng cared for her, his 67-year-old stepmother washed the clothes and the linens and prepared the meals. Xia Bogen, who could neither read nor write, shared the work during these days with her stepson. For Deng, these days of exile served as a reminder of the hard times of war and struggle. He quickly conceived of his exile as a fresh challenge to strengthen himself physically and spiritually.

The three awoke one morning to find the air filled with dust and a strong wind playing through the bamboo. They all rejoiced over this, for the wind was a harbinger of spring. A few weeks later, green sprouted everywhere through the red laterite soil. Zhuo Lin recovered, regaining her strength gardening. Together they prepared a bed of Chinese cabbage, broad beans, peppers, and squash. When Xia Bogen was permitted also to keep a small flock of hens, good spirits returned to the little red brick house.

Though as General Secretary, Deng had received the princely salary of more than 340 yuan, now, as "despot on the capitalistic path," he had to be satisfied with a fraction of that. Zhuo Lin, too, had to reconcile herself to financial privation. Since, of course, they did not have to spend anything on rent and food, they were able to give over the entire remaining sum to their children. The crippled Pufang alone required at least 80 yuan a month.

In the summer of 1970, a change came into their lives; the "transformation" by the masses began. Sweltering heat lay across the country as Deng and his wife were allotted work in the district's tractor factory. From now on, they descended the hill every morning around 7:30, making the 20-minute walk to their workplace. The workers, particularly the younger ones, were not a little surprised to see the aged couple nonchalantly mixing among them, for normally men retire at 60, women, at 55.

They would never have dreamed that standing at the next work bench burnishing and adjusting threads on newly turned screws would be the former General Secretary of the all-powerful Communist Party, while his wife cleaned and mounted cable spools. The astonished workers soon perceived that Deng worked quite skillfully, though they were not to find out that he had learned the ABCs of metal-working at Schneider-Creusot and Renault. Since the venerable old couple proved convivial, not overbearing, the barriers fell, and the reticence of their fellow workers evaporated.

Whether Deng worked particularly assiduously at his "reeducation" is not known. In any case, his fate so moved several of the older workers that they helped him grind unhusked rice and gave him a bottle of wine spirit from which he was able to ferment his own rice wine. Whenever the rainy season set in, the same spot in the muddy road from the infantry school to the factory flooded. Deng slipped and fell once, and after the little accident people started worrying about that dangerous stretch of road.

Although the two veterans worked in the factory only in the mornings, they soon felt at home among the employees. Deng and Zhuo came gladly and never missed a day of work, either in the sweltering heat of summer or in the cold and damp of winter.

Xia Bogen had prepared the meal by the time they arrived home around 12:30. Following a noontime nap, the afternoons and evenings were their own. Deng lived a life of discipline and remained laconic, never letting himself be rushed. He appeared to be preparing himself for some great task. On his work-free afternoons and evenings, he studied assiduously the "Red Banner of the Mao Tsetung Thoughts," the classics of Marxism-Leninism, ancient Chinese works, and books about other countries. He was fortunate in that Peking had permitted him to take his entire library with him.

Zhuo Lin, the attentive mother, came nearer despair than her husband, for she missed her children more than anything. The parents knew the terrible story of Pufang, but could only guess how things were going for him in the home. In an effort to have their favorite son join them, they sent a formal petition to the Central Committee.

In 1971, Pufang received permission to travel to his parents in Jiangxi and live under their care. The 28-year-old son first had to be nursed back to health, for he was afflicted with sudden fever spikes. While the women saw to his nourishment, his aged father took his helpless son to the toilet and lifted him out of his cumbersome wheelchair to be washed.

One day, the red brick house filled up like a beehive; Maomao walked through the door, and then their son Zhifang. Zhifang had a long, strenuous train and bus journey behind him, for he had come not from Peking, but from the western province of Shaanxi. Such a reunion after all those years of uncertainty and chaos! In 1969, in accordance with Mao's instruction "Educated Youth Should Go to the Countryside," he had been sent to the windy loess mountains of Shaanxi to be reeducated by the peasants there.

The parents spent lovely days with their children; now they could speak openly and frankly about the old quarrels and political differences with the former members of the Red Guard without engendering a feud. It was drizzling when father and mother accompanied their youngest son to see him off on the bus. After a sorrowful parting, they headed straight for the tractor factory, for work there was about to begin. Hardly had Deng carried out his first tasks when he was overcome by sickness. His face went white as chalk, and large beads of perspiration gathered on his forehead. Suddenly his legs gave way, and he sank unconscious to the oil-covered floor of the work hall. The next moment, his attentive fellow workers rushed to his aid. One quickly fetched a glass of sugar water, the universal Chinese elixir. When Deng had been brought to himself once more with the aid of this tonic, he was driven to the infantry school on a tractor. Parting from his son had devastated the father.

Over the course of time, the factory developed into an information exchange for Deng Xiaoping, to whom the reading of news media at home had been prohibited. Only on the national day, October 1, 1971, was he officially allowed for the first time to share in an important party communication via the radio broadcast—truly a landmark for the ex-General Secretary, politically isolated for the past three years. In complete astonishment, he heard over the air that Mao's most intimate comrade-in-arms was absent from the festivities. What had happened? He was unable to make sense of the fact that Lin Piao's name had been passed over in silence. Not until the afternoon of November 5 were Deng and his wife to be enlightened.

As usual, the two came home from the factory at lunchtime, but their faces wore unusually grave expressions. Since their guards sat quite near them during the noon meal, only the clatter of chopsticks was to be heard. Not until the table was being cleared did Zhuo Lin draw her daughter into the kitchen and write—to maintain security—with her index finger on the palm of her hand, "Lin Piao is dead." When the guards had withdrawn, she repeated the announcement in a few words: Lin Piao had attempted to overthrow Chairman Mao and institute a coup. As would soon be learned through the "little channel," he had crashed over Mongolia fleeing to Moscow. While Zhuo Lin spoke, her husband sat at the table in silence. When she had finished, he uttered only the single sentence: "Lin Piao's fate was sealed by providence."

Was he moved at this moment by shame or satisfaction? On the one hand, in his sweeping self-criticism, he had praised Lin Piao to the skies, extolling him as Mao's worthy successor. On the other hand, the relationship of tension between the two had long ceased to be secret, for in their protracted political struggle Lin Piao had often used dirty tricks against Deng.

Putting himself above personal feelings, he drafted the following cooly calculated statement:

> I did not know Lin Piao well, but I am nonetheless prepared to take part in the campaign of criticism against him. Earlier, I pursued a revisionist line and committed errors. Now I wish honestly to accept the criticism of the masses and never again deflect it. At the moment, I am in good health and hope that the party will assign me some simple post in which I can devote the rest of my life to the service of the party and the people.[3]

Deng achieved success with this statement directed to the Central Committee and the Great Chairman. Mao instructed the party to circulate Deng's humble letter to the training sessions of all the Danwei.

Overnight things improved for the exile, for in the context of a national wave of purges, Lin Piao's provincial governor was forced to vacate his post in favor of the new leaders Bai Dongcai and Huang Zhizheng. Soon after taking up their offices, these high-ranking cadres paid a courtesy visit to the little red brick house and arranged for the guards to be replaced by watchmen who would lend the Dengs assistance.

Even before the International Day of Struggle of the Working Class, Mayday, 1972, Pufang, accompanied by Maomao, was permitted to travel to Peking for special therapy. An ambulance took him directly from the railway station to Hospital Number 301. Behind this noncommittal number is concealed the most modern hospital in China. Patients treated here can count on the best doctors and the best Chinese and foreign medications and therapies. But who comes here? Only a few privileged people, military as a rule, for Number 301 is an army hospital. It was here on January 8 that the famous Marshal and Foreign Minister, Chen Yi, persecuted by the Red Guard, died at the age of 71 under obscure circumstances.

Concurrently with Pufang's special treatment—which, however, failed to cure him—the fortunes of the Deng family began to brighten. The children were permitted to visit their parents. Lin, married by now, came with her husband and her young son; Zhifang, too, made another visit. The father began to enjoy a modest reconciliation. In the fall, on the invitation of the provincial Party Committee, he was allowed to visit the birthplace of porcelain, Jingdezhen, where in one of the factories he was given four vases in the traditional style as a present. Today, these vases decorate his office in Peking as a symbol of his connection to the working class.

With his family and his devoted secretary, Wang Ruilin, he also visited the places of bygone days. They traveled in comfort to the former "Red Capital," Ruijin, and to the Jinggang Mountains where a good forty years before the "Red Bandit" had established the first soviet.

During the days in Jiangxi, Deng had become accustomed to walking with firm steps, lost in thought, around the red brick house after dinner. He did this daily, rain or shine, with the perseverance peculiar to him, so that in the course of time, a hard-packed, shiny track was dug in the red earth. Maomao wrote later:

> I often observed my father, how he always made his round, seriously, calmly, and with quick but sure steps. I thought to myself that with each step his belief, his ideas, and

his conviction became clearer and firmer, preparing him for the struggles that lay ahead.

Maomao's premonition would soon become reality.

Between that October 20, 1969, the first day of their banishment, and February 20, 1973, the last day of their exile, lay not just three years and four months, but worlds: the New China had passed the zenith of the Cultural Revolution. Maomao wrote of the journey home:

> The train sped off, its signal horn sounding long blasts, and the icy northwind struck us in the face. The history of China was on the move. A new phase, a political upheaval that would shake the hearts of the Chinese was already visible on the horizon.[4]

Friendly spirits had solved the first big problem already before the the tough Szechuanese's return: an appropriate residence had been found for his extended family. The Dengs received a building complex no less imposing than before in the north of Charcoal Hill. They still live there today, in a secret location behind high barbed-wire reinforced walls to which the tiny, grey gabled houses of the old town cling like swallows' nests. The neighbors in the Hutong (narrow lanes) know that China's most important man lives there. But they confront strangers with a conspiracy of silence. Deng never leaves his concealed estate, which is guarded by the military, on foot—always in a discreet limousine, either through the gates of the main entrance, or through one of the iron side portals.

For the family, a fresh start now gradually began. Maomao, who had taken up studies in medicine at the Institute of Nanchang, moved to Peking and transferred to the Medical Institute there, where she passed her examination. She is Deng's most elegant and attractive daughter, and lives today in Peking. She is a party member, works at her profession, and is married. In 1986, her daughter was of school age.

Zhifang took the most unusual course. At the age of 21, he matriculated in the department of physics at the Beida. After his examination, he worked at the Optical Electronics Research Center. From there, he made the leap to America. He did not go to the city of cities, New York, as is often erroneously maintained, but to Rochester, in the state of New York. Less than two hours by car from Niagra Falls, the former Red Guard devoted himself to an ambitious doctoral program.

When he registered at the University of Rochester in January 1980, neither his doctoral advisor, Professor Joseph Eberly, nor the Dean knew that they now numbered a son of Deng Xiaoping among their student body. After a short term of service at the Chinese Embassy in Washington, and a longer stay back home, he completed his studies in physics with a dissertation on quantum theory. Zhifang, to this day not a member of the party, and his young wife Liu Xiaoyuan surprised the world public by choosing American citizenship for their son.

The artist of the family developed into a traditionally oriented painter in brush and ink of considerable skill. When the Cultural Revolution had faded away, Lin continued her career as an artist. She worked on her own, then studied further, and organized several successful exhibitions. Her debut abroad took place not in Hongkong, but in a true metropolis of art: in December 1981, her florals in ink were exhibited at the Wally Findlay gallery in New York.

In 1986, Deng Lin was much talked about when she announced her entrance into the Communist Party.[5] "I applied because I feel that in the years of reform, one can play a greater role as a party member." She admitted candidly that she actually was not much interested in politics. And it was because of all the "empty words" and the "careerists" that she wished only now—at the age of 45— to join. "What's wrong with my not yet being a member?" she asked. "That doesn't even bother my father. He never forced any of us to enter the party." Asked about her relationship with Deng Xiaoping, she replied, "I am an artist; my father is a statesman. And in spite of that we have something in common—we both love children." Lin has been married longest of all the daughters, and has a son who by 1986 was attending middle school.

Doubtless, she values her father's judgment, but she is not so persuaded of the old gentleman's comprehension of art. "Whenever I show my father pictures I like, he says that these are better than the last, and then asks in the next breath whether all the praise for my work is meant sincerely." Lin's entrance into the Communist Party marked the beginning of a career as a functionary in art and culture. She works today as the Director of the new-fledged "Oriental Art Exchange Association."

Deng's daughter Lin in 1986.

Deng's place of exile during the years 1969–1973: the infantry school of Wang Cheng Gang in the county of Xinjian near Nanchang (see page 211).

Her younger sister, Deng Nan, lost her heart in the country; to be precise, in the district of Shiquan. In the autumn of 1969, she had been sent for reeducation to the barren western province of Shaanxi. Many urban young people had to make do with the wretched peoples' communes in remote mountain valleys, but not Nan. She was assigned to the peoples' commune Chengjiao, in the fertile valley of the Han Shui. There, she worked and lived like a young peasant girl. For two years, no one discovered that she was the daughter of the overthrown "number two despot." Only through an accident did her secret leak out.

At the corn harvest in the fall of 1971, Nan cut her arm with a sickle, severing an artery. Unable to stanch the profuse bleeding in the fields, her friends rushed her to the commune's infirmary. The orderly on duty bandaged the gaping wound and released Deng Xiaoping's daughter, the accident victim, without administering a tetanus shot. The wound became infected. Now, only the better equipped district hospital could help. But how to get there? Without an ambulance, without a donkey cart, without a bicycle? Too weak to walk, Nan had to be carried. Anan, the only son of An Daliang, in whose cottage Deng Nan lived, brought her to the hospital. He stayed with her until she recovered—not out of altruism, but out of love.

She returned his affection and displayed no inclination, even after Lin Piao's death, to return to Peking. In 1977, through the help of her mother, with whom she always had a special relationship, Nan succeeded at age thirty in moving to the industrial city of Tianjin. In 1986, she was living there with Anan and their two children.

The academician of the family was to develop into a politician of a quite extraordinary sort. After Pufang was admitted to Hospital 301 in May 1972, his condition improved to the extent that four years later he was able to work from his wheelchair. He found employment at "East Wind," a factory that manufactured television sets just three bus stops from his home. His health remained stable until 1980; then it deteriorated to the point that Pufang could no longer sit upright. The family decided to send their eldest son for an operation abroad. In October, he flew to Ottawa for treatment; there, Canadian specialists performed two operations on him. Although after four months of rehabilitation he was able to sit upright in his wheelchair again, he remained paralyzed from

**Deng Xiaoping swimming near the resort Beidaihe with
his daughter Deng Nan, accompanied by security
officials.**

the waist down. Against his doctors' advice, he cut short the protracted treatment, and returned to his homeland in the spring of 1981 with an idée fixe: to help China's 15 million handicapped.

How was he, wheelchair-bound, going to help these hordes of people on the fringes of society? Unquestionably, as the son of China's strongman, he exerted some influence, but from 1949 to the present, not even the Communist Party has been able to solve the problem of the handicapped. From time immemorial, the physically and mentally handicapped had been pushed around. Unless they remained in the bosom of their families, they ended in misery.

On March 15, 1984, after seven months of preparation, Pufang and Wang Luguang, paraplegic as a result of an automobile accident, founded the Chinese Welfare Association for the Physically Handicapped. Deeds followed words: he made calls on the authorities of the Ministry of Labor and Education and the State Planning Commission to obtain study and work permits for 301 physically handicapped students. Later, he demanded tax abatements for enterprises that employed the handicapped. In the wake of his father's politics of opening to the west, he advocated lowering tariffs on imported goods for the handicapped. The Welfare Association has in the meantime established branches in other cities, and publishes the journal "March Wind." Its ambitious project, financed by Chinese and foreign monies, is the renovation of the once notorious Qinghe home into a modern rehabilitation center.

Deng's strong-willed son, who now unofficially stands at the rank of minister, is the driving force of the association. Despite weak health, he devotes himself perseveringly to the building of the organization. He regularly undertakes goodwill tours within his own country, and, since 1985, increasingly abroad as well. How popular he has become in Hongkong is indicated by the results of a fund-raising campaign: on his last visit there, he received the equivalent of over 9.5 million U.S. dollars. An idée fixe has turned into impressive accomplishment—an aspiring nuclear physicist has become a politician of a very special sort.

When Deng Pufang makes an appearance, every Chinese is remined of the Cultural Revolution—a chapter which today, many would rather repress. Not so Pufang.

The generation of the Cultural Revolution is in no sense a lost generation, as is often said. Quite to the contrary. All those who passed through that testing have been toughened. These people think a great deal, and have their own ideas. They are firm in their convictions, and show initiative. To my way of thinking this generation represents a trump card for China and for the reforms which they have set in motion. I am sure that in time, we will be clear about this.[6]

Pufang's optimism is the optimism of his father. To both, as to the whole family, the Cultural Revolution was a profound turning point in their lives. In those turbulent years, family cohesiveness determined their mutual fate.

FOURTEEN

Perilous Tug-of-War

"**I**SN'T THAT? . . . No, that's not possible!" The puzzled guest was not mistaken. The elderly little man in the caramel-colored "Mao suit" was none other than Deng Xiaoping. His custom-made suit hung poorly on him, nor was his step spritely. In the massive chandelier's cold light, the returnee seemed still stamped by his exile. He stood off to the side as the leadership collective as a group entered the ceremonial lobby of the Peoples' Congress Hall, running straight into the arms, as it were, of their beaming host: Prince Sihanouk was giving a state banquet.

Even before the first course had been carried to the circular tables, the illustrious guests, Chinese party functionaries and foreign diplomats, were invited to view some photographs. Just back from his former Khmer empire, the Prince was indicating with a pointer on charts the successes of the Khmer Rouge in the "liberated zones" of Campuchea. Although Deng kept to the sidelines, word of his appearance spread through the group like wildfire. The foreigners reacted with confusion, the Chinese, with astonishment. From the very start of the festivities it was clear that Deng—not the Prince—would become the uncrowned king of the twelfth of April 1973.

As Zhou Enlai began greeting the diplomatic corps of the capital shortly after seven o'clock, Deng still kept apart. This was deemed unacceptable by a certain young woman, taken by unknowledgable foreigners for a lady from protocol. Going up to him, she encouraged him to join the Premier. Her word carried weight, for she was Mao's niece, Wang Hairong, the Deputy Foreign Minister. Deng smiled now. And then hundreds of hands were extended to him which he shook with mounting enthusiasm.

When Deng sat himself at one of the tables of honor, it was clear he had once more been installed as Zhou Enlai's deputy, as Vice Premier. Who had reinstated him? Surely Zhou Enlai, his old comrade-in-arms, many must have speculated. Seven years later, Deng was to make the disclaimer:

> . . . It wasn't Zhou Enlai; it was Chairman Mao. At that time, Zhou Enlai was gravely ill, and the entire work of government rested on his shoulders. That was why the Chairman recalled me and reinstalled me as Deputy Premier.

If one is to believe his words, the leadership recalled him from banishment for a very simple reason:

> At a certain point in time they thought I could once again make myself useful and therefore they brought me back from the grave. There is the whole mystery.

The ailing, 79-year-old Party Chairman had by then acknowledged that it was no longer a battlefield on which he stood, but a rubble field. Now he strove for unity and stability. Many of the most capable party functionaries were disempowered, imprisoned, or dead. Great names like He Long, Chen Yi, Peng Dehuai, and Liu Shaoqi had been obliterated. Mao had weakened the party during the Cultural Revolution, but had also purged it and brought new energies to it: beside the veterans Zhou Enlai, Zhu De, and Ye Jianying in the leadership now sat Mao's wife, Jiang Qing, the Shanghai propagandist Zhang Chunqiao, and Yao Wenyuan, as well as the factory worker Wang Hongwen.

After Lin Piao's coup attempt, Mao surrounded himself with only a small coterie of dedicated revolutionaries which, however, lacked people of specialized expertise. He could no longer fully burden the shoulders of the most capable among them, for by then it was clear that Zhou Enlai was suffering from incurable cancer. Mao, then, had to look around for a loyal and at the same time capable collaborator. He swallowed his resentment and recalled his old follower with the words:

> Comrade Deng Xiaoping has a talent such as one rarely comes across. He has rendered service on the battlefield and is an aggressive fighter against Soviet revisionism. In addition, he knows something of economics and military science.

This praise from the mouth of the highest was not intended for the masses, but for Jiang Qing, from whom he had lived estranged the past seven years, as well as for her left-wing hangers-on. These four radicals were dead-set against Deng's return to the leadership, for he was their proven enemy.

There was another reason Deng was recalled: the Party Chairman used him as a tool to solidify his greatly diminished support in the army. Since Lin Piao's death, the leaderless Fourth Army had maintained a wait-and-see posture. Mao could not rely on the First Field Army at all—in fact, it offered opposition because he had brutally eliminated its Commander in Chief, Peng Dehuai. So only the Second and the Third Field Armies were left him. Politcommissar Deng Xiaoping had once commanded the Second, which had evolved from the "Liu-Deng Army." It remained loyal to him. The Third was also loyal, for the Battle of Huaihai they had fought together lived in the memories of the old commanders of both armies. Thus, Mao needed Deng's prestige to draw the influential military men over to his side. Probably, the real reason for Deng's second comeback is to be sought in Mao's loss of military power.

To placate his left-wing partners, Mao did not give Deng any party offices, only government ones. In the wake of the Cultural Revolution, in addition to party committees, ministries and government offices, too, had been debureaucratized. The Council of State, which in 1966 had still comprised ten Deputy Premiers, now had only four. And of these, only one functioned actively in that year, namely Li Xiannian. Mao installed Deng as the fifth Deputy to Zhou Enlai.

In his well-known style, Deng now rolled up his sleeves and got down to work, as in his best years. Through the end of 1973, he appeared publicly on fully 120 occasions. Especially at the reception of foreign guests of state he proved a seasoned, witty, and well-informed interlocutor.

The diplomatic arena had meanwhile become more multilayered and complex, for the Peoples' Republic had turned away from Moscow towards Washington. With the resumption of Chinese-American relations, Deng now fought on two fronts: against socialistic imperialism, which was renewing ancient territorial claims, and against U.S. imperialism, which regarded the southern Chinese island of Taiwan as its unsinkable aircraft carrier. That the Peoples' Republic, dug in for years, now opened a crack in the bamboo curtain is to be credited to the agile, 69-year-old Deng.

His brilliant successes between April and August of 1973 impressed Mao so much that, for the first time in more than a decade, he sought personal advice from his Szechuanese comrade-in-arms. In the fall, he summoned him to Zhongnanhai, and asked him laconically, "What will happen in China after my death?" The great old man saw the end approaching, and his strategical instincts had not been affected by his illness.

Mao ruled enthroned on a heavenly pedestal, idolized, unreachable—alone. Plagued by his old suspicion, he sought counsel not only from Deng, but also from his protégé, the token proletarian on the CC, Wang Hongwen. To get an answer, the old fox dispatched his "right-wing" counselor together with his left-wing counselor on an inspection tour throughout the country. On their departure, he reminded the unlikely pair of his early research in the Chinese village and impressed upon them, "The only way to get to know the situation is social research, the investigation of conditions on the individual levels of society in actual life."

On their return, Wang Hongwen presented an apologetical report: "The whole country will follow the revolutionary line of Chairman Mao strictly, secure unity, and pursue the revolution to its conclusion." An amazing finding of research into actual life! On the other hand, Deng's finding sounded a bitter warning: "Warlords will war on one another; the whole country will sink into chaos."

Mao agreed with Deng, and recommended him to the military heads as the new Chief of Staff of the PLA. For the first time in nearly a decade, the two old warriors were at one again. With irony, but in a thoroughly friendly spirit, Mao said, alluding to the fate of an ancient emperor, "You will not come to a good end. After death, they will flog your corpse." Astonished, Deng asked, "Why should they do that?" "Because you have committed too many errors during your life," Mao replied. "Your virtues and your shortcomings have to be assessed in a ratio of 70 to 30." Deng displayed relief, and answered, "If that is so, then thank heaven. I am quite satisfied to be judged at this ratio. Wasn't the preeminent Marxist Stalin assessed at 70 to 30?" Then both—so the story goes—laughed heartily.

In just two sentences, Deng had thrust to the core of the

problem Mao had addressed; the Party Chairman grasped this at once—and acted. With newly won authority, he summoned the commanders in chief of all military districts to a national conference in Peking. Since he personally presided over the high-level meeting in the Peoples' Congress Hall, he could launch his famous "surprise attack" at the very outset: he had the military leaders, at odds with one another, sing a song, a melody from those days of deprivation of the Long March: "Obey orders in all you do." After this searingly relevant admonition, Mao announced a far-reaching reshuffling of the PLA command, in which even several of Deng's followers lost their posts. That his measures were intended to establish peace would soon become apparent. Once again, Deng's assistance had proven very valuable to the party. But Mao, whose mistrust of the moderate remained deeply ingrained, was incapable of valuing it properly.

While many already foresaw the end of the Cultural Revolution, Mao suddenly recalled a letter of July 8, 1966, from his estranged wife. She had written, "In seven to eight years, the movement against the cattle demons and the serpent gods will be revived again. This should occur often."

Exactly seven years after this declaration, Mao initiated simultaneously two mass movements against his enemies, the "demons," who dared raise their heads once more. One campaign of criticism was directed against the irrepressible influence of Confucianism, a second against the so-called "Wind from the Right." By this means, the people, driven for years from movement to movement, were to be remobilized and prepared for the Xth Party Congress.

The congress, held between August 24 and 28, 1973, was dominated by consolidation of Cultural Revolutionary accomplishments. Mao had his eye on economic development, but maintained simultaneously his commitment to the class struggle, for he thought he detected a "revisionist current" in the party. Although fully 60 moderate veterans returned to the Central Committee, the left-wing occupied the Standing Committee and the twenty-one man Politburo with five and thirteen representatives respectively. The Party Congress left the impression that Mao was handing the left the succession on a silver platter.

For the first time the Shanghai clique—Zhang Chunqiao, Yao Wenyuan, Wang Hongwen, and Jiang Qing—ascended as a group

**Mao Tsetung and Deng Xiaoping after Deng's second
rehabilitation in 1974.**

to the party Olympus, the Politburo. Zhang and Wang rose to the Standing Committee, in which the worker Wang, extraordinarily young by Chinese standards, took his place as third man in the party after Mao and Zhou Enlai. A sensational ascent! On June 12, 1966, Wang had criticized the "capitalistic management" of his factory, the Shanghai Cotton Spinnery Number 17, and thereafter had risen higher and higher as child of the Cultural Revolution. Ultimately, Mao had stretched out his hand to the 38-year-old man, in whom he saw his potential successor.

While Wang Hongwen basked at Mao's side, and Zhang Chunqiao received Deng's old post of General Secretary, Deng sank in the ranks of the 195 CC members. This situation was only to last four months, however. In December, Deng quietly rose once more: Mao had arranged for him to be named one of the Deputy Chairmen of the Military Commission of the CCP, which made him a member of the Politburo ex officio. In February 1974, Deng must already have belonged to the leadership core, for his name appears on the wreaths for the deceased Vice Minister of Defense Wang Shusheng in the ninth place after Mao's.

In fact, Deng by then commanded the second pillar of Chinese power, the government apparatus. For this reason also, he flew in Zhou Enlai's stead to New York for the 6th Special Session of the U.N. General Assembly. Mao had given him the manuscript of an important speech to take with him on his first appearance before this important body.

On April 10, Deng would celebrate one of his greatest international triumphs when for the first time in the history of the CCP he presented publicly the program of Chinese foreign policy: no longer did there exist a worldwide Communist camp, or a capitalist camp—rather, the world had become divided into "three worlds." The two superpowers, the U.S.A. and the Soviet Union, represented the first world—he referred to them as the two "great international exploiters and oppressors." Countries like Japan, France, and Canada he characterized as powers of the middle, numbering them among the second world. As independent industrial nations, these countries strove for independence from the superpowers. To the third world belonged his motherland, Asia, the Dark Continent, and Latin America. These countries formed the main force in the struggle against imperialism, against the two superpowers. Deng's words, "China is no super-power, and never will be one!" were overwhelmed out by the tumultuous applause of the assembly.

As once before after the ideological quarrel in Moscow, the entire top echelon of the party leadership welcomed him, among them even his enemies, with flowers and a triumphal parade at the Peking airport. If eleven years earlier Deng had ushered in the open schism in world Communism, he had now helped socialist China to a new position of prestige in the world. In New York he had succeeded in breaking through China's self-ordained isolation, making his socialist motherland overnight the most powerful advocate of the Third World.

In May, Deng profited from a tragic turn in the life of an old friend. Zhou Enlai's cancer had become so much worse that he had to be admitted to the "Peking" hospital. Until his death, it would—with only brief interruptions—be his home. By this stroke of fate, Deng advanced to acting Premier and, by May 11, had assumed the seat reserved for Zhou Enlai beside Mao at a meeting with Pakistan's President Bhutto. From then on, this seating order became the rule at receptions for foreign visitors.

To the total bafflement of foreigners, at this time a campaign arose from Peking to Canton to "criticize Confucius and condemn Lin Piao." Long-winded, aphoristic articles appeared concerning a quarrel between the "reactionary" Confucians and the "revolutionary" legalists carried out fully two thousand years before; here one could suddenly read marvelous things about a certain Empress Lü of the Han Dynasty and an Empress by the name of Wu of the Tang Dynasty. By their ingenious resort to history, the left-wingers sought to develop a cult around Jiang Qing and stigmatize the pragmatists around Deng as regressive Confucians.

It was not the events of antiquity that triggered the conflict, however, but a quarrel over a current event. At the Politburo meeting of October 17, the laconic Deng and the verbally dextrous Jiang Qing crossed swords for the first time. While Jiang Qing took the launching of the Chinese deep-sea freighter "Feng Qing" as an occasion to attest to the world-class achievement of the Chinese ship-building industry, Deng contradicted her, saying it ranked far below the world standard. Comrade Jiang became enormously agitated, thinking she had unmasked him as a "national traitor." From now on, the lone woman in the Politburo mounted open opposition to the old realist. She wished at all costs to prevent her mortal enemy from becoming First Deputy Premier.

That very evening, therefore, she ordered Wang Hongwen to travel to Changsha to report to Mao, who had been recuperating in his homeland since July. The young worker presented himself to the aged Chairman and maintained that Deng and Zhou Enlai were hatching a conspiracy. As proof, he offered the fact that Chou often received visits at his sickbed. Deng, Ye Jianying, and Li Xiannian came and went almost daily at Chou's sickroom, often staying until late in the night. Wang's brazen accusation peaked in the assertion that Chou was only feigning illness.

Jiang Qing's factionalism had assumed a definite shape. She planned to assume chairmanship of the party after Mao's death. Zhang Chunqiao was, after Zhou Enlai's fall, to become Premier, and Wang Hongwen, Chairman of the Standing Committee of the National Peoples' Congress. In the post of General Secretary, she wanted to install Yao Wenyuan.

On November 12, 1974, she received a letter from her husband telling her she was not popular enough to institute a large-scale reshuffling in the party or the government. "You have too many enemies," he wrote. "You must be careful to win over the majority to your side." Though ideologically and instinctively, Mao was close to the left, he nonetheless condemned their schismatic manoeuvre nevertheless. He had criticized them already in July, admonishing them not to create any "faction of four." And in May of the following year he would once more, more pointedly this time, warn, "I have already told you not to form any 'gang of four.' Why do you persist in doing so?"

The Chairman shook his finger, growled—and drew back again. Since the tug-of-war between left and right did not touch him particularly, he stayed away from the 2nd Plenary Session of the Xth CC. At the meeting from January 8 to 10, 1975, moderates and radicals alike won critical posts. Zhang Chunqiao became leader of the Main Political Division of the PLA, and Deng Xiaoping became one of the five Deputy Party Chairmen[1] and Chief of Staff of the PLA.

Deng's reascent was accomplished quickly. And that seemed to annoy Mao, for a few days later the IVth National Peoples' Congress reconvened in his absence. Zhou Enlai, present despite advancing cancer, excused Mao's absence by illness. But for all that, the Party Chairman was well enough to receive Franz Joseph Strauss, Chairman of the West German Christian Social Union, "in a friendly atmosphere." While the Congress declared the innovations of the Cultural Revolution constitutional law, abolished the post of State President, and gave the Party Chairman in Article 15 of the Constitution the power of command over the armed forces, the left-wing saw itself forced to retreat. Jiang Qing, Wang Hongwen, and Yao Wenyuan had to pull out of the Council of State and the Standing Committee of the NPC; only Zhang Chunqiao was named Second Deputy Premier. Of 27 ministerial posts, the radicals were able to assume only five. Zhou Enlai and Deng Xiaoping achieved the greatest success with their future-oriented economic program. They wanted by 1980 to have set up a "relatively complete industrial and national economic system," and by the year 2000 to have catapulted China to economic world leadership. Since this program envisioned the modernization of agriculture, industry, defense, as well as education and science, it was called succinctly "the four modernizations."

Deng, the favorite of the moderates, finally achieved what the left had tried with all its might to prevent. He was named Zhou Enlai's First Deputy, in other words, acting Premier. For the first time in his party career, his power now rested equally on the three pillars, party, government, and military, for in addition to the new government office, he occupied the post of Chief of Staff and Deputy Chairman of the Military Commission, as well as that of Deputy Party Chairman.

Almost tangentially to the session, another vote took place, the significance of which would be discernible only later. A man by the name of Hua Guofeng was named to the post of Minister of Public Security and to one of the posts of Deputy Premier. This rather unlikely comrade was yet to play a large role in the further course of Deng's life.

Scarcely had Mao studied the documents of the two sessions, when a new movement made its appearance: "Study the theory of the dictatorship of the proletariat." The storm warnings were up again. Was the Cultural Revolution flaring up again? In the theoretical party organ "Red Flag" one could read, "Also some of our comrades in one way or another harbor confused ideas about the dictatorship of the proletariat. They persist in confusing capitalistic things with socialistic ones." And in the "Peoples' Daily" of February 10, Liang Xiao wrote, "The proletariat must exercise its dictatorship over the bourgeoisie." Behind this name hid the authors' group "Two Schools" of the universities of Beida and Qinghua. They would soon launch anonymously the central article of criticism against Deng.

The moderates sent their spokesman Deng to the front, and he countered the attacks from the left with the words, "There is no basis for a bourgeoisie in China." Proceeding from this fundamental principle, Deng denied the necessity of treating the class struggle as the main task, or, as Mao put it, the master link in the chain. At a national conference of the iron and steel industry on March 25, he appealed to the assembled workers and functionaries, "to regard the three directives as the master link." Mao was very annoyed at him for this declaration: "What is this supposed to mean? Have you fabricated your 'three directives as directional line' because the class struggle, this directional line, is dead or obsolete?"

Suddenly, Deng found himself the central target of criticism for his overvaluation of the three Mao directives—first, studying the theory of the dictatorship of the proletariat, second, strengthening stability and unity, and third, promoting the national economy. The radicals reproached him for preaching, as during the fifties, the theory of the extinction of the class struggle and for regarding successes in production as the measure of all political success.

Deng withdrew from the growing polemic, traveling from May 12 to 18 to the country of his youth, France. But he avoided old venues such as Montargis, Chalette, and Le Creusot. In Paris, he did not even manage to look up the suburb La Garenne-Colombes.

In highly developed Europe, Deng seemed to have received new impetus for his economic reform, for, after his return, he organized many national conferences of up to seven thousand participants. He wanted to win over China's old and new economic elite to the "four modernizations" and thus pull the rug out from under the radicals' sloganeering.

On July 18, his colleague Hu Yaobang, formerly General Secretary of the Youth League of the CCP, was appointed Deputy Director of the Chinese Academy of Sciences. Deng commissioned him to prepare the so-called "report" on the situation in the educational sector. While the left rhapsodized about the great accomplishments of the Cultural Revolution in instruction and education, Hu insisted there was a deep-seated crisis. And while the left demanded the reeducation of the petit-bourgeois intellectuals, the "report" characterized the intellectuals as "a part of the working class," and "research as production." Much in this report seemed appropriated from the "60 Articles on Higher Education" of 1961.

Likewise in July, Deng commissioned his theoretician Hu Qiaomu, once Deputy Chief of Propaganda, to work out the so-called "General Outline." While the left regarded the class struggle as the directional line for all work of the party and the entire country, Deng's political structural program stated:

> Chairman Mao gave out the directives concerning the study of the theory of the dictatorship of the proletariat, concerning the strengthening of stability and unity, and concerning the promotion of the national economy. These three important directives of the Chairman form the general program of all work of the entire party and the whole country . . . The realization of these three important directives means the realization of the fundamental line of the party as well, the line of victory through unity and the general line of socialist development.

Finally, Deng mandated the so-called "Twenty Points" for stepped-up econonmic development, which sounded like a new edition of the "70 Articles on Industrial Work" of 1961. All three documents represented, in the eyes of his opponents, the worst of the "three poisonous weeds," for here Deng's economic treatise advocated everything against which the Red Guard had mounted its assault: economic incentive, the piece-work system, professional instead of Red management of enterprises, close collaboration with other countries, and profit-oriented national industries.

Jiang Qing could not stand by and watch as Deng's influence grew from day to day with each of his gigantic realignment conferences. On September 15, the two clashed at the "National 'Learn from Dazhai' Conference," but Deng was to refer to the event only two years later:

Jiang Qing came with a troup of actors and attempted to disrupt the meeting. She gave a talk in which she labeled Hua Guofeng's speech as "revisionist."[2]

Shortly after the conference in the district Xiyang of the province of Shanxi, where the agricultural brigade Dazhai is located, the public learned that Deng Xiaoping and Jiang Qing had given important talks—nothing more. After a ten-day wait the anxious public was able only to study the talk of the brigade secretary in the party organ—for the masses, accustomed to reading between the lines, indication enough that there had been a falling out between the participants. Likewise in Peking, the second venue of this conference, only one speech appeared on October 20. It was by Hua Guofeng, the colorless Minister of Public Security, who earlier had once busied himself with agriculture in Mao's home province. As became known months later, his appearance was on Mao's initiative. The Party Chairman personally had positioned Hua as a buffer between the two enemy camps.

On October 1, organizer Deng could risk carrying out a remarkable action without consulting Mao which the radicals later construed as preparation for a coup d'état. At the reception for the National Holiday, which he led in the place of the deathly ill Zhou Enlai, forty-nine "right-wing" veterans celebrated their comeback with the appropriate number of toasts to their spokesman and his bold politics. Deng had not only given the "old masters" from the Long March their political civil rights back, but had also reappointed them to their earlier—which is to say their higher—functions. Thirty-one of his old comrades he placed in ministerial posts, fifty-eight in chief-of-division posts, and forty-four in offices in provincial administration. The powerful Deng succeeded even in appointing seven people once vilified as "cattle demons" provincial First Party Secretaries.

The counter-attack of the radicals followed on November 3, still articulated in code and confined to the campus of the Qinghua University. In a guarded area of the University grounds specially set aside, students denounced the "wind from the right" in the educational system on long paper banners. They attacked the new Minister of Education by name, as well as the Deputy Party Secretary of the Qinghua, because he had complained to Mao about the "children of the Cultural Revolution" and had written him that "the College graduates can barely read." A few weeks later, the rice-straw panels set up in the marked-off area would be papered with attacks against the "wolfish, snarling Khrushchev of China."

"There will be a battle in the party!" This premonition was expressed by the fatally ill Party Chairman on New Year's Night, 1976, to a foreign visitor. Mao would be correct. The Year of the Dragon became a fateful year for the Peoples' Republic; the tug-of-war between the group surrounding Jiang Qing and the Deng faction assumed dangerous proportions.

To bring in the New Year, Mao had thought of something special. To delineate his own position in the critical internal party power struggle, he released for publication two poems of his from 1965. In the "Conversation of Two Birds" Mao ridiculed Khrushchev's "goulash Communism." An anxious sparrow is terrified by the turmoil throughout the world. Turning to the giant bird, the little one says he wants only to get to the Jade Palace on the mountain of the gods, for "There's also plenty to eat there, potatoes, steaming hot, and goulash, too." The giant bird replies "Stop your farting! Look, the world is being turned upside down." No one could miss the allegorical reference to Deng's pragmatism.

The voices of millions of mourners broke the wintry silence in the capital on the eighth of January 1976. The Chinese people had lost their beloved Premier. Deng Xiaoping was keeping watch nearby when Zhou Enlai died at dawn, and a little later, when the members of the Politburo entered the room, Deng remained standing silently, his head bowed, by the bier of his old friend. Deng said later:

> [Zhou Enlai was a man who] worked very hard and never complained. There were days when he worked even 12 or 16 hours out of 24. I can tell you because I knew him since France where we were together and I regarded him as my elder brother. We joined the revolution almost at the same time. Zhou Enlai was much respected by all, friends and enemies, people and comrades, and this partially explains why he wasn't wiped out by the Cultural Revolution, why he always remained at his post of premier: something which was a great fortune for many. It also explains why he could exercise his influence as moderator and act as a pillow cushion which softens the blows. Many losses could be avoided thanks to Zhou Enlai, many people could be spared thanks to his role.

But, in those years, he found himself in the most difficult position. And he often said things that he would have wished to have not said, he often did things that he would have wished to have not done. This in spite of the fact that people forgave him all. For instance, when Liu Shaoqi was expelled from the party and jailed, it was Premier Zhou Enlai who read the report of Liu's so-called crimes . . . Of course, the report had been written by others. But it was Zhou Enlai who read it. He had to. He could not avoid it.[3]

The Cultural Revolution destroyed Liu and knocked Deng to the canvas, but the truly tragic figure of this difficult epoch is Zhou Enlai. His boundless loyalty to the great Chairman and to the party put him into a nearly schizoid state. On the one hand, he served Mao like a courtier; on the other, a thousand threads tied him—on account of his aristocratic origins and his socialization—to the "despots on the capitalistic path."

What didn't he do for Mao! At the negotiations with the Kuomintang in 1945 he tasted the banquet wine ahead of Mao, lest it be poisoned. Before every large gathering, he tested the seat on which momentarily the Chairman was to take his place. He saw to it for Mao that the elevator was working, and that the red carpet had not bunched anywhere to trip him. In short, he sacrificed himself to Mao, who for his part did not even bother to make an appearance at Chou's burial.

Had not the sensitive, diplomatic Zhou Enlai time and again exerted his moderating influence in the internal party quarrels at the beginning of the sixties, Mao, with his coarse, peasant hands, would have smashed even more china than he did. Most probably too, Deng would no longer be alive. Chou never defied Mao; party discipline forbade that; on the contrary, he always looked up to him. No statement could delineate the relationship between the two better than this: "We are all his pupils, but we can never equal him."

The funeral took place on January 15 at the Hero's Cemetery Babaoshan. As the hearse rolled along the expansive Chang'an Boulevard, hundreds of thousands said farewell to a great man. Deng insisted on delivering the funeral address. Presumably, he already sensed this would be his last public appearance. Chou's death must have unbalanced the 71-year-old man somewhat, for eye-witnesses report seeing him at three in the morning in silent meditation on Tiananmen Square. There, he is supposed to have been standing directly in front of the monument to the Heroes of the People on whose south face a speech by Zhou Enlai is chiseled in gold letters.

The death of the legendary politician had an effect like the bursting of a dam that was to sweep Deng away. Shortly after the funeral ceremonies, the Central Committee called a conference of all the provincial Party Secretaries at which the criticism of the "capitalistic despot" was sanctioned and standardized on the national level. On February 3, the CC published within the party the Document Number One, in which Hua Guofeng was named Acting Premier. The Party Chairman personally had chosen him as a compromise candidate, thereby passing over the legitmate claimants, Deng and Zhang Chunqiao.

Mao, on the uncertain search for a golden middle course, issued confused instructions. On the one hand, he demanded renewed public criticism of Deng; on the other, he said, "Deng Xiaoping has a very good head; he has substance that ought to be sought out." More jocularly, he added that Deng was a "needle packed in cotton." Mao so confused the lower echelons of the party that they either froze in passivity or fell to quarreling among themselves.

Since the left controlled the mass media and the universities, they were able to influence the bitter tug-of-war for power after Chou's death in their favor. They even dared to use the former U.S. President Nixon as a tool in their anti-Deng campaign. On February 25, Jiang Qing took the unsuspecting visitor into the center of the campaign—the Qinghua. The university cadres explained to him that the caption gracing all the wall newspapers, "Capitalistic Despot Opposed to Improvement," meant Deng Xiaoping. And at a mass rally on the same day, acting Premier Hua Guofeng criticized this "despot" with the words:

> He slandered the Great Proletarian Cultural Revolution led personally by Chairman Mao as petit-bourgeois, regularly recurring fanaticism. . . He rejected the revolutionary line of the Chairman in pompously occupying himself with the Four Modernizations. Behind that is concealed a whole series of contemplated conspiracies to usurp the power of the Central Headquarters of the Party with the Chairman at its head. In conclusion, I should like to deal with Deng Xiaoping directly:

he has committed grave errors. Nevertheless, the party hopes that he realizes them, and that he will examine himself scrupulously. That in addition he will accept the help of the party and his revolutionary comrades and return to the correct line of the Chairman and rejoin our ranks.

In the Year of the Dragon, Mao's compromise candidate stripped off his neutrality like an old skin and joined the ranks of the left, exactly as his foster-father would have wished.

Twenty-four hours later, the party leadership released the name of Deng Xiaoping for general criticism. As though on command, on all Dazibaos, paper strips with the three characters for Deng Xiaoping were pasted over the eight characters for "The Never-to-Repent–Capitalist-Roader." Because of the support from the party leadership, the universities Beida and Qinghua evolved into the Meccas of the anti-Deng movement. Tens of thousands came to the campus by army trucks, bicycles, and buses to educate themselves about the "150 counter-revolutionary revisionist quotations of Deng Xiaoping." Young and old, men and women, in quilted blue and green winter coats, crowded around the rice-straw mats set up with the Dazibao, the "Large Character Newspapers." They carried small notebooks with them, and almost everyone, their fingers numbed, wrote down the Deng quotation: "People who are professionally capable and useful to China are more valuable than those who monopolize the toilet because they are constipated. They are also better than all those who practice cronyism." The following quotation from 1953 also had a provocative effect: "The Chinese capitalists have emerged from hard struggles. They are capable people. Since some of them have studied in America, they understand more about management than we."

A person looking over the shoulders of the readers of this wall newspaper whose ears were open might have observed, rather than noisy vilification of Deng, a busy copying of his statements. The behavior of the population might have nourished the suspicion that the campaign against Deng was transforming itself "at the grass roots" to a pro-Deng atmosphere. In February it was clear that the criticism movement against the man "opposed to improvement" had no decisive bite—something the left-wing in the party's top echelon quickly registered. Therefore, they resorted to the notorious forced mobilization from which not even foreigners could exempt themselves. The German lecturer, Florian Mausbach, still remembers well the "onset of frigid weather" at the press for foreign literature after he had hung up a photograph of Deng Xiaoping over his desk on February 27.

> No Chinese colleague dared exchange a word with me or my wife. I was promptly summoned to the departmental leader. There, the atmosphere was nervous and tense. The deputy leader of the "Peking Review" opened the session with a long speech about the criticism movement against Deng, the gist of which was: as a foreigner, I am not in a position to understand these internal Chinese matters properly. Then he exhorted me urgently to remove the Deng photo from my workstation. Though well versed in German, he spoke in Chinese to underscore the seriousness of the situation. The interpreter translated sentence by sentence and recorded my answer.[4]

This event took place in an office building in the northwestern part of the capital while Hua Guofeng was pulling the wool over ex-President Nixon's eyes at the Peoples' Congress Hall, raving about a "Great Debate" going on throughout the country. Lecturer Mausbach described the situation at his press:

> Wall newspapers had to be written, even if no one read them. The Dazibao were strung one after another like beads on a rosary. The only important thing about them was the signature of the author.
> I also contributed. In an allusion to Deng's slogan about the mouse-catching cat with which his opponents used to embellish their wall newspapers, I decorated my poster with a number of scurrying mice, so to speak as warning: Watch out that the cat doesn't eat you up after all! And so I hung it up next to the others, regardless of a colleague's imploring attempts to dissuade me from my intention. It was a success! The news of the "mice-Dazibao" spread rapidly throughout the press. A mute migration of people began. All day, and also the following days, they came from every department of the press to have a look at the little poster . . . As I was to learn later, the story went all the way to the top, to CC Member and Press Supervisor Feng Xuan.

The tug-of-war within the quarreling party leadership now assumed dangerous outlines. The faction around Jiang Qing, later

Woodcut with Deng's signature (1976).

accused as the "Gang of Four," saw in Mao's dissociation from their archenemy and Hua's siding with them against him the time for a putsch. At the end of March, a session of the enlarged Politburo was convened. The most important item on the agenda: criticism of Deng Xiaoping. The left had brought their followers from Qinghua and Beida as agitators. They belabored Deng with long familiar reproaches and long-winded accusations. He remained silent, however, giving no thought whatever to conceding any errors or acknowledging his guilt. His opponents had not reckoned on such obstinacy: they exploded; one of them pounded the table with his fist; others screamed throughout the hall. Deng finally put an end to the conference by standing and taking his leave with the curt words, "I am deaf; I couldn't hear a thing."

He did not doubt the correctness of his politics for a second, for his economic program of the Four Modernizations corresponded to the interests of the workers and the farmers, of the academics and the professionals. The radicals around Jiang Qing for their part knew they had to set a trap for Deng to break his enormous influence inside and outside the party. This trap would be laid during the Peoples' Day of Mourning, the Qing Ming Festival.

In the spring of 1976, there were increasing hints of a mass memorial rally to take place on Tiananmen Square on April 4. The Pekingese were planning to bid farewell to Zhou Enlai in their own way on this traditional day of remembrance of the dead. The rumors concerning this mass rally intensified after March 19, when the first paper wreaths appeared on the monument to the Heroes of the People. The Qing Ming Festival fell this year on a Sunday, so that working people had time enough to get to the gigantic "Square of Heavenly Peace," the heart of the New China.

The people of Peking came by the tens of thousands. To the obelisk in the middle of the square, they brought wreaths they had spent days weaving out of white silk paper. They pulled hundreds of little cards on strings with poems on them. The elegies were anonymous:

> In my grieving, I hear demons shriek.
> While wolves and jackals laugh, I weep
> Tears shed to mourn a hero.
> Head held high, I draw my sword.

The caution was not exaggerated. The author of these "counter-revolutionary" verses would later be hunted from Harbin to Canton—though never found.

The entire Sunday long, there was coming and going in the square; half the nine million inhabitants of the city seemed to be on the move. Of course foreigners could not be absent. Gerd Ruge, at that time correspondent for the daily newspaper "Die Welt," was on the spot, and reported later:

> It was exciting to see how thousands of wreaths came— with a photo of Zhou Enlai, with the characters of his name, with a dedication. We all knew, of course, that it was a silent protest against Mao Tsetung's wife, Jiang Qing, and her friends, who were later called the Gang of Four. Then the first poems made their appearance in which Deng Xiaoping was mentioned as the man in whom Zhou Enlai had trusted, whom he had loved. And one could see that something was happening.[5]

On Monday, many passersby must have rubbed their eyes bewildered, for the square looked as though it had been given a spring cleaning. Overnight, the wreaths had been carried away on 200 trucks, and wanton hands had ripped off the elegies. An eye-witness of this action said disparagingly, "Things went very feverishly at night. The police picked up many."

The masses now did something that had never happened before: they demonstrated spontaneously, without and against the leadership of the party. No deed could exemplify their determination better than the unusual protest action of the workers of the Peking factory for Electrical Engineering. From scraps of metal, they forged a six-meter high wreath, weighing 500 kilograms, which they conveyed the fifteen kilometers from the factory to Tiananmen Square on two freight bicycles. "We had no political motives," one of the workers said ten years later, "we were simple workers and did not know what was going on in the party leadership."

On the afternoon of April 5, more than a hundred thousand Peking residents gathered on the square and remained there in silent protest. Up to then, socialist China had known only officially ordained demonstrations and rallies. The Tiananmen Incident, as the events surrounding Qing Ming now were officially called, would go down in the history of the New China as the first truly democratic mass movement.

Gerd Ruge experienced the progress of events firsthand:

> . . . a gigantic mass of people who did not know exactly why they were there except in collective protest which they could not organize. At the university, as well as in almost all industries, it had been forbidden to go to this square, because the event was construed as a demonstration against the leadership ruling at that time.

On Monday afternoon the party leadership still held back. Even when agitators set fire to a car of the garrison of the guard, the security police looked the other way. At 17:00 hours on the dot, the sea of people froze. Spellbound, they all listened to the crackling voice that announced through nearly a hundred loudspeakers, "Today, evil elements are in the square . . . The revolutionary masses will now vacate the area at once." While march music blared, the audience guessed at who that could have been. Deng Xiaoping's or Hua's voice? No, this high-pitched voice belonged to a man known popularly only as "Without Morals." The command came from Wu De, First Party Secretary and Chairman of the Revolutionary Committee of Peking. Over and over, Wu De's demand to the "revolutionary masses" resounded throughout the square.

A large part left; but many also stayed, among them, the German correspondent Gerd Ruge. He reported:

> Towards evening, when the Tiananmen slowly emptied, the Peoples' militia surrounded the square. Then suddenly the huge lights were flashed on, and one could see how the last people still demonstrating at the Hero's monument were beaten up and taken away.

Overnight, the customary emptiness conducive to the state had returned to the Square of Heavenly Peace. Now heavily protected police cordons forcibly held the people back. The purportedly "counter-revolutionary" Tiananmen incident had shaken China. Had the trap sprung shut on Deng?

The wave of mourning was succeeded by one of terror. Citizens had to provide alibis at their place of employment for the days around Qing Ming; in the Danwei, interrogations by the respective security divisions took place. Everywhere, the authorities hunted down poems directed against the party, and the prisons filled with "counter-revolutionaries." The people held their breath, kept their mouths shut, purloined the copied verses in flowerpots or sent them to relatives in the countryside.

The dire situation came to an end on the night of April 7. Shortly before ten o'clock, a cacophony of crackling, crashing, and drumming shattered the silence of the night streets. In the city center, the first trucks got under way filled with students, soldiers, and workers waving red flags and making noise with firecrackers, gongs, and drums. Though their proficient performance lacked real exuberance, their noise-making having been commissioned by the leadership, they were nonetheless bearing a far-reaching CC decision to the people.

During the course of the day, the party leadership had met without Deng and on Mao's recommendation formulated the following resolution:

> The Politburo of the Central Committee has deliberated on the counter-revolutionary incidents on Tiananmen Square and the latest behavior of Deng Xiaoping. It has come to the conviction that the problem of Deng Xiaoping has become an antagonistic contradiction. At the suggestion of our great leader, Chairman Mao, it has decided unanimously to remove Deng Xiaoping from all his offices inside and outside the party. He is permitted to retain his party membership, so one may see how he behaves in the future.

FIFTEEN

Turn of an Era

DENG'S THIRD FALL from power came at a time when despotism and chaos reigned anew. His last disempowerment went hand in hand with a grievous breach of the Constitution: though appointment of the Premier is reserved to the National Peoples' Congress, this time the Politburo conferred that significant state office. By this double-barreled decision of April 1976—the demotion of Deng Xiaoping and simultaneous promotion of Hua Guofeng—the party leadership placed itself above the Constitution.

With Deng's renewed exit from the political stage, many of his adherents had to submit their resignations. His most capable collaborators, Hu Yaobang, Hu Qiaomu, and Wan Li, lost their influential positions overnight. "Down with the Deng Xiaoping gang!" blared the agitprop loudspeakers, and the slogan appeared in large characters in all the regional and national newspapers. "Down with the despot opposed to improvement on the capitalistic path!"—this and similar slogans were to be heard at rallies taking place throughout the country.

On April 30, 1976, Premier Hua Guofeng and Mao had a meeting. On this occasion the Party Chairman, half paralysed by a stroke, pressed a piece of paper into the hand of his compromise candidate on which he had written in almost illegible characters, "If things are in your hands, my mind is at ease." What did this sentence mean? . . . a question that would be much puzzled over.

Following this encounter, the anti-Deng campaign continued to escalate. The tone set by the top echelon of the party was already dangerously shrill; the ultra-left wanted to see the man "opposed

The wall newspaper from 1976 documents the "anti-Deng campaign" after Deng Xiaoping's third fall and illustrates tortures of Deng adherents.

在专题审讯我保护邓小平问题时，将我上着绳，堵上咀，多次吊到铁管子上严刑拷打血染公堂！近十种惨无人道的法西斯暴刑折磨我

to improvement" sacrificed at last. Deng, sitting tight in his secret house, guarded like a fortress, knew this scenario only too well—his life was once more at risk.

There are two versions of the further unfolding of the events coming to a head. The one comes from Deng Xiaoping himself. At his meeting with Franz Josef Strauss in 1982, Deng said that he remained in Peking from his fall to his reinstatement. The other unofficial version comes from Cantonese and Hongkong sources; it probably corresponds to the facts. Since the radicals around Jiang Qing had elevated Deng to archenemy of socialism, his life hung by a silken thread. But through the help of the powerful Marshal Ye Jianying, Deng was able to flee south secretly on a military plane. Unrecognized at the Cantonese airport, "White Clouds," he boarded a modest limousine that took him to the headquarters of the Guangdong military region. He was now in safety, 2,300 kilometers south of the capital, for the most powerful man on the scene was one of his followers. Commander Xu Shiyou had fought under Politcommissar Deng in the 129th Division during the Sino-Japanese War.

Deng Xiaoping, it is said, spent the hot summer months alternately at the thermal baths of Zhongshan, 75 kilometers southeast of Canton, and in the provincial capital. Since soon after his disappearance the Jiang Qing group guessed he was in the city on the Pearl River, they dispatched the Deputy Security Chief of the CC with several secret agents. But Canton was not to be infiltrated by the left. The spies had to depart again without having accomplished a thing. From then on the radicals harbored the suspicion that Deng was hiding in his Szechuanese homeland.

They would never learn that Marshal Ye Jianying and the First Party Secretary of Szechuan, Zhao Ziyang, had taken part in a secret meeting with Deng. At this encounter in the Canton underground Deng is supposed to have said:

> Are we supposed to stand here impotently waiting for them to slaughter us? Are we supposed to let four people set our country back a century? Or should we fight them so long as we have breath? If we win, all our problems are over. If we lose, the survivors can go into the mountains and fight on, or flee abroad and await another chance. At the moment, we have bases in Canton, Fuzhou, and Nanjing from which

we can fight them. But we lose everything if we don't fight them now.[1]

Deng was not exaggerating in the slightest. His military instincts told him that only a counter-attack could save them.

Now it was up to the 79-year-old Ye Jianying to act. He returned secretly to Peking to win allies at Central Headquarters. First he took Premier Hua Guofeng into his confidence, then together they brought the left-oriented Wang Dongxing, leader of the CC apparatus, into their conspiracy against Jiang Qing and her allies. Ultimately, however, two natural events independent of their compacts were to decide the success of the conspiracy.

On July 28, a catastrophic earthquake devasted the region of Tangshan to the east of the capital. According to unofficial figures, 600,000 people are supposed to have died as a result of this disaster. The people now learned who was running things in the top echelon of the party. To surmount the overwhelming destruction, the CC telegram of condolence instructed them, the population was to "orient itself to the class struggle as directional line and to develop and deepen the criticism of the counter-revolutionary and revisionist line of Deng Xiaoping." Deng, once more disempowered, would have mobilized the army immediately, organized transports of relief goods, and arranged for emergency shelters. Not so the ruling of relief goods, and arranged for emergency shelters. Not so the ruling ultra-left; they saw the most efficacious relief measures in the class struggle. With their agitational telegram of condolence, they divested themselves of the last sympathies of the masses; now the abyss yawned before them.

To this day, earthquakes are a heavenly sign of the ruler's imminent passing. Mao Tsetung died on September 9. The earthquake and Mao's death hastened the course of subsequent events. While the giant empire still lay wrapped in deep mourning, the group around Jiang Qing, later styled "the Gang of Four," circulated a "Last Will and Testament" of the great Chairman. Internally it was said that Mao had assembled the party leadership around his deathbed and placed the succession in Jiang Qing's hands. In addition he had ordered that everything was to proceed "according to the directional line laid down." Was there not, however, already a designated successor? According to Jiang Qing, Mao's note to Hua Guofeng, "If things are in your hands, my mind is at ease," represented only a fragment of his testament. Mao is supposed, namely, to have added, "If you have any questions, turn to Jiang Qing."

Premier Hua insisted on taking up the legitimate succession. Jiang Qing, contrariwise, maintained that Mao's cryptic sentence of April 30 had referred only to the anti-Deng campaign, not to the succession. While everyone put on a good face to the outside world, publicly displaying profound grief, the conflict swelled further within the party. Not till September 18 did Hua seem to have gained the upper hand, for on that day he delivered the funeral address. Deng was forbidden to take part in the ceremony.

With his death at 82, the founder of the New China left behind a land ruled by chaos. In August 1980, Deng said:

> It's imperative for me to make a clear distinction between the nature of Chairman Mao's mistakes and the crimes committed by Lin Piao and the Gang of Four. . . . Chairman Mao devoted most of his life to China and saved the party and the revolution in the most critical moments. In other words, he gave such a contribution that, without him, in the least the Chinese would have spent much more time in groping their way in the darkness. Then let's not forget that it was Chairman Mao who combined the principles of Marxism and Leninism with the realities of China.

So long as Deng lives, he will personally guard against anyone's dealing with Mao the way Khrushchev once dealt with Stalin.

"With cold eye, now, I survey the world beyond the seas," the great Chairman had written in a 1959 poem about the banks of the Yangtze, revealing his emotions admirably. In the young romantic Mao, the democrat and the anarchist were still in equilibrium; in the Mao "with cold eye," the balance had tipped toward the anarchist, the radical. While he revered Kropotkin, at the same time he admired the important empire builder, Emperor Qin Shi Huangdi (259-210 B.C.). The aged Mao was no pure anarchist, then; rather, in his mind anarchistic and monarchistic ideas were intertwined. With increasing age, he was fascinated by the coupling of destruction with development. This dualism explains his virtues and his errors. The Chinese people, ruled by emperors for two thousand years, are submissive to authority and yet ungovernable, at once conservative and radical. They wish to preserve their civilization. To this end they resort from time to time to radical means. Mao was able to grow into an idolatrously revered cult figure because these contradictions repeat themselves within every Chinese. The great Party Chairman, this genius of strategy, intrigue, and leadership, remains an unforgotten son of his people.

His words, "Jiang Qing has a power-hungry heart; after my death she will sow unrest," would soon come true. At a meeting of the Standing Committee at the end of September, Mao's widow proposed that she herself should be elected Chairman of the CC instead of Hua, who, in her view, was incompetent. Since the moderates nevertheless strongly resisted this audacious demand, Jiang Qing was forced to promote her politics by other means.

In Shanghai, the Revolutionary Committee began in total secrecy by arming the Peoples' Militia. The Jiang Qing faction wanted to consolidate the armies of the military districts Shenyang and Shanxi in Peking on October 2, in order to accomplish a coup seven days later with the help of the 38th Army. But this massive troop movement foundered on the opposition of the powerful Ye Jianying. The old Marshal had meanwhile operated successfully against the four radicals, bringing Li Xiannian, Wang Dongxing, as well as the military leaders of northern China, Chen Xilian and Li Desheng, over to his side. In southern China, he was guaranteed Xu Shiyou's support. With this civilian and military lobby behind him, he convinced Hua Guofeng to order the arrest of the four.

On October 6, towards 22:30 hours, a special armed unit forced its way into Jiang Qing's small house, quickly disarmed her bodyguards, and surprised the old lady in bed. By now, though she ranted and raved, flight was out of the question.

Meanwhile, Wang Dongxing summoned her three accomplices to a nighttime emergency session in the Peoples' Congress Hall. Since the unusual order had come from the proper source, they dutifully, and without the least suspicion, boarded their black luxury limousines and were driven through the empty streets to Tiananmen Square. To dispel any hint of suspicion, the gigantic hall of columns had been illuminated bright as day, something that normally occurred only on extraordinary occasions. As usual, the automobiles drove up the tree-lined entrance and pulled to a stop in front of the main gate. Things now happened with lightning speed. Scarcely had Zhang Chunqiao, Yao Wenyuan, and Wang Hongwen passed through the swinging door when the trap was sprung shut. Apparently, only the powerfully built Yao Wen-yuan put up any resistance. Their long-planned palace revolt came to a bloodless end. The four were led off in handcuffs like common criminals. Already the next day, the Politburo elected the 55-year-old Hua Guofeng to be the new Party Chairman, and thereby successor to the late Mao.

On October 10 Deng Xiaoping, well informed about the drastic events in the capital, wrote the following letter to Hua Guofeng and the Central Committee:

> I support with all my heart the decision of Central Headquarters to appoint Comrade Guofeng Chairman of Central Headquarters and the Military Commission. I rejoice over this decision, which is of great significance not only for the party but also for socialism itself. With respect to politics and ideology, Comrade Guofeng is the most appropriate successor to Chairman Mao. His age guarantees that the leadership of the proletariat will remain stable for fifteen or twenty years. Truly, a great decision for party and people! Is this not inspiring to all?
>
> The most recent battle against the foundered takeover attempt of the careerists and conspirators occurs at an important moment after the death of the Chairman. The Party Central Headquarters with Comrade Guofeng at its head has brought down this group of hoodlums and come away with a great victory. This was a victory of the proletariat in the battle against the bourgeoisie, a victory of socialism over capitalism. Finally, the dictatorship of the proletariat was thereby secured and a capitalist restoration prevented. The great things of the party prevailed—the Mao Tsetung ideas and the revolutionary line of the Chairman. Like the people, I rejoice with all my heart over this important success and must cry out over and over, "Hurray for the victory!" By these brief words I try to express my deepest feelings. Long live the great victory of the party and socialism!

Hua Guofeng reacted with considerable reservation to this rhapsodic epistle. Curtly and cooly he answered, " . . . You have committed errors and must therefore be criticised further."

Unrest spread through the diplomatic quarter of Peking when late on the evening of October 20 loud, staccato firing ripped the silence over the guarded embassies. Since the noise sounded like the firing of a pistol, the correspondent for one of the British newspapers telegraphed home that adherents of the "Gang of Four" were being executed under sentence of a court martial. While this erroneous report ran around the world, the true state of affairs made the rounds in the capital. The Pekingese were celebrating the arrest of the four with firecrackers and cherry bombs. On the afternoon of the following day, Party Document Number Sixteen was circulated in all the Danwei. Now it was official: the "Gang of Four" was behind bars.

The whole country reacted in a transport of joy scarcely ever seen. When the sensational news was broadcast over the radio, even the corridors of the Peking prisons where participants in the Tiananmen incident were incarcerated rang with "Shengli! Shengli!"—"Victory! Victory!" A certain He Yanguang, Assistant Director of a factory, was at this time behind bars for refusing to initiate an anti-Deng campaign in his unit. Forty-nine times they had interrogated him; forty-nine times he had refused to denounce Deng. Now he could return to his family a free man, though he had lost his position at work.

On October 24, a "gigantic political carnival parade" wound through Peking's streets. "The giant drums they carried along with them were being beaten as though they were the hindquarters of the arrested four," eyewitness Florian Mausbach reported. They all met up tumultuously on Tiananmen Square. The Comrade "Without Morals," Wu De, could not resist adding several drops of bitterness to the overflowing mood of the multitude. For the last time in the context of the condemnation of the "Gang of Four" he demanded the continuation of criticism of Deng Xiaoping. Of course thereby he isolated himself finally from the people, whose mood that eventful autumn is expressed by the following slogan:

> Down with Liu Shaoqi—
> all join in
> Down with Lin Piao—
> all are amazed
> Down with Deng Xiaoping—
> all are perplexed
> Down with Jiang Qing—
> all clap hands.

Jiang Qing—the brains of the "Gang of Four"—and Deng had from the beginning been open enemies. So it is not surprising that

Deng, even four years after her arrest, spoke very derogatorily of Mao's widow.

> [Jiang Qing] is a very, very evil woman. She is so evil that any evil thing you say about her isn't evil enough, and if you ask me to judge her with the grades as we do in China, I answer that this is impossible, there are no grades for Jiang Qing, that Jiang Qing is a thousand times a thousand below zero. Yet Chairman Mao let her usurp power, to form her faction, to use Mao Tsetung's name as her personal banner for her personal interests, to use the young ignorant people to build her private political base on them. . . . Even after, when he was separated from her. Yes, separated. . . . Yet, not even after the separation did he intervene to stop her and to prevent her from using his name.[2]

In using these harsh words, he did not shield the Party Chairman either. Deng characterized Mao's marriage to this woman for whom he felt the most profound hatred as one of the Chairman's many errors.

After the arrest of the ultra-left faction, the purged Politburo declared the Cultural Revolution at an end, without—to be sure—rehabilitating Deng Xiaoping. Over his return, a violent quarrel would break out in the top party leadership. While Ye Jianying, Li Xiannian, and Tan Zhenlin, as well as the Commander Xu Shiyou spoke out on Deng's behalf, Hua Guofeng, Wu De, Wang Dongxing, and the Commander Chen Xilian opposed his reinstatement.

Independently of the tug-of-war over his person, Deng turned his back on the "Gateway to the South," and returned to the frigid north. While he occupied a post shielded from publicity in the State Council, the new Party Chairman declared on December 25:

> Because we have hardly alluded to the campaign of criticism against Deng Xiaoping, some people doubt we mean to continue this campaign initiated personally by Chairman Mao . . . Deng Xiaoping stood in sharp contrast to the Gang of Four, but they are all revisionists. . . The smashing of the Gang of Four does not mean that Deng Xiaoping will be spared.

Nevertheless, the crucial battle had basically been won. Since the people saw the anti-Deng campaign as nothing more than a skirmish, they could now laugh once more. The situation relaxed to the point that soon political jokes were circulating. The nub of one of the best about Deng was at Mao's expense: Deng and his grandson go to visit the Chairman. Patting the little boy's cheek, he says, "Feel free to call me Uncle Mao." The boy shakes his head and says nothing. So Mao takes an apple from a bowl next to him and hands it to the child. The boy takes it and says politely, "Thank you, Uncle Mao!" Then Deng says, "There you see, Chairman, what a little material incentive can do."

At first, people merely laughed at this kind of joke—then they began demanding their rights. One year after Zhou Enlai's death over a million people gathered in Tiananmen Square between January 6 and 15, 1977, to demand the rehabilitation of Chou's protégé, Deng Xiaoping.

So Hua now felt his way carefully towards a reassessment of the "despot opposed to improvement." At a CC labor conference in March 1977, he stressed Deng's merits and certified that the deposed Deng had had no connection to the Tiananmen incident.

Since his third "absolution" was at hand, on April 10 Deng wrote his last petition:

> Chairman Hua, Deputy Chairman Ye, and the rest of Party Headquarters!
>
> Without reservation, I support not only the latest speech of Chairman Hua at the labor conference, but also his directional line, to proceed with the master link and govern the state. I support fully and completely the manner in which Hua Guofeng attacks the problems and tasks. Even though I was able to make myself useful during the year 1975, I was subject to inadequacies and errors. I accepted sincerely the criticism and the teachings of the great leader and teacher, Chairman Mao.
>
> I thank Central Headquarters for certifying that I stood in no relation whatever to the incidents in Tiananmen Square. I am particularly happy that Chairman Hua has characterized the mass activities of the people on the Qing Ming Festival as justified. As to my duties: what offices and the question of when I will begin working depend on the deliberations and the instructions of the Central Party Headquarters.
>
> When the great leader and teacher, Chairman Mao, died, I committed my great grief and my deepfelt sympathy to paper. To advance the concerns of the party, of socialism,

and of world revolution victoriously, our generation and the following generations must view the Mao Tsetung Thoughts in their wholeness and their correctness as the guiding thread for the tasks of the party, the army, and the people.

After I learned that Central Party Headquarters had appointed Chairman Hua Guofeng Chairman of the party and the Military Commission and had won a swift and convincing victory over the Gang of Four, I expressed my sincere support and enthusiasm for Chairman Hua Guofeng and Central Party Headquarters in a letter. If the party leadership deems it appropriate, I should like to propose that this document and that letter be circulated within the party. How this question will be decided is entirely up to the deliberations and decisions of Central Headquarters. With respectful esteem.[3]

On May 3, the Politburo considered this letter, approved it, and had it circulated within the party as Deng had proposed.

At the 3rd plenary session of the Xth CC, held from July 16 to 21, Deng was reinstated to all the posts he had lost fifteen months before. The CC document in question stated, "The plenary decided to reinstate Comrade Deng Xiaoping as CC member, Politburo member, member of the Standing Committee, as well as Deputy Chairman of the CC and the Military Commission, and also as Deputy Premier of the State Council, and as Chief of Staff of the PLA." The delegates officially confirmed Hua Guofeng in his office as Chairman of the Party and the Military Commission. The radical quartet permanently lost their party membership.

Since in the summer of 1977 Mao's proverb "Order follows disorder" had become reality, the XIth Party Congress could take place during a phase of peace and stability. While Hua Guofeng and Ye Jianying delivered major speeches that lasted hours, Deng was unusually brief. One of his main statements was, "We must renew and develop the practical tradition that Chairman Mao founded for our party." No one dreamed that from this would grow a new political line.

The Congress again promoted Deng to the upper echelon of the leadership, electing him—after Ye Jianying—Second Deputy Party Chairman. Simultaneously, his followers Hu Yaobang, Wan Li, and Zhao Ziyang entered the Central Committee. Later in the same year, the diminutive Hu Yaobang would be appointed leader of the organizational division of the CC.

Four weeks after this mammoth event from August 12 to 18, the writer Han Suyin met a man "who is lively and agile in his movements, spits copiously, and smokes constantly."[4] He impressed her because he "seems so absolutely direct, candid, and completely unaffected that it is impossible not to like him or not to be fascinated by the total candor with which he hurls himself against a fact." The face of this man she described as a face without lines in which only "one eyelid is somewhat slack." Han Suyin, the daughter of a Chinese and a Belgian, could well be proud: she was the first foreigner Deng received for a private interview after his third rehabilitation. He expressed himself on the most important aspects of the current situation, coining a phrase that was by the standards of the time unusually courageous: "Only when we recognize that we are backward will we progress."

On the subject of the "Gang of Four" he said that while this faction had ruled for eleven years, it would take another twenty to eradicate their influence. They had sabotaged science, "with the result that we are now fifteen years behind . . . And it has rendered an entire generation mental cripples." Asked about his new superior, Deng said:

> It is very good for China, for the party, and for the future of the country to have a young chairman who will remain in office a long time. I am only his assistant; I work as Chairman Hua's helper. I want nothing more than just to work.

The developments that took place soon afterwards would unmask this declaration as a big bluff.

On February 26, 1978, Deng opened the meeting of the Vth National Peoples' Congress. In his capacity as Executive Chairman, he called for "modernization in this century of agriculture, industry, defense, as well as science and technology, in order to promote our country to a position among the most advanced countries in the world." To the accompaniment of rousing applause, the delegate added, "We can probably develop China in the next twenty years, in any case within this century, to a modern and powerful socialist country." Shortly thereafter, the Congress appointed him First Deputy to Premier Hua, and at the same time Marshal Ye Jianying President of the Parliament.

This short-lived phase of order was to be followed by renewed disorder. When the party leadership got down to the translation

Deng Xiaoping on a tour of inspection. The dedication is inscribed by him personally and reads: "Deng Xiaoping, September 6, 1977."

and concretization of Deng's strategy, the contradictions between Hua and Deng stepped boldly into the limelight. At the National Science Conference in March, Deng based the difference between manual and intellectual work on the social division of labor, and not, like Hua, on the division of society into classes. While he stressed that one could perfectly well characterize a patriotically minded scientist as "Red," Hua maintained that every academic had to be reeducated with the Mao Tsetung ideas and that only under the primacy of the party could he work his way up to "Red" expert.

The conflict grew sharper as at Deng's instigation the unorthodox newspaper "Guangming Ribao" wrote on May 11 that not every Mao quotation could be regarded as unassailable and that only reality was the measure of all things. Immediately after their appearance, the left-oriented Wang Dongxing characterized these statements as "destructive and aimed against the Mao Tsetung Thoughts." Representing a whole group in the Central Committee, he said that only the Mao Tsetung ideas could be the criteria of truth. Without attacking him by name, Deng countered with his sharp tongue:

> There are comrades who day in day out talk about the Mao Tsetung Thoughts, forgetting, as they do so, the fundamental Marxist concept of the Chairman and his basic method which is to seek the truth in facts. Furthermore, they often neglect—at times even intentionally—to proceed from reality and to connect theory to praxis. Yes, many even consider seeking the truth in facts . . . a grave crime.

Five weeks after Deng's first public appearance since his rehabilitation, at which 80,000 people in the Peking Workers' Stadium gave him a standing ovation, the conflict peaked in a censorship of the press. In the first edition of the journal "Chinese Youth," Deng's close associate Hu Yaobang had written under a pseudonym that it was not exclusively the sayings of Mao that were necessary to discover truth. Deng Xiaoping, in North Korea at the time, was unable to prevent his new opponent Wang Dongxing from confiscating the sought-after journal for this critical observation.

Since Deng ordered the reversal of this dictatorial measure immediately on his return from abroad, on September 20 the issue could be distributed uncensored. That late summer's day was to be a milestone in party history, for now the power struggle between the Deng group and the last dedicated Maoists in the top echelon of the party began. It would be a spontaneous battle, sparked by three current factors: the establishment of a "wall of democracy" for wall newspapers featuring citizens' free and uncensored expressions of opinion, the growing economic problems occasioned by the increasing foreign debt, and China's war of retaliation against Vietnam.

Screened off by the imperial walls of Zhongnanhai, the opponents met in a small circle of seven participants[5] to prepare the 3rd plenary session of the XIth CC. What was unusual about this preparatory meeting was neither the venue nor the restricted number of participants, but the strident controversy between Maoists and moderates and the unvarnished behavior of Deng Xiaoping. Because one of the factions sought thereby to inflict injury on the other, the minutes of this secret session surprisingly made their way abroad. Thus, the chance presented itself to follow the course of this explosive meeting in detail.

Deng used the small group to throw the switches of the important plenary session. As no one else, he demonstrated his leadership qualities. From the very start he elicited confrontation with the words, "Certain people maintain that I behave like a criminal and will one day step from behind the scenes as the person pulling the strings of some heresy."[6] Irritably, he complained of the continual carping of certain people, and said:

> Although the economy is making swift advances, some people complain that the budget balancing is not proceeding quickly enough. Then many deplore the democratic window [the "wall of democracy"] which has caused a bit of mischief. Many even think the sky is about to fall. Now they are tripping over one another looking for scapegoats. How is it possible to get anything important done with so much scaremongering?

When Deng had expressed his annoyance, Hua Guofeng took the floor. He demanded iron-fisted measures to counter the "mad attacks of the counter-revolutionaries" on the publicly posted wall newspapers. The newly founded human-rights organizations and the attractive "wall of democracy" on Chang'an Boulevard on which nonparty members had written criticism of the party and socialism were a thorn in his side. Deng tried to calm him:

> Everyone is saying that the human-rights organizations ought to be disbanded, the right to demonstrate abolished, and the counter-revolutionaries suppressed. A prohibition of the "wall of democracy" is even being discussed. All right, if that is what everyone wants, I will bow to the will of the majority.

The Party Chairman Hua countered him gruffly, "Why shouldn't the disruptive actions be prohibited? That at least is what Central Headquarters has decided!" Deng did not give in, but responded:

> Doubtless, the counter-revolutionaries are being suppressed for good reason. Nevertheless, it would be a mistake for us to prohibit divergent opinions and criticism. We cripple the initiative of the people by censorship, and the enthusiasm of the masses is kept from developing. Therefore I think that continued posting of wall newspapers should be permitted. As soon as there is evidence of criminal activity, the evil elements in the human rights organizations must be arrested.

Wang Dongxing tried to switch the heated debate onto another track by turning to the economy:

> Chairman Hua has proposed a ten-year plan. Although some target figures are set too high, we were able to achieve initial successes in development. This was possible only because, in accordance with the teaching of Chairman Mao, a large-scale mass movement had been developed. We must hew to the directional line for economic development outlined by Mao Tsetung.

Now the economic expert Li Xiannian felt called upon to contradict:

> What Chairman Mao said corresponded to the situation at that time. He hasn't left us magic any envelope with a strategy one needs only open to find the solution. One cannot solve all the problems that come up in practice with the teachings of Chairman Mao.

Deng, who meanwhile was dominating the conference, could control himself no longer. He criticized everything that failed to suit him.

> Before, it was just a couple of pounds of pork, a couple of pounds of sugar, a couple of railway tickets or ration coupons for three yards of cotton for which one went through the "little backdoor" [corruption and retail blackmarket]. Today, people use the "big backdoor." Today, we are dealing with relations among enterprises, among Danwei. Since corruption is more complex and is coupled with theft, the national economy is undermined in large measure. This all takes place under the guise of "development of the Communistic spirit of mutual aid."

And then he attacked his superior Hua Guofeng with biting ridicule:

> There is a comrade who went abroad once. He flew on a Boeing 747, rode in American limousines, slept in luxury hotels, drank exotic liquors, and fancied he understood the foreign world. He learned how to speculate in bull market or in bear, and played the role of wealthy magnate. With the monies of the state, he always ran around munificently.

As these words illustrate, Deng had long since ceased considering himself "Chairman Hua's helper." He leveled serious rebukes in connection with China's new politics of openness. He said:

> At his own discretion, many a small department head signed a contract with a foreign firm at a value of more than ten million U.S. dollars. He did this only to embarrass Central Headquarters . . . If all of last year's orders are reckoned up, we have a mountain of foreign debt in the amount of 1.8 billion U.S. dollars. An emphatic stop must be put to this way of doing business, and these transactions must be reduced.

With an eye to the past he said in conclusion:

> Thirty years of autocracy have forced our spirit into isolation. Behind us lie more than ten years during which our horizons narrowed and during which we behaved very vainly. We sat at the bottom of a well, judging heaven to be as large

as the opening of the well. Then the door was opened, and things were turned upside down. The economy reared up like an unbridled horse. Politically speaking, the wall newspapers and demonstrations made us completely lose our composure. Although militarily we were victorious in the Vietnam War, success was balanced equally with loss . . . In this war, nevertheless, we showed the rascals and the hoodlums. True—our heads were bloodied, but ultimately we conquered . . .

With a view to summation, I have to say we lacked experience . . . Another reason for the problems was that there was not enough time, and we were able to prepare ourselves only inadequately. The burden we took on was too heavy. We behaved too impatiently and tried to play the hero. As a result, our plans were unfulfilled. When errors cropped up, people muttered things about heaven and human nature. Whenever responsibility was sought, it was shifted onto a higher authority. On whom can I now shift my responsibility? At the moment, I can only suggest to Chairman Hua that we sit down and take counsel together, so we can peacefully discover the origins of the problems and draw up solutions.

Deng laid bare the problems, then, but he remained silent as to their solutions. Those he did not want to yield up prematurely.

Helpless, with a dwindling power base, the last Maoists stood aside as Deng accomplished the turn of an era. On December 18, 1978, a new era began: on that memorable day, Deng Xiaoping stepped before the 3rd plenary session of the XIth CC to announce the beginning of a new chapter in Chinese history. For the first time in over twenty years economic development and the modernization of the country—not the class struggle—stood at the center of the party's politics. Now, at last, China's second, her industrial, revolution could begin.

The slogan the "New Great Leap Forward," issued at the XIth Party Congress by Hua Guofeng, was shelved. Deng criticized Hua's concept of the "two alls," by which he meant Hua's formulation of March 1977: "All political decisions made by Chairman Mao must have our determined support and all his instructions must be unswervingly followed." Now nothing stood in the way of Hua Guofeng's removal.

No one denied Mao's great services to the Chinese Revolution, but the session came to the decision that even leaders make mistakes. Peng Dehuai was rehabilitated posthumously; Yang Shangkun and Tao Zhu were given back their party membership. Now, finally, the party assessed the Tiananmen incident as a revolutionary event and rehabilitated in addition many of the so-called "rightists" who had fallen victim to the great wave of purges in 1957.

The new orientation of the party policies was accompanied by countless changes in personnel. China's most experienced economist, Chen Yun, Zhou Enlai's widow, Deng Yingchao, the former youth leader Hu Yaobang, and Wang Zhen entered the Politburo. Chen Yun won the most impressive promotion: he was elected Fourth Deputy Party Chairman. Now he ranked above the Maoist-oriented Wang Dongxing, who, though he remained in the Politburo, had to relinquish all additional offices. From now on, Deng's followers ran the departments and the organs of the Central Committee. In the military realm, too, Deng extended his position considerably. His adherent General Yang Yong took over command of the elite troop "8341," the body guard of the Central Committee, and the Peking garrison of Chen Xilian.

The citizens of the capital celebrated the session of changes more radically than any party meeting in the past. In wall newspapers they bluntly demanded the resignations of Hua Guofeng, Wu De, Wang Dongxing, and Chen Xilian, the "oppressors" of the Tiananmen incident.

At last, at the ripe old age of 74, the indefatigable Deng had after all accomplished the long wished-for renovation. Since that plenary session in December 1978, he has steered China a new course. Today, economic development is the focus. The country has opened to the west and instituted special economic zones. Despite many relapses, democratic rights are being extended and a system of justice established. For the island of Taiwan and the British Crown Colony of Hongkong, a policy holds good under the rubric, "one country, two systems," while a reduction of one million soldiers in the troop strength of the gigantic army has been announced.

Sixteen

Dogmatic Here, Pragmatic There

SATELLITES AND SUPERSONIC jet fighters in the sky, satellite stations on the ground: an artist's rendering of the Deng era on a poster at the monument to the Hero of the People. Hardly a person cast a glance at this futuristic painting; Peking's citizens were pressing on westwards past Tiananmen Square. There, where Chang'an Boulevard crosses the shopping street Xidan, lay the focus of everyone's interest. Stretching for 200 meters was a whitewashed brick wall on which layers upon layers of printed sheets of paper had been pasted.

The "Wall of Democracy" drew them like a magnet. Here the thoughts of the people were to be read. In the fall of 1978 the political "Peking Spring" had bloomed in the capital. Thanks to Deng Xiaoping's tolerance of free expression of opinion, the Maoist leaders dared not order the wall newspapers, large and small, torn down. Even when informers not order the wall newspapers, large and small, torn down. Even when informers reported ugly attacks against the party and socialism, they did not intervene. They tolerated Mao's being called a despot and the demands of newly founded human-rights organizations for the institution of a parliamentary democracy along western lines. To all appearances calm, they looked on as demonstrating youths drew more and more people to their ranks and as the incited mob drove party cadres from their offices with blows.

Suddenly, the political barometer fell below zero, and a cold wave set in overnight. On December 8, 1978, police roped off access to the wall of opinions. They directed the waiting masses further west towards the tiny Moon Temple Park which had, meanwhile, been established as the locus for expression of critical opinions.

A 29-year-old man refused to be diverted, insisting on his right to sell his newspaper, which he had printed himself, in front of the "Wall of Democracy." The peace officers knew the persistent Wei Jingsheng quite well, for the worker came to the wall almost daily. Even after the eighth of December he made provocative speeches here and sold his paper, "Investigation."

Even though Deng only passed by the wall on Xidan Street in his black government automobile, he knew precisely that the human-rights activist Wei and his like-minded comrades represented oppositional democratic ideas. That is why on March 29, 1979, handcuffs snapped shut on Wei Jingsheng's wrists.

The dissident had irritated the new leader by his article "Democracy or Despotism?" challenging him personally. Under the pseudonym "Voice of Today," Wei had written:

> It is clear to everybody that the social system in China is undemocratic and that during the past thirty years this lack of democracy has impeded development of the society as a whole. Today, we have the choice between social reform that will lead to a quick upturn in production and living standard, or the continuation of a dictatorship like Mao's with all its negative consequences for production and living standard . . . Does Deng Xiaoping deserve the people's confidence? No leader deserves the unconditional confidence of his people. If he pursues a policy that brings the people peace and a better life, then he deserves their confidence—otherwise not. Deng was quick to stress that without Mao there would have been no New China, and then he said that Mao's errors were mere bagatelles. Is Deng perhaps afraid of investigations that might touch former co-workers of Mao, himself, for instance? Or does he intend to persevere with Mao's political directional line?
>
> In case the first of these questions applies, Deng can rest assured. We will not throw any old errors up to him, but he must lead our country towards democracy and a better life. In case the second question applies, however, there can be no compromise. The fact that a short time ago Deng was still the best is irrelevant if we are now once more to be subject to despotism—with its terrible consequences. . .

Sharply formulated observations and questions that to this day have lost none of their explosiveness. Not twenty-four hours after Wei's arrest, Deng Xiaoping provided an answer which left China numb. On March 30, he announced categorically four fundamental principles of socialist development: holding fast to the socialist path, to the dictatorship of the proletariat, to the leadership of the Communist Party, and to Marxism-Leninism and the ideas of the leadership of the Communist Party, and to Marxism-Leninism and the ideas of Mao Tsetung. With these four fundamentals he defined for the first time the framework—a narrow one—of his policy of renewal, and he has persevered in these to the present day.

Now the new era was connected to a doctrinaire line that might as well have originated with Mao. Disillusionment could be read in the faces of the young after Deng had already been celebrated as a tolerant liberal. The old merely nodded in silence; old memories revived for them. They could never forget Mao's perversion of the "Hundred Flowers Movement" into its opposite and his transformation of democracy into despotism.

Deng's position in the spring of 1979 seemed rooted in Mao's old maxim, "You have to let the poisonous weeds sprout before you can pull them out!" As he had twenty-three years earlier, he now proved an uncompromising opponent of a "Great Democracy," the manifestations of which were the wall newspapers and spontaneous demonstrations. His initial tolerance showed itself to have been a tactic relying on the ancient Chinese battle strategy, "Lure your opponent onto the roof, then take away the ladder."

Four months later, Deng took drastic action. The human-rights organizations were outlawed and their leaders arrested. There were show trials. After nearly seven months of interrogatory detention, Wei Jingsheng, his head shaven as was usual only in capital cases, was put on trial on October 16. The public prosecutor accused the army veteran of having sold military secrets to a British correspondent on the fourth day of the Chinese war of reprisal against Vietnam for the equivalent of 535 U.S. dollars[1] and of having called in his journal "Tansuo" for the overthrow of the dictatorship of the proletariat. In a trial before 400 specially selected onlookers, Wei Jingsheng was condemned to fifteen years in prison and to an additional three years' loss of all political rights

**Deng Xiaoping hiking in the mountains of Huangshan
(Anhui Province) in 1979.**

to warn "the monkey"—in this case, the people. Despite the strenuous efforts of Amnesty International and other democratic forces throughout the world, not even special privileges could be arranged for the seriously ill Wei until 1986. "Democracy or Despotism?"—had that not been his question?

The party made a further example of two other dissidents. In February 1980, the Honkong citizen Liu Shanqing was condemned to ten years' imprisonment. Although the newly instituted code of criminal procedure limited dentention pending trial to a maximum of three months, Liu remained in detention thirteen months before coming to trial. Another instigator of the "Peking Spring," Ren Wanding, was condemned to four years in prison because, as cofounder of the "Chinese League for Human Rights," he had demanded free elections, the combating of corruption, abolition of the secret police, and the conversion of the Mao mausoleum into a museum.

While feelings ran high over the abrupt end to the "Peking Spring," Deng worked secretly at assuming total power. To achieve this he had to be sure of his support in the military. From the inception of the new era it had been clear to him that so long as he did not have the loyal backing of the 4.2-million man Peoples' Liberation Army for his course, the accomplishment of his reforms remained uncertain.

After the precipitous end to the "Spring" and the turnabout engendered by the four fundamental principles of "pure" socialism, Deng could now act all the more peremptorily towards the Maoists for having depicted himself the true Grail Knight of the Mao Thoughts. In February 1980, he demanded his tribute. At the 5th plenary session of the XIth CC, from February 23 to 29, the former mayor of Peking, Wu De, the leader of the CC apparatus, Wang Dongxing, and the Commander Chen Xilian were expelled from the Politburo. Deng Xiaoping's closest collaborators, Zhao Ziyang and Hu Yaobang, by contrast, ascended to the Standing Committee of the Politburo. The delegates elected the 65-year-old the new General Secretary. He was to function for six years as nominal party leader—as the long arm of the *éminence grise*, Deng Xiaoping.

After the trend setting February plenary session[2] the situation in the top echelon of the leadership grew more complex from day to day. Each innovation proposed by Deng's collaborators at Central Headquarters was greeted by the hoary Marshal Ye Jianying with skepticism. With his great authority, he resisted Deng's reforms in the military, which sought troop reductions of a million soldiers, an end to the thirty-year long "infantryism," and a reduction of defense expenditures, as well as a radical reduction in the average age of the officer corps. Thus in the spring of 1980 Deng had no choice but to declare war on his brother in arms from the Long March. He had to strip the 82-year-old Ye of power in order to secure his long-term reforms through the military arm of the party.

Shortly before the February plenary, Deng handed in his resignation as Chief of Staff of the PLA. He had not conveyed his request personally to Ye, but rather had had it transmitted through the "neutral" economic experts Chen Yun and Li Xiannian. To underscore his line of rejuvenating cadre staffs, he led the way demonstratively by his good example—or so the resignation seemed outwardly.

By this tactical "step into the second rank," however, he was in reality taking the offensive by presenting Marshal Ye with his chosen candidate to succeed him. As soon as Ye heard the name Yang Dezhi, what his 75-year-old adversary had planned was clear to him. Deng wanted to secure the PLA leadership's commitment to his reform course beyond his own death. The veteran of the Long March remembered of course that Yang Dezhi[3] had served in the Sino-Japanese War under Politcommissar Deng. The Marshal wanted for cogent arguments against the appointment, for Deng's hand-picked candidate had distinguished himself during the Sino-Vietnamese border war by meritorious service. At last, grudgingly, Ye agreed.

After this successful action, Deng flew to Shenyang to meet with Li Desheng, China's most powerful regional commander, and win his commitment to his new course. General Li's very prominent position came from his command of the 400,000-man elite PLA troops shielding China's industrial center from the Soviet Union. He, too, had fought in the "Liu-Deng Army" and thus numbered by tradition among Deng's followers. But before Li pledged his old superior loyalty, he set two conditions. He demanded a promise that Deng would not divide the country and that he would undertake nothing to diminish Mao's accomplishments. Deng agreed, thereby winning important backing for his second step forward.

As Mao had done in the fall of 1973, to everyone's astonishment he announced a shake-up in the army leadership on his return from the northeast. Taken by surprise, Ye had to look on as Deng, backed by the most powerful regional commander, replaced the commanders in chief of all ten military districts,[4] thereby aligning the backbone of the Peoples' Liberation Army with his line. How stiff a resistance Deng had to crush in doing this, however, is illustrated by the fact that it took him the entire year of 1980 to put Yang Dezhi through as his successor. But having laid the foundation for his course, Deng could now contemplate radical political changes.

Especially in need of reform was one area in which the Confucian maxim "Not legally, but mannerly!" still predominated. After more than thirty years of uncertainty—without a penal code, a code of criminal procedure, or economic laws—Deng ended a juridical practice at the mercy of political tides. In a protracted trial in July 1979, the development of a judicial system along western lines was begun.

In August 1980, at the 3rd plenary session of the Vth NPC, Deng laid down his office as Deputy Premier, contenting himself with membership on the "Constitutional Revision" committee. His resignation paved the way for the 61-year-old Zhao Ziyang into the government: Zhao replaced Hua Guofeng—long since fallen into discredit—in his office as Premier. It would be naive to believe that Deng had once more stepped down only for reasons of age. By his demonstrative abnegation he sought to exert pressure on his most influential adversary also to retire. The 83-year-old Marshal Ye Jianying was, according to Deng's plan, to hand over chairmanship of the NPC to a younger man, thereby opening the way for governmental reforms. Since Deng's strategy foundered on the stubbornness of the crafty old soldier, he had to "go through the back door" by subterfuge.

Four years after their arrest, he had the four radicals reemerge from obscurity. In November, the Supreme Court of the People put the "Gang of Four" on trial. Originally, the court proceedings were to have taken place much earlier and behind closed doors, but Deng firmly opposed this. After smashing the dissident movement, he wished to demonstrate to the people and to the international public the state-stabilizing sense of justice of his era. And another thing—the media-oriented show trial, organized for internal as well as international consumption, was to accomplish the final overthrow of Hua Guofeng, politically isolated but still functioning pro forma as Party Chairman.

It suited Deng's purposes perfectly when, standing before the bar, the highly verbal Jiang Qing told the court that the left-oriented Mao follower Hua Guofeng had been a participant in the radicals' activities. Hua now had to choose between testifying openly as a witness or remaining silent. Fearful of unmasking himself, Hua refused to testify, wrapping himself in silence until December 16.

Anyone happening to pass by Tiananmen Square around two-thirty on the afternoon of that stormy winter's day could see at once that something big was up, for dozens of the heavy party limousines "Red Flag" congested the entrance drive to the People's Congress Hall. The following day, readers of "Renmin Ribao" were able at least to surmise what had happened, for in curt sentences the party organ reported that a labor conference of the Central Committee had begun under the leadership of Hu Yao-bang. That Hu occupied this position was surprising, since everyone had expected Party Chairman Hua to preside over the meeting. Instantly, Xiao Dao, the "little channel," filled with speculations about Hua Guofeng's deposition. And the rumors were to prove true this time, too.

At the center of the labor conference was Zhao Ziyang's report about the extremely critical economic situation. His exposition of a rapidly rising rate of inflation, a menacing energy shortage, an annual increase in the deficit of 52 percent, and a drastic decline in oil production triggered great consternation among the CC members. Great unrest stirred in the hall when he turned to Hua Guofeng and laid to him the following errors: bad investments in the amount of ten billion yuan in the Shanghai steelworks Baoshan, continuation of the Mao cult, violence against the people at the Tiananmen incident, and the sabotage of Deng Xiaoping's reinstatement.

Hua broke his silence and went on a feeble counterattack in criticizing Deng's economic reforms as a policy of "free enterprise," demanding the investigation of the new economic course.

Surprisingly, many Party Secretaries of the provinces and cities greeted these words with sustained applause. Nevertheless, Hua's hour had struck. He saw himself forced to abdicate the Party Chairmanship and the Chairmanship of the Military Commission unprotestingly. The crafty Deng knew perfectly well that Hua still controlled a power base to be reckoned with; therefore he spoke on behalf of his election as Deputy Party Chairman—under the circumstances, purely a token post.

Anyone who believed that with the stepping down of the last Maoist the power struggle had ended, however, was to be disillusioned. Ever new hurdles blocked Deng's course of reform. He had actually intended building up his closest associate, Hu Yaobang, as Hua Guofeng's successor, but this was protested, not, to be sure, by the hoary Marshal Ye, but, nonetheless, by the 75-five-year-old economist Chen Yun.

The economic planner, shelved by Mao already in the fifties, warned against the well-known dangers of concentrating party, government, and military power in the hands of one person. Instead of Hu, therefore, he proposed Deng Xiaoping as the new Chairman of the Military Commission. Deng declined at once, saying that he would soon have to "go to be with Marx" and that he could not possibly assume this high office after only a year earlier having stepped down as Chief of Staff. Irritated, Chen Yun reproached him with evading a historic duty. After a brief debate there was a vote which Deng lost, being, in June 1981, elected—counter to his strategical goal—Chairman of the Military Commission of the CC.

Everyone who knew Deng's robust nature suspected that his ever recurring allusion to his age only served him as a ploy. In this case he had wanted to place the power over the party and the army in Hu Yaobang's hands to assure that, even after his death, the reform course would be pursued without interference from the all-powerful army.

After Hua Guofeng's resignation from the two most important party offices, Deng's position was considerably complicated, for his remaining opponents allied themselves and pursued a confrontational course. The first wall newspaper against "Dengism" appeared on February 8, 1981, in south China, in Mao Tsetung's and Hua Guofeng's home province of Hunan. Students from the First Teacher Training Institution of Changsha accused Deng

Xiaoping of pursuing undisguised capitalism, and of creating a gap between rich and poor. In addition, they said, the people were suffering from unheard of inflation. The situation was serious; the spark threatened to jump from Hua's "independent kingdom" over to the cities of Shanghai, Wuhan, and Canton.

On February 12, students occupied a building of the People's Stadium in Changsha, depending from the roof a fifteen-meter long banner with the inscription visible from afar, "Down with the bourgeois headquarters of Deng Xiaoping." This challenge spread like wildfire throughout the country. The banner action was followed by demonstrations in the provincial capital and other large cities. On March 6, the theoretical party organ, "Red Flag" had to concede that factions confronted each other within the top echelon of party leadership.

No Chinese citizen believed the official announcement that Marshal Ye Jianying had left Peking purely for reasons of health and had gone for a cure to the spa Zhongshan, south of Canton. Everyone knew that the hoary Ye sought by his departure from Central Headquarters to make the tension between him and Deng public.

But Deng was not disconcerted; on the contrary, the orthodox military leader's opposition seemed rather to confirm him on his course of reform. Thus, he was able in 1981, the "Year of the Complaints," among various innovations in the economic sphere, to present his much admired Taiwan initiative. In August, he had concretized his concept of "one country, two systems," stressing that Taiwan need not practice socialism and could retain its social system and its fighting forces unaltered, if it agreed to be incorporated as a province in the People's Republic.

A year's preparation was necessary to develop this new Taiwan doctrine, first and foremost a confrontation with the prevailing China policy of the United States. Deng Xiaoping personally undertook this formidable task.

"As for our two nations, today is a time of reunion and new beginnings. It is a day of reconciliation when windows too long closed have been reopened," said President Jimmy Carter, receiving the Chinese Deputy Premier at the White House on January 29, 1979. Deng's pioneering visit did indeed bring to an end half a lifetime's estrangement and enmity between China and the United States.

The previous day, a cold, lead-grey winter's Sunday, the Chinese Boeing 707, after a calm flight round half the globe, had landed safely at Andrews Air Force Base near Washington. All the turbulence, meanwhile, was enacted on the ground: led by Senator Barry Goldwater, the Taiwan lobby agitated against the Communists. They had placed a full-page ad in "The New York Times" accusing the Peking regime of having killed 70 million people. In addition, before his departure, the Chinese guest had himself stirred up a great controversy in branding the Soviet Union the breeding ground of war. Party Chief Leonid Brezhnev promptly cautioned the West against "another Munich." The President was compelled to reassure him by letter that China would receive none of his country's weapons.

Everyone wanted to throw open the window to China at last, but no one wished to jeopardize the scheduled Carter-Brezhnev summit. Finally, Carter lost his temper. If Congress forced the administration to submit an official certification of security for Taiwan, or otherwise attempted to block the resumption of diplomatic relations with the People's Republic of China—retroactive to January 1, 1979—he would employ his right of veto.

The "Peppery Napoleon," meanwhile, acted the moderate, smiling inscrutably over the confusion among his hosts. He made an obligatory condemnation of all aspiration towards hegemony and called for an alliance among the United States, China, Japan, and Western Europe against the "Russian Bear." Then, however, with great conviction, Deng revealed China's real desire. In Seattle, the visitor of state explained to 500 business people that despite their divergent social systems, the two countries had common interests. China was an impoverished developing nation, desperately in need of American economic assistance. With his aphorism that "It makes no sense for an ugly woman to fancy herself pretty," he summarized the economic situation of his country and invited investment.

After a strenuous week with stops in Washington, Atlanta, Houston, and Seattle, the unorthodox Communist left behind an America infected with China fever. His "visit of the year" relegated even the death of former Vice President Nelson Rockefeller to the status of a second-rank news story and would go down in the history of East-West relations as a pioneering achievement.

After years of important activities in foreign affairs—his spectacular visit to the United States serves as an example—Deng devoted himself from 1982 to domestic reforms. This phase began with rejuvenation of personnel within the party and government apparatus. On February 20, 1982, the Central Committee decided on a retirement regulation for veterans of the revolution in order to rejuvenate, intellectualize, and professionalize cadre personnel. When he drafted this plan, the 77-year-old Deng knew perfectly well that these old soldiers who went back to the earliest days of the revolution were not just going to fade away into retirement. For this reason, so-called "consultant committees" were instituted on many levels for the original revolutionaries. Deng, their initiator, did not at that time foresee that these "Old Masters' Groups" would in the course of the coming years develop into shadow cabinets.

The reformers presented the meritorious seniors with the "iron rice bowl," that is, their salary and their many privileges, but drew up simultaneously a three-tiered, long-range plan for the dismissal of one-quarter of the 600,000 government functionaries. In August 1982, "skimming the dross" from the central agencies began; in 1983, from the provincial organs; and in 1984, from the district agencies. With the retrenchment came a reduction in posts, by which thousands of deputy positions in the bureaucratic hierarchy were abolished. If Deng was to achieve success with his economic reforms, he had to render the governmental colossus, which at the beginning of 1982 still comprised 902 vice ministers in 98 ministries and state committees, leaner and more transparent. Since many graybeards with their "iron chairs" seemed rooted in their posts, however, the campaign of debureaucratization flagged before achieving its goal.

Not until 1985 could Central Headquarters revive the fight against the gerontocracy by its own good example: in September, 141 long-term functionaries retired from the Politburo, the Central Committee, the Consultative Commission, and so on. Ten members left the twenty-five man Politburo on grounds of age, among them Zhou Enlai's 81-year-old widow, Deng Yingchao, and the 87-year-old Marshal Ye. The guidelines issued for new appointments to government offices stipulated an average age between 35 and 55 years and a college degree or the equivalent professional training.

Between September 1 and 11, 1982, one month after the second

Deng Xiaoping on an inspection trip to Xinjiang in August 1981. He is holding his granddaughter in his arm, the child of his daughter Deng Nan.

offensive of the rejuvenation campaign, the XIIth Party Congress took place. In his opening address, Deng outlined the three tasks for the eighties: hastened economic development, reunification with Taiwan, struggle against hegemonism. The greatest innovation in terminology consisted in the abolition of the offices of Party Chairman and Deputy Party Chairman. The post of General Secretary was restored to the favor it had enjoyed before 1945. On Deng's initiative, party power was divided three ways among the Central Committee, the Consultative Commission, and the Disciplinary Control Commission.

Among the lower priority items on the agenda was expulsion of Hua Guofeng from all leadership offices. The former Mao follower would in the year 1984—though he retained CC membership—disappear from public view, not to appear again until May 1986, when, after protracted illness, he was seen as an ordinary visitor at the imperial Ch'ing graves northeast of Peking.

Deng Xiaoping was elected to the Standing Committee and appointed Chairman of the Military Commission at the 1st plenary session of the XIIth CC, convened immediately following the Party Congress. Outwardly, however, not he, but General Secretary Hu Yaobang, appeared as China's most powerful man. Beside Deng in the Standing Committee sat his two comrades in arms, Hu Yaobang and Zhao Ziyang, his adversaries, Ye Jianying and Chen Yun, as well as Li Xiannian, the economic expert who remained open to both sides. On September 13, Deng was elected Chairman of the newly instituted Consultative Commission, and Chen Yun First Secretary of the Disciplinary Control Commission.

The Deng era was already entering its fifth year when, in July 1983, Deng Xiaoping's "Selected Works," in an edition of twelve million copies, filled the bookstores from Harbin to Canton. The five-volume Mao edition had to be pushed only slightly aside for Deng's forty-seven speeches and lectures to take their place on the shelf of Marxist-Leninist classics.

A time span of eighteen years lies between Mao's last and Deng's first published speech. Nevertheless, Mao's fifth and Deng's first volumes complement each other in many points. For example, Deng refers fully five hundred times to Mao and scarcely twenty times to Liu Shaoqi, while the name Hua Guofeng, except for a few references, fell victim to the red pencil. Indeed, Deng's writings have been rewritten in familiar Chinese fashion, and thus no longer correspond in many points to the original text. Thus, his remarks on foreign policy have been altered, since the CCP in the meantime no longer operates on the assumption of the inevitability of a new world war—a view it still held in 1977. The August-1980 interview with the Italian writer Oriana Fallaci, too, is reproduced only in abbreviated form. Despite all the falsifications, one must recognize that this collection of writings breaks for the first time with the unwritten rule that speeches a leader delivers to party committees are held confidential until after his death.

The selected writings show once more that Deng is a tactical thinker, but no Marxist theorist, and that one can by no means characterize his policies of openness as an independent, sovereign line. Since the edifice of his thought lacks consistency, it would be incorrect to speak of "Dengism."

Deng avoids complex theoretical problems. As in most of the works of the Chinese Communists, here, too, Marxism-Leninism, deprived of its philosophical core, is reduced to its methodology ("The Manual of Action"). Deng's lack of willingness to deal theoretically with controversial viewpoints is illustrated by the following event. In mid-December 1984, a lead article appeared in the party organ of the CCP, the gist of which was that Karl Marx and Friedrich Engels had said much of general validity to be sure, but that several of their theories did not correspond with the times and were even false because they had had access only to the experiences of their own epoch. The text then reads, "One can therefore not expect the works Marx and Engels wrote to solve the problems of today." Truly a remarkable thesis for the mouthpiece of the CCP to voice.

Already the following day, however, the "People's Daily" printed an unlikely three-line correction: correctly, it should have read, with the works of Marx and Engels one "cannot solve all problems of today." No ideological "lapse" was blamed, but a simple typographical error. In reality, however, the phrase "the problems" concealed an unresolved controversy.

The centerpiece of the "Selected Works" elucidates Deng Xiaoping's dichotomous view of society. With his "four fundamental principles" (holding fast to the socialistic path, to the dictatorship of the proletariat, to the leadership of the CCP, as well as to Marxism-Leninism and the Mao Tsetung ideas), he divides the "socialism with Chinese characteristics" into two halves. The one he calls the material, the other, the spiritual, civilization. The material gets his principal attention; the spiritual he can define only vaguely:

> We are developing a spiritual civilization of socialism, which means in the main that our people possess Communist ideals and moral integrity and are to be educated and disciplined. Internationalism and patriotism belong to it as well.[5]

In each of these two worlds Deng acts quite differently. While in the material civilization he acts like an unprincipled pragmatist, in the spiritual civilization he confronts us as a dogmatic Marxist. Let us recall: in 1979 he prohibited the "Wall of Democracy" and had human rights activists condemned. In the year 1983 he ordered a campaign against "spiritual pollution," against eccentric hairstyles, slit skirts, and the existentialist philosophy of a Nietzsche and a Sartre. The spiritual civilization received a further rebuke on December 30, 1986, when Deng declared, "The struggle against bourgeois liberalism must be waged another twenty years at least." If it has to do with culture, ideology, morality, or politics, then he holds rigidly to his four fundamental socialistic principles of March 1979. If it is a question of the economy, business, or earning money, then the leitmotif is, "No matter whether it's black or white, so long as the cat catches mice."

Deng's politics, then, has to be content with the objection that while it greatly advances the economic base, it allows the spiritual "superstructure" of society on the other hand only a pitiful individual existence. The party ideologues never tire of blaming the outside world for the threat of the westernization of the culture, mores, and morality of the Chinese people. Just as tirelessly they refer to the Mao Tsetung Thoughts, but appear to have forgotten Mao's philosophy of contradiction. There he states, "The fundamental cause of a thing's evolution lies not outside but within itself; it lies in its inner contradictoriness." Deng Xiaoping, Mao's pupil, opened the door to the west; now he must master inner contradictoriness.

Today, Chinese socialism is not threatened by capitalistic influences from without, but by the one-sidedness of the reforms within: while the material civilization blooms and flourishes, the spiritual civilization lives on "thin air." One dissident defines the dilemma perfectly: "He who preaches capitalism is criticized; he who practices it is protected."[6]

SEVENTEEN

Trekking the Unknown

THE COMMUNISTS DEFEATED the thousand-year-old feudal tenancy system in the countryside by a land reform, while they nipped the fledgling urban market economy in the bud by expropriation. On their accession to power in 1949, they instituted communal property on the Soviet model. Dispossession of land owners and proprietors of factories evolved into a far-reaching social revolution. Until then, no popular uprising had succeeded as fundamentally as Mao's revolution in transforming the Middle Kingdom.

Until 1958, socialistic development corresponded to the interests of the people and the social and economic conditions; up to the year of the "Great Leap Forward" and the people's communes, the welfare of the nation increased. But then—with the announcement of the "Three Red Banners"—economic decline set in, for the victory parade of left-wing radicalism had begun. Eight years of great economic losses and internal party power struggles followed, climaxing in the Cultural Revolution. In 1977, the People's Republic teetered on the brink of ruin. Mao alone is not to blame for her bankruptcy, for not he but his successor Hua Guofeng, clinging to the "class struggle," must answer for the disasters of the two preceding years.

Thirty years of socialistic development in peace time—with what result? The balance sheet is not devastating, but it is sobering; China was unable to root out poverty and backwardness.

With Mao's death, a new path opened for Deng Xiaoping. After a turbulent life as partisan, soldier, and statesman, he recognized that praxis was the only criterion for assaying truth. In

1978, acting in the interests of the people and according to the ancient proverb, "Poverty demands reform," by sheer strength of his will he reversed rudder. Decisively, he terminated Mao's course of adventurism.

With his economic reform he was pursuing just one goal—to build China into the strongest socialist system in the world. And yet this course does not appear credible to everyone; his pragmatic line seems too unprincipled, too procapitalist. At the same time, many, even some of those closest to Deng, would rather shut their eyes to his irrevocable principle: economic opening, yes; ideological opening, no!

The great battle within the party leadership is constantly rekindled by the so-called "cage" politics. Reformers and orthodox alike agree that socialism—allegorically a bird—belongs in a cage. Their differences arise over the dimensions of the cage. The reform Marxists measure out space for freedom of movement far more liberally than the orthodox economic planners. Deng has no intention of giving the bird its freedom, just space enough to spread its wings. Already adversaries accuse him of abandoning socialism. But what could portray his intentions better than his deeds?

Since 1979, the Deng era has provided the 800 million peasants greater independence in tillage and a better life; since 1982 they have enjoyed the fruits of a new, private system of tenancy. On January 1 of that year, the CC approved the separation of the farm households from the prescribed collective work of the people's communes. For private cultivation, individual families were issued plots of arable land commensurate to the number of hands available—younger children not included. Fields, meadows, and pastures—communal property as before—are now leased to the farmers for a minimum of fifteen years. In return, the family has to deliver on the average of a third of its harvest at a contractually stipulated price to the state, receiving cash or tax abatement in exchange.

An additional portion of the harvest must be relinquished to the state as so-called quota surplus at a price that fluctuates with market conditions. The farmers may dispose of the remainder according to supply and demand on free markets uncontrolled by the state in the villages and cities. The overwhelming majority of the 450 million rural able-bodied workers operates by now on this system of tenancy, which has led to an astonishing raising of their living standard.

Parallel to the private households, in 1986 there were 3.7 million Zhuanye Hu, specialized households comprising ten million able-bodied workers. This type is to be found especially in the areas surrounding the cities or the grasslands, where principally vegetable and fruit cultivation or animal husbandry are pursued, for it is equipped for the production of just one product. In addition, households specializing in the delivery of services, transport, and building trades are increasing in numbers. It is these that are so much talked about because their annual income is around 10,000 yuan or higher. When the nouveaux riches of China are spoken of, it is the Zhuanye Hu in the suburbs of the large cities that are meant.

Out of the amalgamation of these "specialists" has evolved a cooperative movement, comprising 4.8 million rural enterprises and 65 million workers, comparable to the 1877 Help to Self-Help of a Friedrich Wilhelm Raiffeisen. Often it is a family clan which amalgamates cooperatively: an uncle raises the pigs, a brother-in-law slaughters them and converts them to sausage, a cousin in the district capital undertakes their transport with his privately owned 7.5 ton truck. Such an enterprise can, meanwhile, employ up to seven salaried workers.

Often, too, the village inhabitants are organized into independent cooperatives by the district or local administrations, which now bear the name "people's commune" only formally, and are furnished with assistance in the form of favorable bank loans to get started. During the years 1984 to 1986, the rural-industrial cooperative sector enjoyed a growth rate on the average of 45 percent, while in the large cities in the state industrial sector it was 11 percent.

Deng's land reforms took account for the first time since the establishment of the People's Republic of the fact that China is an agrarian country and that, as such, agriculture has to stand at the center of the national economy. In the large farm families, the bowls fill lavishly as never before with rice, rich pork, and sundry vegetables. Chairman Mao was worshipped; the new leader Deng Xiaoping is loved, for he has been able to raise the living standard of the farmers. The average net income of the rural population amounted in the year 1987 to 356 yuan—an increase of around 140 percent over 1978. Thanks to his agrarian reforms, in 1986 "only" 60 million rural inhabitants still suffered from grain shortages and poverty. The annual harvest yields were increased. If in the year 1981, 305.3 million tons of grain—rice, wheat, and corn—were harvested, in the following years it was fully 400 million tons.

In addition, the simplified private household system has the advantage over the people's communes of the Mao era that the farmers no longer have to finance the inflated administrative apparatus necessary for the planning, book-keeping, and control of the large collectives. These important advantages of the agrarian reform, however, entailed serious disadvantages as well.

Since the bureaucratic people's commune apparatus has been reduced to a few administrative posts, new positions have to be created for these 106 million people. The acreage cannot be further parceled, because in the areas of greatest unemployment, the land already resembles a garden plot colony: statistically regarded, there is a plot of a thousand (!) square meters for every Chinese person. New employment can be created only in the industries just now developing in the villages and municipalities.

The leasing of fields and plots to private households makes mechanization, so highly praised by Deng, impossible if after all it is unprofitable to work fields of such small area with machines. Actually, one could only contemplate voluntary cooperative cultivation similar to the business enterprises in the villages if large numbers of farmers were to switch their profession. Today, only the beginnings of this trend exist: by 1986, 60 million peasants had partially or wholly given up tilling the fields, migrating into the village industries.

A further disadvantage of the reforms lies in the neglect of the commonweal. If during Mao's time too great an investment was made in construction, today too few canals, roads, reservoirs, and bridges are being built. To make quick money, natural resources are being exploited to an extreme: the soils are being leached, the forests killed off through indiscriminate lumbering, and the environment burdened with toxins to a dangerous extent. Add to this that since 1949 tillable acreage has diminished by more than 12 million hectares in favor of the construction of housing and industrial plants and that it continues shrinking unabated.

Social tensions among the rural population, equal for the last thirty years, are growing. Deng consciously promotes the differential between rich and poor when he declares:

> The creation of a number of private enterprises corresponds to the general demand to develop the socialistic economy. Encouraging a number of regions and private individuals to become rich in advance of others is only to let more and more people become rich and so achieve the goal of the well-being of all.

But the wheat and rice farmers are not getting rich, only the owners of the melon, peanut, and fruit plantations in the climatically favored regions, and all those who would rather drive a minibus than work in the wheat field. So Deng's critics blame this conception, too, for the fact that after record harvests, the grain yields in the year 1985 suddenly fell by more than 53 million tons. They already saw Deng's throne wobbling, and reminded people—not without malice—of the historic wisdom of past dynasties: "Without grain, there is unrest in the kingdom."

The agrarian reform is the basis of Deng's industrial revolution, or, as he says himself, a fundament of the "socialism of Chinese stamp." For the first time on August 20, 1980, the weekly "Liaowang" attempted to give a definition of this individualistic socialism in declaring that stimulating the economy internally and opening to the outside world were its specific hallmarks. By "stimulating" the author meant the agrarian reform, and by "opening," the establishment of so-called special economic zones for foreign investors.

Deng Xiaoping's personal achievement is the opening of the country, not only to the west, but also to the east. In giving an accounting of the Mao era he declared, "The reason China's development stagnated and remained backward so long was the autocracy. Our experience proved that development behind closed doors has to come to grief."

On July 11, 1979, the State Council approved the establishment of four special economic zones situated opposite Hongkong and Taiwan, Shenzhen, Zhuhai, Shantou, and Xiamen. In March 1984, the government decided to open fourteen coastal cities[1] as well as the island of Hainan as special zones for investors from Hongkong and abroad. In January 1985, the Central Committee announced that additional areas open to foreign capital were being established in the delta of the Yangtze and the Pearl River as well as on the coast of the province of Fujian. In the wake of this gradual opening, today an entire chain of economic zones stretches along the 18,000 kilometer coast, offering various investment opportunities.[2]

Up to the year 1986, the goal of attracting foreign capital in large amounts could not be achieved. The bureaucratic socialistic system and the absence of laws and regulations scared off many capital investors. In the years 1983 and 1984 alone, the Chinese government invested fully 1.2 billion U.S. dollars in the four zones opposite Hongkong and Taiwan, while foreign investments amounted to barely 800 million U.S. dollars. The government had diverted a handsome sum[3] from its relatively meager foreign exchange budget for the ailing "miracle zones."

Originally they were supposed to produce goods for export with foreign capital. In the meantime, the internally produced goods flooded the domestic market because they could find no outlets on the world market. The goal of the zones was thus transformed into its opposite: they function as middlemen, buying valuable consumer goods on the world market with the foreign exchange of the provinces and passing them along to the financiers after deducting a high commission. In February 1986, the Peking government admonished the Shenzhen zone to return to its original designation of foreign trade base; it was to furbish products from the countryside and offer them on the world market meticulously packaged.

Finally, the future of the zones is uncertain also because they have not fulfilled expectations relative to the transfer of technology. Foreign firms, primarily Hongkongese and American investors, without exception prefer the light industrial sector, because here high returns can be expected quickly. Besides, many foreign firms put their depreciated, often obsolete, machines into the waiting factories.

Hainan, situated 3,000 kilometers south of Peking, also known as "China's Hawaii," had been open to Hongkong's sun-seekers only a short time, when the greatest consumer goods corruption scandal in the history of the People's Republic broke. The party leadership of the tropical island had, without the knowledge of the central government, illegally imported foreign automobiles and consumer goods at a value of two billion U.S. dollars, reselling them to factories, offices, and private individuals throughout the country at an enormous profit. In this affair, as in many other cases, high party functionaries were involved.

These disadvantages of the economic reform and its no longer to be hushed up black market summoned the orthodox to the scene. Two men were prominent for their very harsh words. "Now special economic zones are established; each province wants one, wants to open itself up. If this continues, foreign capitalists and domestic speculators will come on the scene, and corruption will rage," said Chen Yun, the old economist of the Moscow school. Deng's former CC collaborator Hu Qiaomu characterized the zones deprecatingly as "foreign colonies," and his former superior's policy of openness as "colonialism without colonial masters."

When Chen Yun implied on June 22, 1985, that the reform had strayed from the socialistic path, Deng found himself in a tight squeeze. Though in February 1984, he had still lauded the development of Shenzhen as trend-setting, on June 29, 1985, he toned down expectations. He told an Algerian delegation:

> The special economic zone Shenzhen is an experiment. At this time we can still not say whether we have taken the correct path. In short, it is an achievement of socialism. We hope that the experiment will succeed, but even should it founder, it will nevertheless have been a lesson.

The enormous initial successes of the agrarian reform and the establishment of the special economic zones as "windows" to the outside world encouraged the reformers to venture the next step. In October 1984, the 3rd plenary session of the XIIth CC decided to introduce the economic reforms into the cities. On the agenda now stood extension of the independence of enterprises, division of property rights and executive power in state enterprises, broadening the private economy, and a wage and price reform.

During the Mao era, the 8,285 collective combines and 430,000 medium-size and small state enterprises had had to pay the profits they had earned to the state. In return they had received investment funds and floating capital. In the Deng era, the treasury has been content to make tax demands; this, however, is not a satisfactory solution, for in May 1985 it became known that only 50 percent of the state and cooperative enterprises payed the stipulated taxes

Deng Xiaoping celebrating his 80th birthday with his
family. Extreme left foreground, daughter Deng Rong
(Maomao), in front of her, her daughter. Next to her,
Deng Nan, holding her daughter up. To the right next
to Deng Xiaoping, his eldest grandson, and far right
(only half visible) his eldest daughter, Deng Lin.

on their profits. And among private industrial and trade enterprises, only between 20 and 30 percent fulfilled their tax obligations.

Whereas in the past all state enterprises had been uniformly rigidly incorporated into the state system of allotment and disposal, irrespective of whether they operated at a profit or a loss, today, after payment of taxes they are free to dispose of their profits themselves—for example, by reinvesting them, distributing bonuses, or enlarging the welfare fund. To be sure, the independence of the enterprise ceases when the figures in the books go into the red. And that, on account of an oppressive surplus of personnel, is the case in most enterprises.

Since the principle of profitability is not forcefully applied, the state, in the framework of the 7th five-year plan (1986-1990), has to subsidize its enterprises at an annual rate of 28 billion yuan. A Shenyan factory manufacturing explosive devices was the first firm in China to signal by its formal declaration of bankruptcy that the times of the "iron rice bowl," that is of risk-free, life-long state subsidy, were over. By 1987, 72,000 medium-size and small state enterprises had shared a similar fate.

Scarcely had the industrial production rate zoomed upwards, when another problem manifested itself—the lack of raw materials. By this, a lack of natural resources is not meant, rather the technological inability to explore for these materials, to extract them, and to transport them given a rail system comprising only 55,000 kilometers. In the future, too, the state will have to allocate goods like steel, concrete, coal, oil, and electricity to enterprises according to the planners' priorities. Doubtless, the enterprises can also buy these goods in small quantities directly—therefore also very expensively—from the concrete factories or mines or the rural cooperatives, but they have still not thereby circumvented the weighty problem of transport. Often only a black market deal can keep the wheels turning—let's say, a thousand steel girders for a hundred tons of coal.

What most fetters plannning in the state enterprises is the tenured, for that matter even inheritable, position, praised under Mao as an accomplishment of socialism. Since in the past the laziest worker was paid the same as the most industrious—being fired for incompetence was not even to be thought of—productivity was significantly limited. In the meantime, social leveling has indeed been curtailed by bonuses and piece-work supplements, but one can still not speak of an open labor and employment market. The much lauded filling of managerial positions by advertisement is nothing more than a gimmick for foreign consumption. Significant, on the other hand, are the successes in installing professionally trained nonparty members as directors of entire collective combines, thus wresting authority from the almighty party secretaries.

The state now also tolerates the partnership of stockholders; in 1987, employee shares were issued on the Shanghai and Peking stock exchanges. That the power structure will in this way yield its control of the means of production to the proletariat seems, however, most unlikely.

The Deng era is notable for seeking challenge. No state trade nation in the world, neither Yugoslavia nor Hungary, gives the private economic sector as much space as does China. While in 1976 only 300,000 city dwellers worked in private service delivery and trade enterprises, in 1987 there were already 25 million—3 million more than work in state enterprises. They call retail stores, craft shops, repair shops, restaurants, medical practices, and drug stores their own, and make taxable profits like any capitalistic business in the west.

Thanks to private, cooperative, and state programs to create jobs, 46 million people found new employment between 1979 and 1986. But hard times still lie ahead in the fight against unemployment: by 1990 another 140 million jobs will be needed. Already, the baby boomers born in the years of the Cultural Revolution are crowding into the labor market; 6 million young people annually seek jobs and training places.

Independence of state enterprises, division of property rights and executive power, broadening of the private economy—all these innovations, revolutionary for a planned economy, are still in their infancy. To this moment, no one knows if they will be crowned with success. Whether Deng's renovation of Chinese society will work crowned with success. Whether Deng's renovation of Chinese society will work depends ultimately on the price reform introduced in May 1985.

After the Communist take-over of power in 1949, the view prevailed in the party that with the establishment of the collectivization of the means of production and an economy governed centrally by the state, the prices of products would no longer be determined by the law of surplus value and the relationship between supply and demand. The Communists regarded the abolition of the commodities economy, which between 1923 and 1949 had developed under the Kuomintang into a kind of state capitalism, as a prerequisite for the development of socialism. In imitation of the Soviet model, the Chinese economists placed the planned economy in diametrical opposition to the commodities economy, denying there could be a socialistic commodities economy. To stabilize prices, they were, like wages, frozen by state intervention. In this way, the typical capitalistic manifestations such as overproduction crises and the rise of monopolies were to be avoided. What were the actual results of this economic policy of the Mao era?

Reviewing the years from 1949 to 1978, one can see that the repertoire of products narrowed, the quality of goods deteriorated, and a consistently low standard of living prevailed alongside a permanent dearth of commodities. Since capital goods industry was preferred in every regard, consumer goods industry and agriculture lagged behind. Heavy industry developed into a behemoth while the other sectors of the national economy atrophied. A tremendous rate of accumulation confronted a low rate of consumption.

Whether a product was good or bad, it always cost the same; besides, the central planning authority set the fixed prices for energy resources and for raw and constituent materials so low that resources were massively squandered. Ultimately, the thirty years of socialist development demonstrated that productivity—despite what Lenin had predicted—was far below that of capitalism.

Deng Xiaoping's historic service is the unsparing revelation of these serious failings. In revolutionary manner, he broke with antiquated dogma, in this case Marxist, and achieved a breakthrough in the fight against orthodox ideology. With the energy of a young man, he applied himself to the task of repairing the building threatened by collapse. In his place, Mao would uncompromisingly have torn it down. In a learning process that lasted twenty years, Deng freed himself from conceptions of Marxist political economy to adopt elements of national economy.

The pragmatist Deng is immune to the reproach "revisionist." He calls his "third way," "socialism of the Chinese stamp," outlining it as follows:

> The socialistic planned economy is an optimal development of the planned commodities economy on the foundation of collective property. This is an ineluctable stage of socialist development, and a necessary condition for the modernization of the economy.

At the same time, he stresses the fundamental difference from the capitalistic commodities economy, to be sought in the fact that the labor force, land, mines, banks, railroads, and state enterprises did not consititute commodities. Besides, in socialism, production of commodities and commodities exchange are for the most part interwoven in state planning.

Commodities production and commodities exchange notwithstanding, the reformers do not wish to abandon the planned economy, even though their "planned commodities economy" restricts the repertoire of offered goods much more. With this conception, however, they distance themselves—without conceding that they do so—from the Marxist idea that in socialism, the supremacy of the relationships of production over the producers is gradually eliminated. They approach the bourgeois economic viewpoint in incorporating bits and pieces of capitalism as well as anarchistic economics into their theory. Viewed historically, the Deng era can accordingly be characterized as a transitional stage between the negation of the law of surplus value and its conscious usage.

Deng's industrial revolution is based on the recognition that the law of surplus value is of major significance in capitalism as well as in socialism. He declares, "Socialism differentiates itself from capitalism, not in bringing the law of surplus value into effect, but rather in consciously employing the law of surplus value proportionally to the society as a whole."

Until 1985, it was reserved to the supreme planning authority to set prices nationwide. In this method of setting prices, political interests played a larger role than supply and demand. The Maoists boasted at home and abroad of their price stability. In doing so, however, they kept quiet about the ever-increasing budget deficit, and the fact that enterprises were producing at only half-efficiency.

The Deng era has to throw all this ballast overboard. Not radically, not overnight, for the withdrawal of state subsidies in the amount of billions would tear the national price structure apart. For example, it is not possible at the moment for the state to abandon grain prices to the whims of supply and demand, for the consumer prices of rice, corn, and wheat have to be subsidized by one billion yuan monthly. Staple foods sold in the cities are accordingly cheaper than those purchased in the villages and municipalities. A price rise would be prohibitive since today city dwellers already pay more than 70 percent of their income for food. An improvement for the grain farmers would accordingly lead to urban unrest. Under these circumstances, the reformers aspire to a partial and gradual decontrol of prices. By 1990, they want first of all to decontrol retail prices to alleviate the scarcity of consumer goods.

Parallel to the price reform, in July 1985 the party began a wage reform. The cornerstone of this accompanying measure is merit pay. By the year 1990, all state enterprises will operate under a wage and bonus system tied to their profitability.

Housing rents and prices of raw materials and electricity still have to be held artificially low by heavy subsidies. Consequently, the employed do enjoy cheap housing, which amounts on the average to ten percent of their salary. As a result, however, the quantity and quality of state housing construction is far below world level. Electricity and coal are rationed, to be sure, but the state distributes them at prices so cheap that they do not cover even the cost of production and delivery. When the upturn in the economy took place in 1980, supply shortages arose in all enterprises that ranked low in the state plan.

As the reformers gradually abolish state subsidies to restore the economy to soundness and establish a price structure in line with market conditions, the rate of price increase—in 1985, between 30 and 50 percent for food—will shoot up. Therefore, the state will have to increase real incomes through so-called "grants," thereby further burdening the state budget. The only way out for the reformers is higher productivity, improved efficiency, and a more frugal use of raw materials and resources.

Let us summarize the advantages of Deng's course of reform. Since today the national economy—after a 30-year delay—has developed in accordance with the order of priorities "agriculture, light industry, heavy industry," it has been possible to raise the living standard of the 800 million inhabitants of the country by leaps and bounds. While as recently as ten years ago, consumer goods such as bicycles, sewing machines, wrist watches, and all food staples were rationed, today ration coupons are required only for grain and cooking oil. The reformers brought about this outstanding achievement in an astonishingly short time. Thanks to their course of action, productivity in industry and agriculture is on the upswing. Finally, the prospering private economy and the opening to foreign countries[4] has brought a wider and improved supply of goods, above all in the sector of consumer goods.

Against these advantages the following disadvantages must be set. During the Mao era, inflation was held in check. Since Deng's accession to power, escalation of prices has seemed to gallop. If the principle of profitability gains further ground, the problem of unemployment will be drastically heightened. If in Mao's day the proposition "All are equal," that is, equally poor, held true, today the slogan "Money rules the world" is in vogue. Polarization between rich and poor advances unchecked. Thus, a privately employed taxi driver today earns four times the salary of a teacher, five times that of a state-employed bus driver. It is precisely between the state and the private economic sectors that income disparity grows most rapidly. Finally, economic crimes have taken on a new dimension. According to investigations of Chen Yun's Disciplinary Control Commission, in 1985 every third economic criminal was a party member.

These disadvantages give the orthodox ammunition to attack the reform course as "playing with fire." They are, to be sure, not fundamentally opposed to Deng's course, but they want to see the freedoms of the economic reforms more narrowly restricted. Their concept "Planned economy first, market regulation second" serves as their general line. The economic planner Chen Yun, under the influence of the Soviet economy, developed this already in the fifties, but was unable to carry it through against Mao's radical left course of the "Three Red Banners."

The controversy concerning the "cage" policies, that is the place of the market economy in the context of the planned economy, has dragged on since the beginning of 1985. The reformers had to make countless concessions to the orthodox before finally, in March 1986, after a twelve-month tug-of-war, the 7th five year plan could be adopted by the 4th session of the VIth NPC. Chen Yun's central criticism was directed against the free play of supply and demand. Were such freedom permitted, a "blind" regulation of the market would arise that would lead necessarily to over-heating of the national economy. He countered the reformers:

> In the year 1984, the value of gross industrial production rose by 14 percent over the previous year. In the first six months of the year 1985, it rose in relation to the correspond-ing period in the previous year by 22.8 percent. Such a high tempo cannot be continued . . . The faster one rushes forward, the later one reaches one's goal.

Chen Yun, just one year Deng's junior, lobbied vigorously for applying the brakes to the reforms and for a long-term, centralized regulation of the national economy.

The orthodox, denounced meanwhile as men of the past, are losing support because they are unable to point the people the way to the future. It is otherwise with the reformers; they awaken great interest among the consumption hungry population with their ideology of growth—by the year 2000, a Chinese citizen will sup-posedly earn the equivalent of 357 U.S. dollars (today, 48 U.S. dollars) per month.

Thereby, the question of victory or defeat for the reform course has not been decided. Deng's trek into the unknown is reminiscent of climbing a mountain in the fog. He and the party roped to him grope their way forward, securing their every toe-hold with socialist terminology. Soon, these courageous avant-gardists will come to a fork in the path where they will finally have to choose a direction. If they hue to the path they have taken, they will help the private economy to a breakthrough and the upturn will continue. If they turn off, then the planned economy will triumph and the upturn will stagnate.

EIGHTEEN

Race Against Death

DURING THE WINTER of 1986, China was momentarily astir as a few "lucky dogs" took to the streets demanding democracy. Many could not understand the protest of the students, who numbered among society's privileged, and for that very reason were called "lucky dogs." So the spontaneous actions remained limited to student circles and included only a fraction of the 1.8 million budding academics. On December 9, at the Technical Institute of Hefei, capital of the province of Anhui, 3,000 students undertook a limited strike under the mottos "No modernization without democracy" and "We want a true, not a false democracy." Incited by their Vice Rector, astrophysicist Fang Lizhi, the indignant students confronted the party leadership with the old demand for democracy called for already in 1979 by the dissidents of the "Peking Spring" as the fifth modernization, alongside the four others of agriculture, industry, national defense, and science and technology.

It was clear by December 22 at the latest that the students were talking about democracy not only on campus, when in the heart of Shanghai more than ten thousand university students sang the "Internationale" and on a large banner recalled the anti-imperialist "May 4th Movement" of 1919: "70 years have passed since then, but where is the democracy?" Instantly, the wave of protest spread to twenty-two cities, not excepting the capital. At New Year, many thousands of students from the reknowned universities Beida and Qinghua headed for Tiananmen Square. On their fifteen kilometer march to the city center they shouted through megaphones, "Down with the conservatives in the Politburo!" and "Xiaoping, hear our voice!"

Deng had long since heard their voice, but had kept silent. He expressed himself on the subject for the first time on the evening of December 30, 1986, at a meeting of a small circle of the leadership, quite cross over the student disturbances:

> . . . because for many years now, the current of bourgeois liberalism has not been fought with determination and clarity . . . When we speak of democracy, we can adopt neither bourgeois democracy nor the tripartite division of governmental power. I have repeatedly criticized the rulers in the U.S.A., telling them that in reality they had three governments.

Deng Xiaoping could insinuate that the indignant students wanted bourgeois democracy along parliamentary lines because their various mottos exhausted themselves in abstractions. Their demands remained formulas that exploded without much effect, leaving behind only depression and bewilderment among the young intellectuals. Like all previous movements for democracy, this, too, showed it lacked any basis. China has no tradition of democracy. And for the Chinese, concepts like freedom, equality, and popular sovereignty are not values handed down as they are for people in the west.

The Middle Kingdom never experienced a bourgeois revolution in the western sense. The short-lived republican revolution of 1911 brought anything but a far-reaching overthrow of the society as it had existed for millennia; it burst only the long mouldering fetters of feudalism. For this reason, before 1920 no word for political or philosophical freedom yet existed. By way of substitute, to this day the terms Minzhu (people rule) or Ge Ren Ziyou (personal freedom) are used, such that the term "individual freedom" is often understood negatively in the sense of "set free."

Mao Tsetung and the founding Communists recognized this oppressive lack in the society marked by feudalism. In Yan'an, Mecca of the revolution, therefore, they experimented with elements of a plebescite and soviet democracy which grew into the "New Democracy" in the Red base areas. But only a few years later, they established their authority throughout China through one-party rule and prematurely announced the end of the New

Democratic phase. Along Bolshevik lines, they adopted democratic centralism with its division between consultation at the base level and decision-making in the top echelon of the party. To this day this form of centralism constitutes the pillars of the dictatorship of the proletariat, which, according to Deng Xiaoping's statement, "means a socialistic democracy for the people; a democracy enjoyed by workers, farmers, intellectuals, and the rest of the working people, in fact the broadest democracy that has ever existed in history."

Since democracy in the Old as well as the New China was always just the by-product of the interests of particular classes and strata, it could never evolve into its actual meaning, namely, government by the people. That is why to this day the basis for a multiparty system with free elections, free trade unions, and an independent press is absent in the People's Republic. In short, the fate of democracy is linked to the fate of the Communist party. Were it to relinquish supremacy tomorrow, chaos, feudal manners, and robber baronry would in all probability spread throughout the land. A glance at history makes it clear why the students who longed for democracy in the winter of 1986 were unable to formulate answers to any of the burning questions of the Deng era.

Professor Fang Lizhi, known since his expulsion from the party as "China's Sakharov," wants to break apart the tragic concatenation of party interests and popular democracy. In the early summer of 1987, he commented on Deng's announced structural reforms with respect to the four absolute fundamentals: "Democracy prescribed from above is not democracy at all in the true sense. It is only a loosening of control."

Fang Lizhi and the dissidents Wang Ruowang and Liu Binyan have become idols of the young intelligentsia because—from a basic position of progressivism—they fundamentally welcome the reform course, but criticize it in the same breath as one-sided, sticking their fingers into the old wounds of the system in a way Deng, for fear of the orthodox, dares not do. In their opinion, his reform course is doomed to founder if in the future a priority is not given the promotion of science and democracy.

The 52-year-old Fang Lizhi reproaches the reform-Marxists for reducing science and technology to a purely technical productive resource, and all the advances in the capitalistic west to a

The secret private residence of the Deng Family near
Beihai Park in Peking.

question of per capita income, know-how, and productive output. His critique is directed against Deng, who said on December 30, 1986:

> We are carrying out a policy of opening to the outside. We are learning from foreign technologies and we employ foreign capital. But that is just a fulfillment of socialist development and does not mean abandoning the socialistic path . . . If we reach an average per capita national product of 4,000 U.S. dollars . . . , the correctness of Marxism will be demonstrated all the more forcefully.

Deng Xiaoping's dogmatically hedged efforts to exploit western technology for the development of socialism of the Chinese stamp is ominously reminiscent of the attitude of the neo-Confucianists of the last century.

During the second half of the nineteenth century, a rift developed in the declining Ch'ing Empire between the high Manchu and Chinese dignitaries and a small group of modernists. The two monarchistic military leaders and victors over the Taiping Uprising, Zeng Guofan (1811-1872) and Li Hongzhang (1823-1901), made many enemies at the imperial court in Peking because they saw the salvation of the empire only in cooperation with the west. Against the opposition of orthodox court officials, they set about modernizing the imperial army and industry with foreign assistance. So the Viceroy of Nanjing, Zeng Guofan, built arsenals and shipyards in Shanghai with the aid of French technicians. The first programs for study in the United States for gifted young Chinese students originated with his initiative.

Governor Li Hongzhang ("China's weakness lies in her poverty") devoted himself more to industrial development of the country. In 1872, with loans from foreign banks, he founded the Chinese Steamship Company and, six years later, the Mining Company of Kaiping and, in 1880, the Telegraph Company of Tianjin.

By these revolutionary measures, two office-holding pioneers opened the door to modernity and gave the hermetically sealed Middle Kingdom new impetus. But ultimately they foundered on their own inconsistencies. Both were, on the one hand, cosmopolitan pragmatists, and, on the other hand, ardent supporters of the revived Chinese orthodoxy, neo-Confucianism. They were taken in by the illusion that they could cure the ailing feudal empire through modern foreign technology alone. Unquestionably, their accomplishments acquired the most modern navy in Asia for the Ch'ing Empire, but they were nonetheless helpless to prevent its devastating defeat in the Sino-Japanese War of 1885.

Since that defeat, which drove the Middle Kingdom to the lengths of self-repudiation, relations to everything foreign have been broken, indeed, characterized by trauma. Since then, China, once the acme of world civilization, has attempted to master its humiliation. Traces of the trauma are still to be found in relations between Chinese and foreigners. Either they lie "on their stomachs" before them, that is behave servilely, or they are exceedingly overbearing. Ever since the failure of the modernists, the country has attempted repeated approaches at an appropriate opening to the outside.

Then, as now, the problem has been the fight against a rigidified and introverted elite. In former times, this elite commanded powerful backing among the corrupt, opium-hungry bureaucracy. Today, it derives its support from the encrusted, privilege-hungry cadre personnel of the middle ranks of government and is thereby no less powerful.

Deng Xiaoping has repeatedly underestimated these forces and has frivolously allowed trump cards to slip from his hand. Had he mobilized the people loyal to him to the fight, today his reform course would be unstoppable. His last kowtow before the orthodox—when in January 1987 he sacrificed his closest associate, Secretary General Hu Yaobang—almost vanquished him.

But in the long term, Deng's concept of reform, "dogmatically here, pragmatically there," will be threatened not from the side of orthodoxy, but from a position like that represented in the twenties by Lu Xun (1881-1936). China's most important poet of the twentieth century called Chinese society "man-eating," and pleaded therefore for its complete westernization. Lu Xun's conception, which today fascinates the young intelligentsia disillusioned with socialism and which is spreading among the newly emerging middle class, derives nourishment also from Gorbachev's political and economic reforms.

If in their contest over the correct general line the Chinese and the Russians once each sought to advance themselves to the avant garde of the world Communist movement, today they are competing for the title "Best Socialist Reformer." When they were still denouncing each other, even threatening each other militarily, all seemed routine and simple. But now that a global trend towards socialist reform has manifested itself, the Chinese are forced to follow, and are becoming visibly nervous.

For Deng Xiaoping and his successor, Zhao Ziyang, the future has long since begun; time runs through their fingers, while the orthodox see time as their ally. It is a race against death for the great old man, for without him, his life's work seems not fully viable. Therefore, he had once more to summon all his strength and all his tactical skill at the XIIIth Party Congress of October 1987 to solidify the basis of his life's work: through a clever pro forma resignation from two offices he managed to compel the orthodox of the old guard—still comprising forty percent of the CC members—likewise to vacate their accustomed places. In actuality, even after the "Gaobie Dahui" (Party Congress of Departure), he is "our true party leader," as the Mayor of Canton said. Deng Xiaoping's reelection as Chairman of the Military Commission, that is as Commander in Chief, confirms this. The power of the reformers, which thereby in the future, too, will come from the barrel of a gun, is guaranteed in the "Party Olympus" by his followers Zhao Ziyang, Hu Qili, and Qiao Shi. But who guarantees that lacking Deng's protecting hand this trio will be able to withstand some future attack of the orthodox behind Premier Li Peng and Yao Yilin?

In fact, his life's work is one of the "greatest experiments of all previous economic history." If it succeeds, Deng will have to rate as an alchemist of genius, able, as it were, to mix oil and water together. If it fails, then schism threatens the Communist Party, and possibly civil war the country. China's renovator knows that "a hundred years do not suffice for building up—but that for tearing down, one day is too much."

Notes

Foreword

1. Deng Xiaoping's official *curriculum vitae* of November 1987, reads:

Deng Xiaoping was born in 1904 in the district of Guang'an, province of Szechuan. At 16, he left his home to study in France. He financed his studies there through work on the side. In France, he took part in the work of the party, joining the Communist Youth League in 1922, and the CP of China in 1924. From France, he went in 1926 to the Soviet Union to pursue his studies. Returned to China, he led two uprisings south of Guangxi, in 1929 the uprising at Bose, and in 1930 that in Longzhou. During the Long March between 1934 and 1936 Deng was General Secretary of the CC of the Party [an accurate translation would read, Head of the CC Secretariat]. In the year 1938, he was appointed Politcommissar of the 129th Division of the Eighth Route Army. Together with Marshal Liu Bocheng, he commanded countless important campaigns. In the year 1947, the troops under the command of Deng and Liu, commonly known as the "Liu-Deng Army," crossed the Yellow River and marched into the strategically important Dabie Mountains, signaling the commencement of the People's Liberation Army's extensive counter-offensive against the Kuomintang troops. Deng Xiaoping, Marshal Liu Bocheng, and Chen Yi led one of the large campaigns in the war of liberation, the battle of Huaihai, which put 550,000 men of the Kuomintang troops out of action, and inflicted a devastating defeat on the fighting forces of the reactionaries. At that time, Deng was General Secretary of the Front Committee of the CP of China, which coordinated the operations of the two field armies of Liu and Chen respectively. Soon afterwards, the troops of the three commanders crossed the Yangtze and liberated Nanjing, the capital of the Kuomintang government. The "Liu-Deng Army" then marched further south and liberated the entire southwest of the country. In 1949, Deng was Secretary of the Southwest China Regional Office of the CC, Politcommissar of the Military district, and Deputy Chairman of the Military and Political Commission in the southwest. Deng is not only a revolutionary, but also a statesman, a strategist, and a diplomat. Chairman Mao Tsetung once characterized him as "a rare talent." During the war years, Deng was Politcommissar of a field army, and following the founding of the New China, he functioned as Deputy Chairman of the National Defense Committee, Chief of Staff of the People's Liberation Army, Deputy Chairman and Chairman of the Military Commission in the CC. In 1945, at the VIIth Party Congress, he was elected a member of the CC, and in 1955, a member of the Politburo of the CC. At the VIIIth Party Congress in 1956 he became General Secretary of the CC. He occupied this position until 1966. Like the earlier State President Liu Shaoqi, he also became a victim of the "Cultural Revolution." In the year 1973, he was reinstalled in his positions. But already in 1976, he again lost all his functions; not until 1977, at the XIth Party Congress, was he again elected Deputy Chairman of the CC. At the 1st plenary session of the XIIth CC, in the year 1982, he was elected member of the Standing Committee of the Politburo, and Chairman of the Consultative Commission in the CC. Between 1952 and 1980, Deng functioned as Deputy Premier of the State Council. In 1953 he acted as Finance Minister. Deng possesses bravery, tactical wisdom, and the courage to solve tricky problems. He advocated recognizing "praxis as the sole criterion for the assaying of truth," and as the key to the liberation of the people from ossified ways of thinking. In the year 1981, the 6th plenary session of the XIth CC adopted the "Resolution on several historical problems of the party since the founding of the People's Republic of China," compiled by him, in which the "Cultural Revolution" was condemned, the errors of Chairman Mao in his last years were corrected, and his great contributions to the Chinese Revolution acknowledged. Deng proposed the concept, "One country, two systems," to resolve questions bequeathed by history, between China and Great Britain of Hongkong, and between China and Portugal of Macao. This concept is a sensible basis for the solution of the Taiwan question and for the realization of the reunification of the motherland. In the years 1956-1963, Deng led many party delegations to Moscow to carry on negotiations with the Soviet party leadership. His great respect in the party and among the Chinese people comes from his important accomplishments and his prominent position. His role in the historical turning of the party's politics is primarily to be stressed. Deng is the initiator of the reforms and the opening to the outside. He showed China the way to the development of socialism of the Chinese stamp, thereby opening a new chapter in the history of the party and the People's Republic. Deng Xiaoping is married to Zhuo Lin. They have two sons and three daughters. In his spare time, he enjoys sports, walking, and swimming, and plays bridge.

2 Father and Clan

1. As late as 1973 and sporadically even after that, many internationally recognized sinologists published incorrect indications of place and date of birth. Respecting his place of birth alone there are three incorrect identifications:

   Jiading Xian: We find this location indicated in Edgar Snow's work "Red Star Over China." Amazingly enough, his biographical data rest on an interview he conducted with Deng Xiaoping in Yu Wang Bao, Shanxi province, on August 19, 1936.

   Da Xian: This location was published by a certain Tang Mingshu in the Hongkong journal *Zhongguo Minzhu Rentan* (The Chinese Democratic Tribune), No. 9, on December 1, 1965.

   Jiang'an Xian: This indication has its source in the reference book published in Taiwan in 1966, "Who's Who in the CP of China?"

   Guang'an Xian: During the Cultural Revolution between 1966 and 1976 much biographical material about Deng Xiaoping was dug up by the Red Guard which still today is accessible only abroad. In 1967, the Peking journal *Red Guard* published in its Number 2 an "Investigatory report on the crimes of Deng Xiaoping." In this article, the Political and Criminal Justice Collective writes, "Deng Xiaoping comes from the production brigade 'Fanxiu' (anti-revisionism), Commune Xiexing, Guang'an Xian, province of Szechuan."

2. Ten households constituted a "Jia" and ten "Jia," a "Bao," at whose head was a village elder. From 1934, this system of control, which provided for punishment collectively of the misdemeanors of a household, was reinstituted on the lowest administrative levels by the Kuomintang. Originally, it goes back to the Song period (960–1279), when by "Baojia," a militial structure was understood constituted of units of ten militarily trained households each.

3. Robert A. Kapp, *Szechwan and the Chinese Republic* (New Haven, London, 1973), p. 25.

4. Author's interview with residents of Xiexing, August 1986.

5. Ibid.
6. Deng Shimin's most renowned candidates were the man of letters and Hanlin Academician Yuan Mei (Yuan Zicai, 1716-1798), and the military strategist Agui (A Guangting, 1717-1797). Cf. Hummel, A. W., *Eminent Chinese of the Ch'ing Period* (Washington, D. C., 1943-44), pp. 955-57 and pp. 6-8; also, Li Huan, *Selected Biographies of Famous Personalities of the Ch'ing Period* (place of publication unlisted, 1891).

3 Precocious Abroad

1. Author's interview with Pater Jean Verinaud of the Missions Étrangères de Paris, December 1986.
2. See Document F 7 12,900, Archives Nationales, Paris.
3. Jiang Zemin, "Reminiscences of the Life of the Work-Study Students in France and Belgium," in *Selected Writings on the History of Tianjin,,* Vol. XIV (Tianjin, date of publication unlisted), p. 34.
4. Li Huang, *Memoirs from the Ignorant Student's Studio* (Hongkong, 1979), p. 23.

   Until 1981 when the Shanghai People's Press published the work *The Movement for Travel to France for Work-Study,* Li Huang's reminiscences were prized as the pertinent information of a still living eyewitness. In the year 1986, Li Huang was living on Taiwan. Today we know that he made many errors. The two groups from Szechuan were led by a certain Yuan Wenqing from Baxian, a work-study student by the name of Wang Xinzhi from Hechun, and by Wu Yusan from Beixian.

   It suggests itself that Li Huang confused Deng Xiaoping with some other person, for—and this is his greatest error—he spoke always of a Kan Zegao. For years, China experts and sinologists throughout the world assumed that Kan Zegao was Deng Xiaoping's birth name.
5. In accordance with the Pinyin transliteration, now officially employed by China, the names are transcribed as follows: Deng Xixian, Sichuan, Deng Wenming, Tan Shi Deng.
6. In question are Li Lisan, Nie Rongzhen, Li Fuchun, and Zhao Shiyan.

4 From Laborer to "Doctor of Duplication"

1. Zhao Shiyan, Cai Hesen, and Wang Rofei.
2. The first proper members were: Li Fuchun, Li Lisan, Li Weihan,

Chen Yi, Nie Rongzhen, and "China's Rosa Luxemburg," Cai Chang, who married Li Fuchun in 1923.

3. *History of the Founding Organization of the CP of China in Europe* (Peking, 1985), p. 123.
4. Li Huang, quoted in Han Shanbi, *Deng Xiaoping: Biography,* Vol. I (Hongkong, 1986), p. 120.
5. See Document F 7 12,900, Archives Nationale, Paris.
6. Nora Wang, "Deng Xiaoping: The Years in France," in *The China Quartery,* 92 (1982), p. 698.

5 Among the Bolsheviks

1. An indemnity of 450 million silver dollars for the so-called "Boxer Rebellion" of 1900, payable with interest within 39 years (effectively 982 million silver dollars) to Belgium, Germany, France, Great Britain, Italy, Japan, the Netherlands, Austria-Hungary, Russia, Spain, and the United States of America.
2. Quoted in Yueh Sheng, *Sun Yat-sen University in Moscow and the Chinese Revolution. A Personal Account* (New York, 1971), p. 32.
3. In 1960, Mao Tsetung told Edgar Snow in conversation that at the beginning of Chiang Kai-shek's counter-revolution there were fully 50,000 Communists, of which only 10,000 survived his "massacre." Cf., Edgar Snow, *Roter Stern über China* (Frankfurt a. M., 1979), p. 427.
4. To be precise, the group was called the "28½ Bolsheviks," for Xu Yixin was so short that jokingly he was reckoned as just half a person. The other 28, listed alphabetically, were: Bo Gu (Qin Bangxian), Chen Changhao, Chen Shaoyu (Wang Ming), Chen Yuantao, He Chushu, He Kechuan (Kai Feng), Li Yuanchi, Li Zhousheng, Meng Qinshu (wife of Wang Ming), Shen Zemin, Song Bamin, Sun Chimin, Tu Zuoxiang (wife of Chen Changhao), Wang Baoli, Wang Jiaxiang, Wang Shengdi, Wang Shengyong, Wang Yuncheng, Xia Xi, Xiao Defu, Yang Shangkun (today, State President and Vice Chairman of the Central Military Commission), Yin Qian, Yuan Jiayong, Yue Sheng, Zhang Jinjiu (wife of Shen Zemin), Zhang Wentian (Luo Fu), Zhu Ahken, Zhu Chushun.
5. Wang Ming, Bo Gu (Qin Bangxian), Luo Fu (Zhang Wentian).
6. Among the prominent fellow students of Deng Xiaoping were Zhu Wu, Zuo Quan, and Yu Xiusong. Zhu Wu was the son-in-law of the KMT hero Yu Yuren. He left the CCP in the thirties, and was later made a member of the Control Yuan, one of the five executive organs of the Chinese Nationalist Government. Zuo Quan, once a

cadet at the Whampoa Academy, remained a Communist, and advanced after 1930 in the Jiangxi Soviet to commander of the 15th Army. During the founding years of the CCP, Yu Xiusong had served as assistant to the Comintern advisor Gregory Woitinsky (Wu Dingcan). After his return from Moscow, Yu founded the Shanghai Foreign Language Institute.

An older fellow student was the teacher Zhou Tianlu, shot in 1949 by secret agents in Shanghai. Shen Zemin, brother of the author Mao Dun, also belonged to Deng's class. Shen Zemin functioned until his death in 1934 as member of the 6th CC of the CCP. He was one of the "28 Bolsheviks," and worked at the university as interpreter and instructor.

7. Here sat the founding fathers of the Kuomintang, like Wu Yuchang, who after 1930 went temporarily as instructor to the Soviet Party School in Vladivostok. Until his death on December 12, 1966, Wu Yuchang was member of the CC of the CCP, responsible for the so-called Pinyin transliteration of Chinese script. Then Lin Boqu, who had worked already on Sun Yatsen's staff. In the thirties, he administerd the finances of the Central Soviet government in the Jinggang Mountains. Until his death in 1960, he belonged to the Politburo of the CCP. Finally, Ye Jianying, who died in 1986, one of the ten Marshals of the People's Liberation Army, and until 1983, Parliamentary President of the People's Republic of China.

8. Qu Qiubai, Li Weihan, Cai Hesen, and Chen Duxiu.

9. Mikhail Borodin, Otto Braun, Gerhart Eisler (elder brother of the composer Hanns Eisler), Richard Sorge, Manfred Stern, Earl Browder, Eugene Dennis, Arthur Ewald (Ewart), and Steve Nelson were the most important.

6 A Tragic Mission

1. Zhang Yunyi, Gong Zhu, and Feng Dafei.

2. Gong Zhu, *Memoires,* Vol. I (Hongkong, 1978), pp. 258, ff.

3. On June 11, 1930, a "rump" Politburo met, consisting of Li Lisan, Xiang Zhongfa, Cai Hesen, and Zhou Enlai. Li Lisan used the meeting to send his opponent Cai Hesen to Moscow for "right-wing opportunistic" errors. Zhang Guotao and Qu Qiubai were already living there in exile.

4. Yuan Renyuan, "The Red Assault of You Jiang in the Autonomous Region of Guangxi—Reminiscences of the Bose Uprising," in *Renmin Ribao,* December 9, 1978.

5. Mo Wenhua, quoted in Han Shanbi, *Deng Xiaoping: Biography,* Vol. I (Hongkong, 1986), p. 149.
6. The Red Guard's information came from the *Short History of the Seventh Corps* by Mo Wenhua (1964). The author was at that time president of the Military Political Academy of the People's Liberation Army, and was reckoned an adherent of Lin Piao. His book about the Seventh Corps was confiscated immediately after its publication. On instructions from Deng Xiaoping and Marshal He Long (1896-1969), Mo Wenhau was relieved of his office and replaced by Cai Xunli.

Since Mo Wenhua was, on Lin Piao's urging, rehabilitated during the Cultural Revolution (at the CC plenary of August 11, 1966), one may assume that his book, which speaks of Deng Xiaoping's "desertion," was launched by Lin Piao in order to attack Deng as "capitalistic despot." Mo Wenhau's statements have to be viewed with caution, for he was not an eyewitness to Deng's flight; his information was based on hearsay.

7 Rough Fall, Tough Climb

1. Cf. Harrison E. Salisbury, *The Long March* (Frankfurt a. M., 1985), Chapter 13.
2. In January 1934, at the Fifth plenary session of the VIth Party Congress in Ruijin, the CC concerned itself extensively with the so-called "Luo Ming Conspiracy," and one month later instituted a far-reaching wave of purges. Besides Deng, the most important cadres accused were: Gu Bo, Xie Weijun, Luo Ming, and Mao Zetan. The CC initiated an investigation against Mao Tsetung, led by the CP founding father Dong Biwu. Mao was forced to leave the Politburo.
3. Li Zuoran, quoted in Han Shanbi, op. cit., p. 173.
4. Document Collection of the Zunyi Conference (Peking, 1985), p. 68.
5. Chen Yun, "Theses of the Circular on the Expanded Conference of the Politburo," in Document Collection on the Zunyi Conference (Peking 1985) p. 42.

These are handwritten notes prepared after the fact by Chen Yun (at the Zunyi Conference itself only Deng Xiaoping, as editor of "Red Star," was allowed to make notes; his notes were lost during the Long March, however). Chen Yun's notes are preserved in the Central Archive of the CC; they were made public by the party leadership only in 1985.

The Military Commission consisted then of the following members: Zhu De, Chairman of the Commission, standing member of the Politburo, and Supreme Commander of the Red Army; Zhou Enlai, his deputy, standing member of the Politburo, and First Politcommissar of the Red Army; Wang Jiaxiang, likewise Zhu De's deputy, standing member of the Politburo, and leader of the Main Political Administration of the Red Army; Mao Tsetung, standing member of the Politburo, and Zhou Enlai's collaborator in the military leadership; Liu Bocheng, Chief of Staff of the Red Army; Li Fuchun, Acting Head of the Main Political Division of the Red Army.

6. In their journal *Red Guard* (2/1967)M, the Red Guard published the following contribution of the State and Justice Science Collective:

> On November 3, 1958, Deng Xiaoping, Yang Shangkun, and Li Jinquan visited the memorial in Zunyi. At that time, the exhibition had been constructed after a painstaking and comprehensive examination. The visitors could view the portraits of the 18 participants. Since Deng Xiaoping had not taken part in the conference, of course no picture of him hung in the exhibition. This careerist was very annoyed when he remarked that the portrait of the General Secretary [his position at the time] was missing. His eyebrows were drawn together, and he started brooding. Then he suddenly remembered, climbed to the second floor and entered the room in which the conference had been held. Now he acted as though rediscovering a familiar place. He said that the Conference had taken place here. Then he had the audacity to point to a corner of the room and claim he had sat there. To convince his companions of his participation, gesticulating wildly he explained all the details, wishing to demonstrate thereby that he was familiar with everything that had occurred there.

7. The post of "Director of the Secretariat of the Central Committee of the CCP" is always equated with the position of "General Secretary of the Central Committee of the CCP." That is incorrect. In the official Chinese Deng Xiaoping biography (see p. 323) it is written erroneously, "After 1927 he worked as . . . General Secretary of the Central Committee of the CP of China." Correctly, this would read, "Head of the CC Secretariat," literally translated, "Chief Secretary of the CC of the CP of China." From the IVth Party Congress of the CCP in 1925 until 1938, the term "General Secretary of the CC of the CP of China" was used for the highest position in the CCP. Later, this position was temporarily abolished in favor of that of

Party Chairman. When at the VIIIth Party Congress in 1956 Deng Xiaoping was actually appointed General Secretary of the CC of the CCP, this post was no longer as important because it was subordinate to the office of the Party Chairman.

8 Front Years

1. Author's interview with Anna Wang in Hamburg, July 12, 1986.
2. The 115th Division, commanded by Lin Piao, the 120th Division, commanded by He Long, and the 129th Division, commanded by Liu Bocheng.
3. Brigadier General Carlson went down in American history as the only U.S. general to train his troops in Communist guerrilla tactics. In the Second World War, these special units became known as "Carlson's Raiders." Evans Carlson died in the spring of 1947.
4. Author's interview with Lu Yi in Shanghai in September 1986. Lu Yi was one of the three most famous reporters in China before 1949. During the "Hundred Flowers Movement" he was iced by Mao.
5. Author's interview with Hans Müller in Peking, August 6, 1986. Hans Müller, born in 1915 in Düsseldorf, numbers among the most remarkable foreign personalities of the history of the Chinese Revolution. In contrast to the Canadian physician Norman Bethune and the American physician of Syrian extraction George Hatem (Ma Haide), Müller never became famous because he always kept in the background. In 1933, he fled Hitler's Germany to Switzerland, attending a medical school in Basel. In 1939, he traveled to Yan'an. Twelve years later, Müller was granted Chinese citizenship, and during the following three decades, numerous important posts in the health administration of the People's Republic of China. There are numerous rumors in circulation concerning the "Chinese" Hans Müller. So for example it is maintained that he taught Deng Xiaoping to play bridge. Müller is a good chess player; of bridge, however, he is ignorant.
6. Huang Dao, *30 Years of the Chinese People's Liberation Army* (Peking, 1957), p. 26.
7. The Red Guard journal *The New Peking University* of April 1967, wrote:

> In 1939, with his mottos "Let us transform the occupied areas to a colony" and "Let us take from the occupied areas what we need," Deng Xiaoping ignored the line issued by the party and by Chairman Mao, "Win over the majority and fight the mi-

nority" . . . indiscriminately making all forces into enemies. He thereby isolated himself.

8. Liu Shaoqi, *Report on the amendment of the party statute* (Hongkong, 1949).
9. Deng Xiaoping, quoted in Zhou Xun, *Deng Xiaoping* (Hongkong, 1983), p. 44.
10. Ibid.
11. Op. cit., p. 49.
12. The CCP had brought this conference into being on September 21, 1949, as a people's front organ, to include important democrats and representatives of the nonparty, urban intelligentsia in the drafting of a constitution for the new state.

9 The Great Leap Upward

1. Liu Wenhui, Commander in Chief of Xikang, in 1954 became a delegate to the NPC. Lu Han, Commander in Chief of Yunnan, became Deputy President of the National Commission for Physical Culture and Athletics.
2. Cf. the Peking Red Guard newspaper *Red Guard* (2/1967).
3. On February 19, 1953, Mao Tsetung inspected ships of the People's Navy on the Yangtze. He assured the young sailors that they would see the emergence of Communism.
4. He functioned as one of Mao's deputies in the Central People's Governing Council and as one of his deputies in the People's Revolutionary Military Council.
5. Ahead of Deng ranked Mao Tsetung, Liu Shaoqi, Zhou Enlai, Zhu De, and Chen Yun.

10 The Break

1. Deng Xiaoping, quoted in *Zhenming* of March 1980.
2. Deng Xiaoping, quoted in *Document Collection for the Socialist Course of Studies* (Peking, date of publication unlisted), p. 270.
3. *Renmin Ribao* of 7/1/1957.
4. Report of the realignment movement, 3rd plenary session of the VIIIth CC, September 1957.
5. *Renmin Ribao* of 2/4/1968.
6. In question are Huang Kecheng, Zhang Wentian, and Zhou Xiaozhou.
7. *Renmin Ribao* of 2/16/1987.

8. Deng Xiaoping, "Remarks on the draft of a resolution of several historical questions since the founding of the People's Republic of China," in *Selected Writings (1975-1982)* (Hongkong, 1984), p. 231.

11 The Dragon Hounds the Bear

1. *South China Morning Post* of 9/15/1986.

12 Like a Reed in the Wind

1. To the "Four Cleanups" belonged: "Cleanup" of bookkeeping, "cleanup" of the granaries, "cleanup" of property, and "cleanup" of the division of labor.
2. That is, Liu Shaoqi, Chen Yun, Peng Zhen, Li Xiannian, Yang Shangkun, Luo Ruiqing, Tan Zhenlin, and Lu Dingyi.
3. "The Ten Grave Crimes of Deng Xiaoping," in *Battle Communiqué of August 25,* 4/10/1967.
4. Ibid.
5. Deng Xiaoping's deputy and mayor of Peking, Peng Zhen functioned as chairman of the "Cultural Revolutionary Group of Five"; the other four members were the political advisor Kang Sheng, the Propaganda Chief Lu Dingyi, the Cultural Minister, Zhou Yang, and the Director of the Xinhua news agency, Wu Lengxi.
6. "Deng Xiaoping's Words Against Mao Tsetung," (Red Guard pamphlet, September, 1967), p. 77.
7. The members of the "Central Cultural Revolutionary Group of the CCP" were Jiang Qing, Chen Boda, Kang Sheng, and Zhang Chunqiao.
8. The circular letter to all party committees, drawn up personally by Mao Tsetung, was presented for a vote to the Politburo of the CC on May 16, 1966, in Hangzhou, and thus received the designation "May 16th Circular." The circular canceled Peng Zhen's "February Theses," explaining that the representatives of the bourgeois line in the domain of culture and education were never to be allowed free expression of opinion: "Their fight against us is to the death; for them there can be no equal rights whatsoever."
9. Ding Wang, *Selected Materials on the Cultural Revolution,* Vol. I (Hongkong, 1972), p. 500.
10. The members of the expanded Standing Committee were, Mao Tsetung, Lin Piao, Zhou Enlai, Tao Zhu, Chen Boda, Deng Xiaoping, Kang Sheng, Liu Shaoqi, Zhu De, Li Fuchun, and Chen Yun.
11. Author's interview with Carl Bürger in Hamburg, July 14, 1986.

Bürger was able to enter only because already previous to 1949 he had lived for many years in Tianjin, and carried on business with China.

12. Quoted in Ching Hua Lee, *Deng Xiaoping: The Marxist Road to the Forbidden City* (Princeton, 1985), p. 147.
13. From the magazine "Ausblick": Red Guard fighting squad "Taming the Tiger" of youths moved to the countryside from the province Guangdong.
14. Quoted in Thomas Scharping, *Mao Chronik* (Munich, 1976), p. 205.
15. Remarks on the VIIIth Party Congress of 1956; the last is from the year 1957.
16. *Zeitschrift für Sportfreunde* (2/1986), p. 52.
17. Interview with Oriana Fallaci in *The Washington Post*, 8/31/1980.

13 A Family's Fortunes

1. "Drag Deng Xiaoping into the Light of Day!" in *The New Peking University*, No. 45.
2. Cf., *Libération* (Paris, 9/2/1985). Many rumors about this event circulated in China and abroad. According to one he had attempted suicide, to another, been pushed out the window.
3. Deng Xiaoping, quoted in Han Shanbi, op. cit., p. 32.
4. *Renmin Ribao* of August 22, 1984.
5. The following quotations from *Jing Bao* of 8/10/1986.
6. *Libération* of 9/2/1985.

14 Perilous Tug-of-War

1. The five Deputy Party Chairmen who replaced Li Desheng were Zhou Enlai, Wang Hongwen, Kang Sheng, Ye Jianying, and Deng Xiaoping.
2. *Der Spiegel* of 11/21/1977.
3. Interview with Oriana Fallaci in *The Washington Post* of 8/31/1980.
4. Author's interview with Florian Mausbach and Ursula Mausbach-Zylka in Frankfurt a. M., May 19, 1987. Florian Mausbach and Ursula Mausbach-Zylka lived in Peking from January 1967 until September 1977.
5. Author's interview with Gerd Ruge in Cologne, West Germany, March 15, 1986.

15 Turn of an Era

1. Chang Pinghua, Head of the Propaganda Division of the CC at a conference on July 23, 1978.
2. Interview with Oriana Fallaci, op. cit.
3. Deng Xiaoping, quoted in Zhou Xun, *Deng Xiaoping* (Hongkong, 1983), p. 111.
4. *Der Spiegel* of 11/21/1977.
5. The participants in the preparatory meeting were, Deng Xiaoping, Li Xiannian, Wei Guoqing, Hua Guofeng, Wang Dongxing, Ji Dengkui, and Wu De.
6. *Zhenxiang* 32 (Hongkong, 1978).

16 Dogmatic Here, Pragmatic There

1. The China correspondent of *Reuters* at that time stated independently of the trial that he had paid Wei Jingsheng ten yuan for a subscription of the journal *Tansuo,* which appeared three or four times.
2. At the plenary session, Liu Shaoqi was rehabilitated and designated a "great Marxist." His expulsion from the party, carried out during the Cultural Revolution on Mao's initiative, was assessed as the greatest error in the history of Chinese Communism.
3. Up to that time, Yang Dezhi, headquartered in Kunming, functioned as Commander in Chief of the border troops of Yunnan and Guizhou.
4. To prevent compacts and intrigues, the commanders of the ten military districts (Peking, Shenyang, Lanzhou, Jinan, Wuhan, Chengdu, Nanjing, Fuzhou, Canton, and Kunming) had to fly with their body guards to the newly assigned command posts immediately after the Peking Conference.
5. Deng Xiaoping, *Building of Socialism with Chinese Characteristics* (Peking, 1985), p. 21.
6. *Frankfurter Rundschau* of 6/3/1987.

17 Trekking the Unknown

1. From north to south: Dalian, Qinhuangdao, Tianjin, Yantai, Qingdao, Lianyungang, Nantong, Shanghai, Ningbo, Wenzhou, Fuzhou, Zhangzhou, Canton, Beihai.
2. The following investment opportunities were offered:

Joint Venture: Cooperative enterprises with shared Chinese and foreign capital. While the Chinese as a rule provide the land, the buildings, and the personnel, the foreigners contribute know-how, machinery, and finance capital.

Cooperative Production: Chinese and foreign enterprises produce on the basis of a mutual agreement, but are not financially tied to each other.

Payment in Kind: The Chinese partner pays for plants or machines supplied by the foreign investor with the products produced thereby.

Finishing Industry: The foreign partner delivers raw materials or unfinished goods which the Chinese partner finishes.

Barter Trade: Trade of goods for goods, whereby the lack of market opportunities for the Chinese is compensated.

3. While the budget reserves of the People's Republic of China still amounted to 16.6 billion U.S. dollars in September 1984, they dropped in September 1986 to 10.37 billion U.S. dollars.

4. From 1981 to 1985, the volume of imports and exports rose to 230 billion U.S. dollars, double that of the previous five years. Between 1981 and 1985, foreign loans amounted to 10.3 billion U.S. dollars, and direct foreign investment in China to 5.3 billion U.S. dollars.

Chronology

22 August	1904	Birth of Deng Xixian (Deng Xiaoping) in the village of Xiexing, District of Guang' an. Reckoned by the Chinese lunar calendar, the birth date is July 12, 1904.
	1904	Russia's incursion into Manchuria and towards Korea triggers the Russo-Japanese War.
10 October	1911	Republican uprising in Wuchang; fall of the Ch'ing dynasty.
1 January	1912	In Nanking (Nanjing), Sun Yatsen founds the Chinese Republic.
11 September	1920	Deng Xiaoping travels as work-study student to France.
1 July	1921	Founding of the "Communist Party of China" (CCP) in Shanghai.
June	1923	Deng Xiaoping is elected to the leadership of the "Communist Youth League of China" in France.
	1924	Deng Xiaoping is coopted into the "Base Organization of the CCP in Europe."
12 March	1925	Sun Yatsen dies in Peking.
7 January	1926	Deng Xiaoping leaves Paris traveling to Moscow to study at the "Sun Yatsen University."
July	1926	Start of Chiang Kai-shek's northern campaign (Beifa).
16 September	1926	After six-year absence, Deng Xiaoping returns to China.

November	1926	
–Summer	1927	Deng Xiaoping stays in Xi'an.
	1927	Chang Kai-shek smashes the Communist Revolution in Shanghai. Start of the Nationalist–Communist Civil war (until 1937).
August	1927	
–Summer	1929	Deng Xiaoping stays in Shanghai.
Autumn	1929	Deng Xiaoping is for the first time appointed Politcommissar.
18 September	1931	The Japanese occupy Manchuria.
August	1931	
–April	1933	Deng Xiaoping works in the Jiangxi Soviet.
Summer	1933	Deng Xiaoping is toppled for the first time.
16 October	1934	Start of the Long March (Chang Zheng).
15–17 January	1935	Zunyi Conference: Deng Xiaoping is editor of the journal "Red Star," Head of the CC Secretariat, and Deputy Head of the Main Political Division of the Red Army.
6 December	1936	Xi'an incident: Chaing Kai-shek is captured and forced to join the anti–Japanese united front.
7 July	1937	Start of the Sino–Japanese War (until 1945).
January	1938	Deng Xiaoping becomes Politcommissar of the 129th Division (the "Liu–Deng Army").
August	1940	"Battle of the Hundred Regiments."
23 April		
–11 June	1945	VIIth Party Congress of the CCP: Deng Xiaoping is elected to the Central Committee (CC) of the CCP.
April	1946	Start of the second Nationalist–Communist Civil War (until 1949).
	1948	In Nanjing, Chiang Kai-shek is elected President of the Republic.
6 November	1948	
–10 January	1949	Battle of Huaihai: Deng Xiaoping functions as highest ranking commander.
1 October	1949	Founding of the People's Republic of China: Deng Xiaoping becomes a member of the Central People's Governing Council, of the Political Consultative Conference,

		and of the Executive Committee of the Sino-Soviet Friendship Society.
	1952	Party campaign against corruption, waste, and bureaucracy.
7 August	1952	Deng Xiaoping becomes Deputy Premier.
	1953	First five-year plan (1953-57). End of the Korean War.
18 September	1953	Deng Xiaoping becomes Finance Minister for one year.
15-27 September	1954	Ist National People's Congress (NPC): Deng Xiaoping becomes Deputy Chairman of the National Defense Council.
April	1955	Deng Xiaoping is elected to the Politburo of the CC of the CCP.
15-27 September	1956	VIIIth Party Congress of the CCP: Deng Xiaoping is elected General Secretary of the CC of the CCP and enters the Standing Committee of the Politburo.
May	1958	Announcement of the "Three Red Banners": general line ("More, faster, better, more economically soundly"), Great Leap Forward, and the people's communes. Liu Shaoqi replaces Mao Tsetung as State President.
	1959	Rebellion in Tibet. Lin Piao replaces Peng Dehuai as Defense Minister.
July	1960	Withdrawal of Soviet development aid.
May	1966	Start of the Great Proletarian Cultural Revolution (until 1976).
14 December	1966	Deng Xiaoping's last public appearance; he is toppled for the second time.
March	1969	Sino-Soviet border incidents at the Ussuri.
1-24 April	1969	IXth Party Congress of the CCP.
20 October	1969	
-20 February	1973	Deng Xiaoping lives in exile in the province of Jiangxi.
12 November	1969	Death of Liu Shaoqi.
12 April	1973	Deng Xiaoping's first public appearance since exile.
24-28 August	1973	Xth Party Congress of the CCP: Deng Xiaoping is reelected to the CC.
8 January	1976	Zhou Enlai dies.

4-5 April	1976	Tiananmen incident.
7 April	1976	Deng Xiaoping is toppled for the third time.
9 September	1976	Mao Tsetung dies.
16 July	1977	Deng Xiaoping is rehabilitated.
12-18 August	1977	XIth Party Congress of the CCP: Deng Xiaoping is elected Second Deputy Party Chairman.
18-22 December	1978	3rd plenary session of the XIth CC: beginning of the "Deng Era."
November -January	1980 1981	Trial of the so-called "Gang of Four" for high treason.
27-29 June	1981	6th plenary session of the XIth CC; Deng Xiaoping is elected Chairman of the Military Commission of the CC.
January	1982	New lease system in agriculture.
1-11 September	1982	XIIth Party Congress of the CCP.
13 September	1982	Deng Xiaoping is elected Chairman by the 1st plenary session of the Consultative Commission of the CC.
March	1984	fourteen coastal cities and the island of Hainan are opened to foreign investors.
26 September	1984	Initialing of the Hongkong Agreement.
20 October	1984	3rd plenary session of the XIIth CC: start of the urban economic reforms.
July	1985	Start of the wage and price reform.
25 March -12 April	1986	4th session of the VIth NPC: adoption of the 7th five-year plan (1986-1990).
December -January	1986 1987	Student unrest in 22 cities.
16 January	1987	Hu Yaobang resigns as Secretary General of the CC of the CCP.
25 October -1 November	1987	XIIIth Party Congress of the CCP: Deng Xiaoping leaves the Standing Committee of the Politburo and resigns as Chairman of the Consultative Commission. He remains Chairman of the Military Commission of the CC.

Genealogy

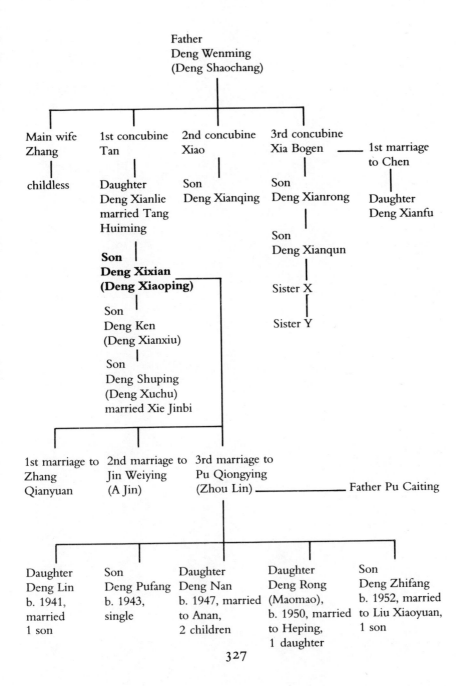

Father
Deng Wenming
(Deng Shaochang)

Main wife
Zhang

childless

1st concubine
Tan

Daughter
Deng Xianlie
married Tang
Huiming

**Son
Deng Xixian
(Deng Xiaoping)**

Son
Deng Ken
(Deng Xianxiu)

Son
Deng Shuping
(Deng Xuchu)
married Xie Jinbi

2nd concubine
Xiao

Son
Deng Xianqing

3rd concubine
Xia Bogen ——— 1st marriage
to Chen

Son
Deng Xianrong

Son
Deng Xianqun

Sister X

Sister Y

Daughter
Deng Xianfu

1st marriage to
Zhang
Qianyuan

2nd marriage to
Jin Weiying
(A Jin)

3rd marriage to
Pu Qiongying
(Zhou Lin) ——————— Father Pu Caiting

Daughter
Deng Lin
b. 1941,
married
1 son

Son
Deng Pufang
b. 1943,
single

Daughter
Deng Nan
b. 1947, married
to Anan,
2 children

Daughter
Deng Rong
(Maomao),
b. 1950, married
to Heping,
1 daughter

Son
Deng Zhifang
b. 1952, married
to Liu Xiaoyuan,
1 son

Bibliography

Association pour l'Information des Chalettois. *Chalette-sur-Loing. Deux Siècles d'Images*. Maury Imprimeur, Millau, 1976.

Ba Jin. *Die Familie*. Oberbaum-Verlag, Berlin, 1980.

Bartke, Wolfgang. *Die grossen Chinesen der Gegenwart*. Suhrkamp, Frankfurt a. M., 1985.

Belden, Jack. *China Shakes the World*. Monthly Review Press, New York, 1970.

Bianco, Lucien. *Das moderne Asien*. Fischer, Frankfurt a. M., 1969.

Braun, Otto. *Chinesische Aufzeichnungen*. Neue Welt, Berlin-Ost, 1973.

Brown, Arthur Judson. *New Forces in Old China*. New York, 1907.

Carlson, Evans F. *Twin Star of China*. Dodd, Mead and Co., New York, 1940.

Chang, David W. *Zhou Enlai and Deng Xiaoping in the Chinese Leadership Succession Crisis*. University Press of America, Boston, 1984.

Chen, Jack. *China's Rote Garden*. Klett-Cotta, Stuttgart, 1977.

Ch'en, Jerome. *Mao Papers*. Deutscher Taschenbuch Verlag, München, 1975.

Ch'en, Jerome. "The Resolution of the Tsunyi Conference," *The China Quarterly* **40** (1969).

Ch'en, Jerome. *China and the West*. Hutchinson, London, 1979.

Chi Hsin. *Teng Hsiao-ping, A Political Biography*. Cosmos Books, Hong Kong, 1978.

China-Buchreihe. *Geschichte*. Verlag für Fremdspachige Literatur, Peking, 1984.

Ching Hua Lee. *Deng Xiaoping: The Marxist Road to the Forbidden City*. The Kingston Press, Princeton, 1985.

Deng Xiaoping. *Der Aufbau des Sozialismus chinesischer Prägung*. Verlag für Fremdsprachige Literatur, Peking, 1985.

Deng Xiaoping. *Ausgewählte Schriften (1975–1982)*. Verlag für Fremdsprachige Literatur, Peking, 1985.

Deng Xiaoping. *Die Geschlossenheit des chinesischen Volkes und aller Völker der Welt*. Verlag für Fremdsprachige Literatur, Peking, 1959.

Ellison, J. Herbert. *The Sino-Soviet Conflict. A Global Perspective*. University of Washington Press, Washington, 1982.

Fischer, Martin. *Szetschuan, Diplomatie und Reisen in China während der letzten drei Jahre der Kaiserzeit*. Oldenbourg Verlag, München–Wien, 1968.

Franz, Uli. *Gebrauchsanweisung für China*. Piper, München, 1987.

Geiss, Imanuel. *Geschichte griffbereit, Weltgeschichte in Daten*, vol. I. Rowohlt, Hamburg, 1979.

Gernet, Jacques. *Die chinesische Welt*. Insel, Frankfurt a. M., 1979.

Gittings, John. *Survey of the Sino-Soviet Dispute. A Comentary and Extracts from the Recent Polemics 1963–1967*. Oxford University Press, Oxford, 1968.

Gray, Jack, and Patrick Cavendish. *Chinese Communism in Crisis, Maoism and the Cultural Revolution*. Fredei (Frederick) A. Praeger Publishers, New York, 1968.

Hamm, Harry, and Joseph Kun. *Das rote Schisma*. Verlag Wissenschaft und Politik, Köln, 1963.

Harrison, James. *Long March to Power*. Fredei (Frederick) A. Praeger Publishers, New York, 1972.

Hinton, William. *Hundred Day War: The Cultural Revolution at Tsinghua University*. Monthly Review Press, New York–London, 1972.

Hookham, Hilda. *A Short History of China*. St. Martin's Press, New York, 1972.

Hudelot, Claude. *Der Lange Marsch*. Suhrkamp, Frankfurt a. M., 1972.

Hummel, A. W. *Eminent Chinese of the Ch'ing Period*. Washington, D.C., 1943–1944.

Kapp, Robert A. *Szechwan and the Chinese Republic*. New Haven–London, 1973.

Klein, Donald W., and Anne Clark. *Biographic Dictionary of Chinese Communism*. Harvard University Press, Cambridge, Mass., 1971.

Krott, Martin. *Programm für Chinas Zukunft*. Institut für Asienkunde, Hamburg, 1978.

Kuan Su-chih. *An Early Chinese Experience in Moscow's Advanced Education Centers*. Institute of International Relations, Taipei, 1975.

Li Yi Zhe, Helmut Opletal, and Peter Schier. *China: wer gegen wen? Demokratie und Rechtssystem im Sozialismus*. Rotbuch-Verlag, Berlin, 1977.

Low, D. Alfred. *The Sino-Soviet Dispute. An Analysis of the Polemics*. Associated University Press, London, 1976.

Mao Zedong. *Ausgewählte Werke.* 5 vols. Verlag für Fremdsprachige Literatur, Peking, 1968–1978.

Mao Zedong. *Gedichte.* Verlag für Fremdsprachige Literatur, Peking, 1978.

Mao Zedong. *Worte des Vorsitzenden Mao Tsetung.* Verlag für Fremdsprachige Literatur, Peking, 1972.

Mehnert, Klaus. *Peking und die Neue Linke.* Deutsche Verlags-Anstalt, Stuttgart, 1969.

Mehnert, Klaus. *Maos Erben machen's anders.* Deutsche Verlags-Anstalt, Stuttgart, 1979.

Meyer, Fritjof. *Nach dem Sturm erhebt sich der gebeugte Bambus. China im Umbruch.* Bertelsmann, München, 1987.

Mohr, Ernst-Günther. *Die unterschlagenen Jahre. China vor Mao Tse-tung.* Bechtle, Esslingen–München, 1985.

Moravia, Alberto. *Die Kulturrevolution in China.* Desch, München, 1968.

Ostkolleg der Bundeszentrale für politische Bildung (ed.) *VR China im Wandel.* Bundeszentrale für politische Bildung, Köln, 1985.

Die Polemik über die Generallinie der internationalen kommunistischen Bewegung. Oberbaum, Berlin, 1971.

Proletarier aller Länder, vereinigt Euch gegen den gemeinsamen Feind! Leninismus und moderner Revisionismus in Westeuropa. Oberbaum, Berlin, 1971.

Richthofen, Ferdinand von. *Tagebücher aus China.* Dietrich Reimer-Verlag, Berlin, 1907.

Robitscher-Hahn, Magdalena. *Im Geist Yanans.* China Studien-und Verlagsgesellschaft, Frankfurt a. M., 1980.

Salisbury, Harrison E. *Der Lange Marsch.* Fischer, Frankfurt a. M., 1985.

Scharping, Thomas. *Mao Chronik.* Hanser, München, 1976.

Schlögel, Karl. *Moskau lesen.* Sielder, Berlin, 1984.

Smedley, Agnes. *The Great Road, The Life and Times of Chu Teh.* Monthly Review Press, New York, 1956.

Smedley, Agnes. *Lebenswege in China, Begegnungen.* Oberbaum, Berlin, 1979.

Snow, Edgar. *Die lange Revolution.* Deutscher Taschenbuch Verlag, München, 1975.

Snow, Edgar. *Random Notes on Red China, 1936–1945.* Harvard University Press, Cambridge, Mass., 1957.

Snow, Edgar. *Roter Stern über China.* Fischer, Frankfurt a. M., 1979.

Stalin, Josef. *Fragen des Leninismus.* Oberbaum, Berlin, 1971.

Verlag für Fremdsprachige Literatur (ed.). *Die Yihotuan-Bewegung von 1900.* Verlag für Fremdsprachige Literatur, Peking, 1978.

Verlag für Fremdsprachige Literatur (ed.). *Die Revolution von 1911.* Verlag für Fremdsprachige Literatur, Peking, 1977.

Wang Hsuan. *About Teng Hsiao-ping*. Institute of International Relations, Taipei, 1978.

Wang, Nora. "Deng Xiaoping: The Years in France," *The China Quarterly* **92** (1982).

Wickert, Erwin. *China von innen gesehen*. Deutscher Taschenbuch Verlag, Stuttgart, 1982.

Yueh Sheng. *Sun Yat-sen University in Moscow and the Chinese Revolution. A Personal Account*. University of Kansas Press, New York, 1971.

Zagoria, S. Donald. *Der chinesisch-sowjetische Konflikt 1956–1961*. Rütten und Löning-Verlag, München, 1964.

Works in Chinese

(Translated, Pinyin transliteration)

Atlas of the Provinces of the People's Republic of China. Peking, 1971.

Chou Enlai. *The Works of Comrade Chou Enlai on His Stay in France*. Peking, n.d.

Chou Xun. *Deng Xiaoping*. Hongkong, 1983.

Collection of Secret Documents of the Chinese Communist Party. Taipei, 1978.

Deng Xiaoping. *Selected Writings (1975–1982)*. Hongkong, 1984.

Ding Wang. *Selected Materials on the Cultural Revolution*, vol. I, Hongkong, 1972.

Document Collection on the Zunyi Conference. Peking, 1985.

Feng Yuxiang. *My Life*. N.p., n.d.

Gong Zhu. *Memoires*, 2 vols. Hongkong, 1978.

Han Shanbi. *Deng Xiaoping. Biography*, 2 vols. Hongkong, 1986–1987.

He Changdong. *Revolt of the Work Students in France and the Formation of the Principal Cell of the CP of China in Europe*, vol II. N.p., n.d.

History of the Founding Organization of the CP of China in Europe. Peking, 1985.

Hu Hua. *Teaching Materials on the Revolutionary History of China*. Peking, 1985.

Hu Qiaomu. *30 Years of the Chinese People's Liberation Army*. Peking, 1957.

Huang Dao. *30 Years of the Chinese Communist Party*. Peking, n.d.

Jiang Zemin. "Reminiscences of the Life of the Work-Study Students in France and Belgium." In: *Selected Writings on the History of Tianjin*, vol. 14. Tianjin, n.d.

Li Huan. *Selected Biographies of Famous Personalities of the Ch'ing Period*. N.p., 1891

Li Huang. *Reminiscences from a Tidy Study*. Hongkong, 1979.

Li Tianming. *The Deng Xiaoping of Tomorrow*. Taipei, 1986.

Nie Rongzhen. *Recollections*, vol. I. Peking, 1984.

Peng Dehuai. *Memoires*. Peking, 1981.

Red Guard of Qinghua University. *Down with the Great Conspirator, Carricaturist, and Despot Peng Dehuai*. Peking, 1967.

Red Guard of Peking University. *The Past of the Counterrevolutionary Deng Xiaoping*. Peking, 1967.

Renmin Chubanshe. *Polemics on the General Direction of the International Communist Movement*. Peking, 1965.

Shu Yang. *Deng Xiaoping's Private Life*. Hongkong, n.d.

Topical Problems of the Chinese Communist Party and the Developmental Direction. Taipei, 1987.

Wang Yungxiang, Kong Fangfeng, Liu Binqing. *The History of the Basic Organization of the CP of China in Europe*. Peking, 1985.

Xinhua Bookstore of South and Central China. *Short Summary of the Political History of Modern China*. N.p., 1950.

Zhang Guotao. *My Reminiscences*, vol. II. Hongkong, 1973.

Zhang Junying. *Short History of the War of the Chinese People's Liberation Army*. Peking, 1961.

Zhenfa Gongshe. *Investigatory Report on the Crimes of Deng Xiaoping*. Peking, 1967.

Zheng Qi. *Our Attitude Towards the Kuomitang after the Breach between Them and the CCP and Our Admonitions*, N.p., n.d.

Periodicals

Guangmin Ribao (Peking). 1950–1987.

Jiushi Niandai (Hongkong). 1985.

Qishi Niandai (Hongkong). 1983.

Renmin Ribao (Peking). 1950–1987.

Wenhui Bao (Shanghai). 1950–1987.

Xin Beida (Peking). February–May 1967.

Zhenming (Hongkong). 1986.

Zhongguo Zichun (New York). 1982–1987.

Index

Chialing, tributary of the
Yangtse, 1
Chiang Ching-kuo, son of
Chiang Kai-shek, 60
Chiang Kai-shek, Kuomintang
leader, 49, 60–61, 74, 78–79,
91, 95–96, 105, 117, 121, 124–
127
Chongyi, town in Jiangxi prov-
ince, 86–88
Combe, Louis, French Jesuit, 22

Deng Ken (Deng Xianxiu),
brother of Deng Xiaoping, 10,
17–18
Deng Lin, daughter of Deng
Xiaoping, 120, 153, 202–204,
216, 218–219, 292
Deng Nan, daughter of Deng
Xiaoping, 133, 153, 202, 204,
220–221, 281, 292
Deng Pufang, son of Deng Xiao-
ping, 40, 120, 153, 202, 204–
210, 220–223
Deng Rong (Maomao), daughter
of Deng Xiaoping, 133, 153,
202–204, 208, 214–216, 292
Deng Shimin (Xunzhai), ancestor
of Deng Xiaoping, 19
Deng Shuping (Deng Xuchu),
brother of Deng Xiaoping, 10,
14, 133, 201
Deng Wemming (Deng Shao-
chang), father of Deng Xiao-
ping, 7–16, 21–22, 28, 135
Deng Xianfu, stepsister of Deng
Xiaoping, 19
Deng Xianlie, sister of Deng
Xiaoping, 4, 8, 132
Deng Xianqing, stepbrother of
Deng Xiaoping, 19

Deng Xianqun, stepbrother of
Deng Xiaoping, 19
Deng Xianrong, stepbrother of
Deng Xiaoping, 19
Deng Yingchao, widow of Chou
Enlai, 268, 280
Deng Zhifang, son of Deng Xiao-
ping, 133, 153, 202, 204, 214,
216–218
Dong Biwu, founding member of
the CCP, 95, 172

Eberly, Joseph, American professor, 218
Engels, Friedrich, 283

Fallaci, Oriana, Italian writer, 283
Fang Lizhi, astrophysicist, 301
Feng Yuxiang, general, 69–72
Fujian, province, 89, 93, 96, 290
Fu Zhong, CP functionary, 49,
55
Fuzhou, capital of Fujian prov-
ince, 252

Gao Gang, CP functionary, 137–
140
Gorbachev, Mikhail, 173, 306
Gromyko, Andrei, 171
Gu Bo, secretary of Mao Tse-
tung, 93
Guang'an, district in Szechuan,
Deng Xiaoping's native region,
1–4, 12, 22–23, 27, 30
Guangdong, province, 10, 65,
84–87, 189, 252
Guangxi, former province, 77–78,
80, 88, 90–91, 97
Guiyang, capital of Guizhou
province, 113, 181
Guizhou, province, 80, 84, 97,
131, 181